CITIES ON STONE

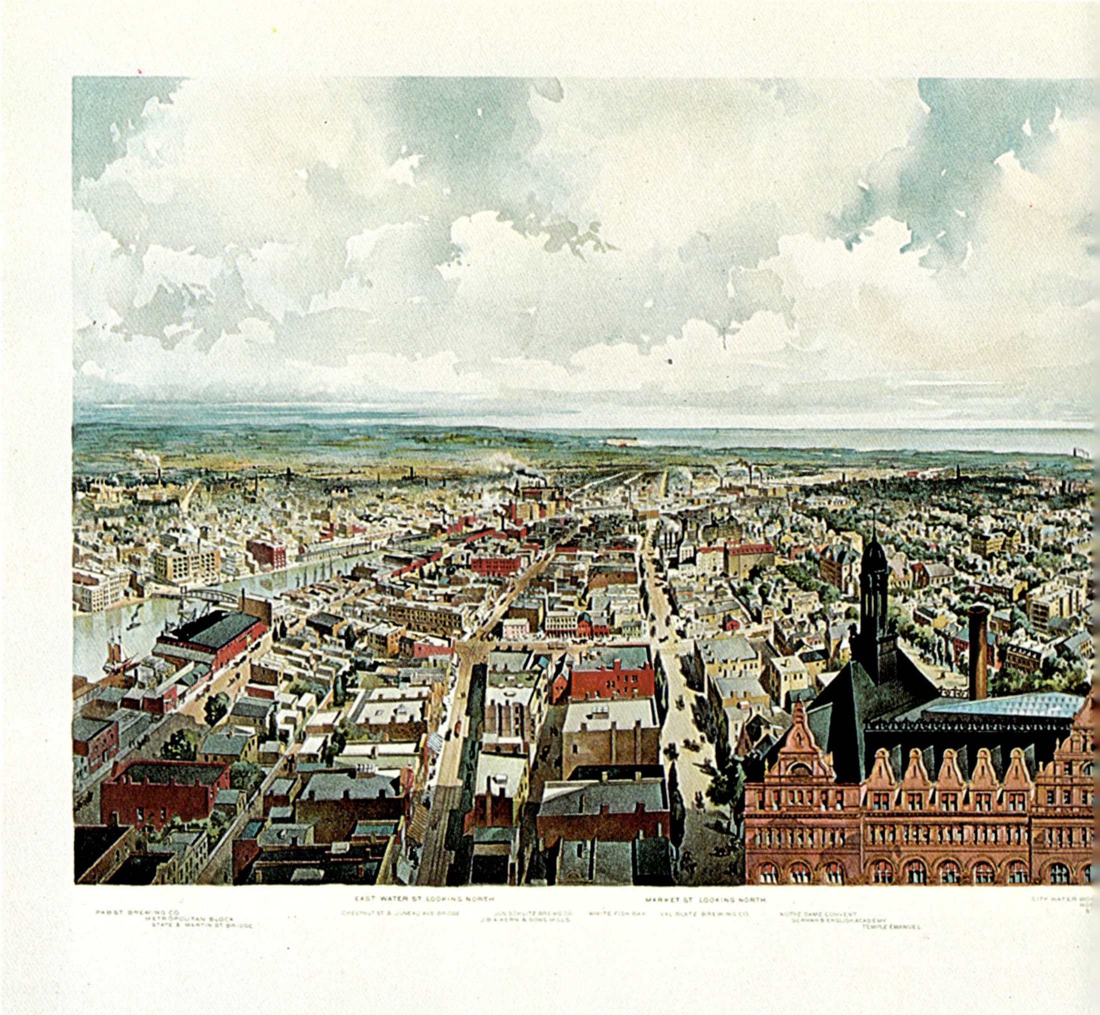

CITIES ON STONE

BY JOHN W. REPS

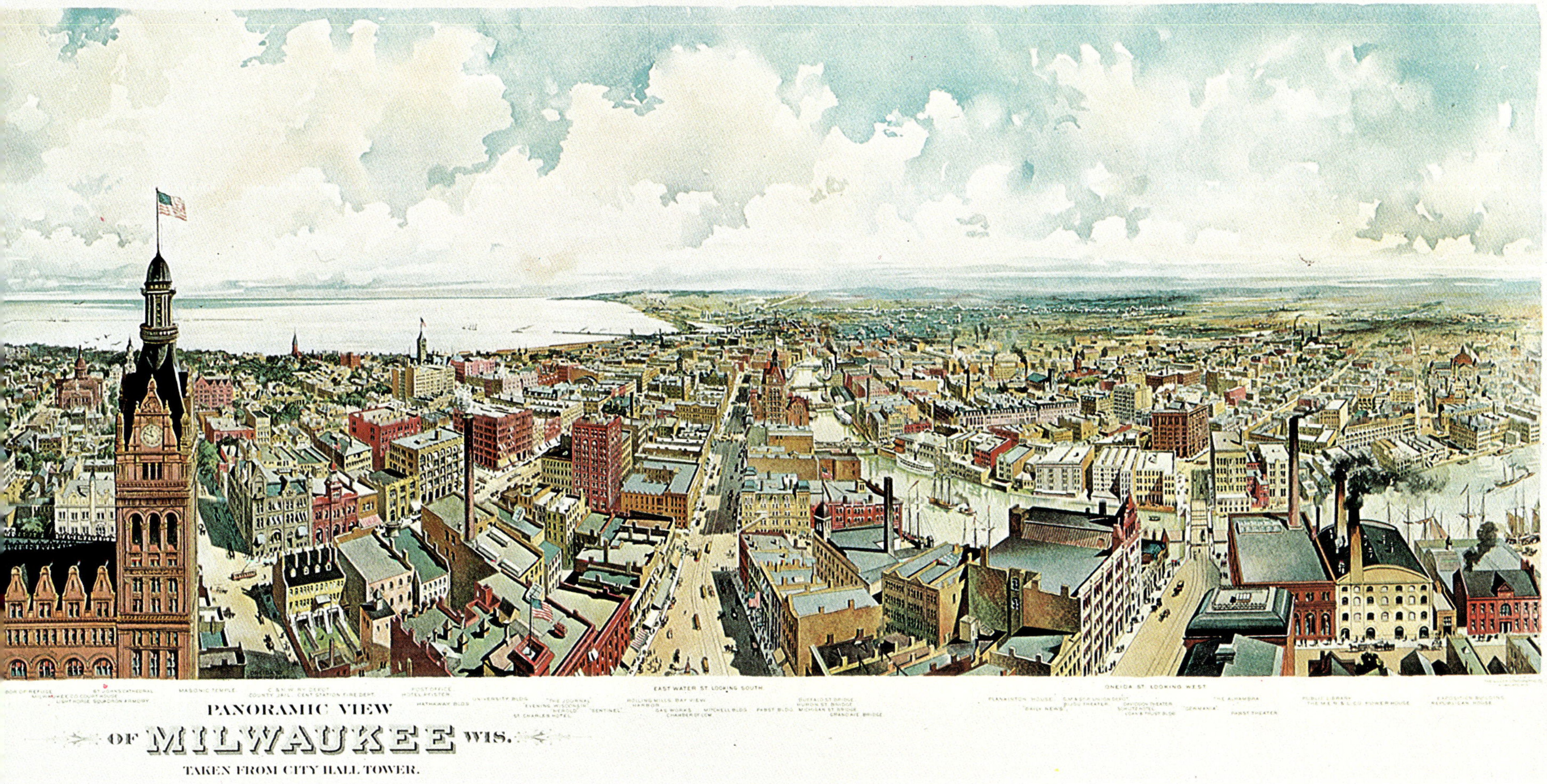

Panoramic View of Milwaukee Wis.

Nineteenth Century Lithograph Images of the Urban West

AMON CARTER MUSEUM FORT WORTH

THE AMON CARTER MUSEUM was established in 1961 under the will of the late Amon G. Carter for the study and documentation of westering North America. The program of the Museum, expressed in publications, exhibitions, and permanent collections, reflects many aspects of American culture, both historic and contemporary.

The Museum has been assisted by the National Endowment for the Arts, a Federal agency, in publication of this catalog and the accompanying exhibition.

Reps, John William.
Cities on stone: nineteenth century lithograph images of the urban West.

Bibliography: p.
1. Lithographs, American. 2. The West in art. I. Amon Carter Museum of Western Art, Fort Worth, Tex. II. Title.
NE2454.R46 769'.973'07401645315 76–12313
ISBN 0–88360–024–2 lib. bdg.
ISBN 0–88360–051–x pbk.

Text set by G & S Typesetters, Austin
Printed by Brodnax Printing Company, Dallas
Design by William D. Wittliff, The Encino Press

CITIES ON STONE

THE RISE OF CITIES in the American West coincided with the introduction and development of lithography as a quick and inexpensive method of producing printed images. The hundreds of new communities that sprang into existence as the West was settled provided attractive subjects for artists and publishers who began to specialize in the business of providing city views. To them we owe much of our knowledge of the nineteenth-century urban scene.

Their output was prodigious. I. N. Phelps Stokes, who formed the great collection of city views bearing his name in the New York Public Library, stated that interest in these views seemed "to have become a universal hobby—almost a mania," adding "that in no other country, and at no other time, were so many views of cities produced as in America, during the five decades between 1825 and 1875."[1] Harry Peters, whose pioneering compilations of information on lithographic artists and publishers did so much to arouse interest in and understanding of the subject, noted the "immense" volume of these urban views and commented that he would "hesitate to pick the most remote and unlikely place . . . in the United States and say that there was no lithographed view of it."[2] While no complete checklist of these views exists, it is possible to make a rough estimate that at least 2,000 different urban views were published between 1825 and 1900, and the number may well run to 2,500 or even 3,000.[3]

Both the medium of lithography and the tradition of depicting entire cities in prints as seen either from the ground or from an imaginary position in the air came from Europe. The older of the two was the artist's vision of the city seen as a whole. Shortly after the perfection of printing itself in the fifteenth century, woodcut illustrations of cities began to be used in books. The most elaborate example was the *Liber Cronicarum* of Hartmann Schedel (Fig. 1), published in 1493 and known more familiarly as the Nuremberg Chronicle. It contained dozens of woodcut views, many showing cities as seen from the air.

Sebastian Münster's *Cosmographiae Universalis* (Fig. 2), published in the middle of the sixteenth century, also included many woodcuts of cities that were less stylized and often surprisingly detailed. This was followed, beginning in 1572, with the six-volume city atlas prepared by Georg Braun and Frans Hogenberg, usually known by the title of its first volume, *Civitas Orbis Terrarum* (Fig. 3). This monumental work included more than four hundred city panoramas, plan-views, and bird's-eye views of cities in the known world, all carefully engraved on copper and based on the work of many artists and cartographers who were asked to assist the publishers.

In the seventeenth century, such men as Mathew Merian in Germany and Jan Blaeu and Frederick de Wit in Holland published, and sold bird's-eye or plan-views of

---

[1] I. N. Phelps Stokes and Daniel C. Haskell, *American Historical Prints*, xv.

[2] Harry T. Peters, *America on Stone*, 39.

[3] The largest single collection of these views is in the Geography and Map Division of the Library of Congress. In a list of their holdings published in 1974, 1,117 items appear. See John Hébert, *Panoramic Maps of Anglo-American Cities*. Forty-nine of them were of Michigan cities. In John Cumming, comp., *A Preliminary Checklist of 19th Century Lithographs of Michigan Cities and Towns*, 160 views of Michigan cities are listed. Since that time the compiler has located twenty additional views. Letter from John Cumming to John W. Reps, April 11, 1975. The Library of Congress checklist includes 112 views of cities in New York State other than those of New York City. With Ms. Carol Branan, I have compiled a preliminary list of upstate New York views that numbers 200 items. If these two states are representative, the total views issued for the entire country might well number in excess of 3,000. The number of cities represented would, of course, be substantially less, since for many cities there was more than one view.

cities showing every building in perspective with great accuracy and attention to detail. John Speed in Britain used small views of this type as insets to embellish his maps of English and Welsh counties in his great atlas of 1611, the *Theatre of the Empire of Great Britain* (Fig. 4).

The discovery of the New World excited all of Europe, and artists and publishers of Europe responded to the demand for pictures of natives, plants, animals, and the landscape. Illustrations of colonial settlements were also produced, many of them, such as the late sixteenth-century engravings of Theodore de Bry, appearing as high-level views or as plans with buildings in perspective. Somewhat earlier was the view of the Indian town of Hochelaga (Fig. 5) on the site of the modern Montreal as depicted in Giovanni Battista Ramusio's *Delle Navigationi e Viaggi* of 1556 from an account by the French explorer, Jacques Cartier. Arnoldus Montanus of Amsterdam and John Ogilby in London, among others, continued this tradition in the seventeeth century with their illustrated accounts of exploration, travels, and settlement in the Western Hemisphere.

The earliest city map to be engraved and printed in the English colonies—that of Boston in 1722—also combined a kind of perspective with a street plan. Its author, Captain John Bonner, knew more about sailing a ship than drawing buildings from the air, and he simply depicted each structure of the city as though it had fallen over backwards leaving its front facade visible from a point directly overhead.[4]

Far more skillfully executed was the view of Savannah, Georgia in 1734 as drawn by Peter Gordon (Fig. 6), one of the first colonists in the community that James Oglethorpe had planned a year earlier. The Trustees of the Georgia colony had Gordon's view engraved in Britain to stimulate further colonization in the infant settlement. It is this type of view, showing from an imaginary point in the air all of the buildings in perspective and revealing clearly the basic street pattern and location of squares, market places, and port facilities, that was widely used by urban artists in the American West.

During the last half-century of English colonization many other city views were drawn in America and engraved and published either in the colonies or the home country. Virtually all of them showed the city as seen from ground level or from only a slightly elevated point of view. Notable among them were the four, multi-sheet panoramas of Boston, New York, Philadelphia, and Charleston, known only by a few surviving impressions.[5]

The earliest nineteenth-century American city views were also drawn from a ground-level or a slightly elevated position. Most of them were reproduced in aquatint, a medium making possible the rendering of tonal values to resemble paintings.[6] They were then usually

---

[4] For a detailed analysis of this and other Boston maps and views see John W. Reps, "Boston by Bostonians: The Printed Plans and Views of the Colonial City by its Artists, Cartographers, Engravers, and Publishers," in Walter Whitehill and Sinclair Hitchings, eds., *Boston Prints and Printmakers, 1670–1775*, 3–56.

[5] Only one impression of the first state of the Boston panorama by William Burgis is known to exist. It is in the Stokes Collection of the New York Public Library which also has the second state of the Burgis view of New York City. An impression of the Charleston panorama can be seen at the Winterthur Museum, Winterthur, Delaware. The panorama of Philadelphia is in the collection of the Historical Society of Pennsylvania. Other views of New York City are reproduced in I. N. Phelps Stokes, *Iconography of Manhattan Island, 1498–1909*. Early views and maps of Philadelphia are described and reproduced in Martin P. Snyder, *City of Independence: Views of Philadelphia Before 1800*.

[6] An early technical description of the aquatint technique appeared in the first American edition of Abraham Rees, *The Cyclopaedia; or Universal Dictionary of Arts, Sciences, and Literature*, II, unpaged entry under "Aquatinta." The tonal grain on the copper plate was produced by coating it

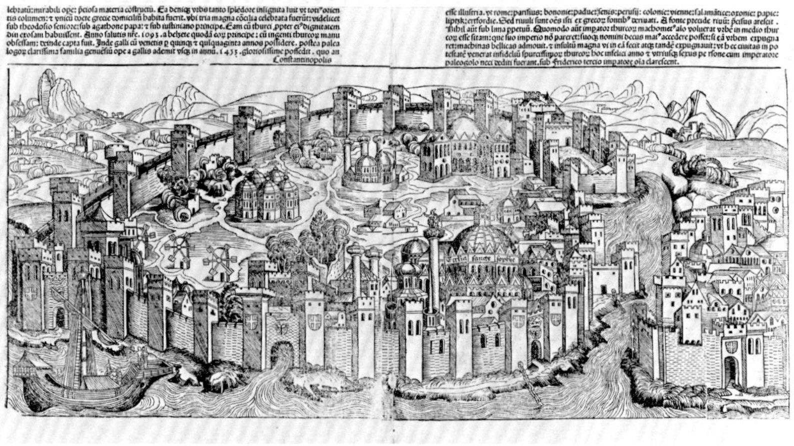

FIGURE 1. *Constantinople*. Hartmann Schedel. 1493, in *Liber Cronicarum* (Nuremberg Chronicle). Woodcut. 9-1/4 x 20-5/8 in. (23.5 x 52.4 cm.) Courtesy Collection of Professor John W. Reps.

hand colored in delicate washes, such as the superb view of Newburgh, New York by William Guy Wall, engraved in aquatint by John Hill and published with many others in the series issued during the years 1821–1825 by Henry Megarey of New York as the *Hudson River Portfolio*.[7]

While the aquatint technique remained popular as a method of printing city views until the 1840s, it was soon superseded by a new, easier, and less expensive method of printing. This system was invented and perfected at the end of the eighteenth century by Alois Senefelder in Germany. Printing establishments using his new process of lithography were soon at work in Germany, France, and England producing a wide variety of prints.[8] Although the *National Intelligencer and Washington Advertiser* reported in 1808 that "Dr. Mitchell of New York received a lithographic stone and inks from Paris and made some experiments in this new art," it was not until a decade later that Bass Otis produced the first surviving true American lithograph. This

with rosin powder and then heating the plate. Etching, engraving, and burnishing provided the design, after which the plate could be inked and printed.

[7] Wall's work is reviewed in Donald A. Shelley, "William Guy Wall and his Watercolors for the Historical *Hudson River Portfolio*," *New-York Historical Society Quarterly*, XXXI (January, 1947), 25–45. For Hill, see Frank Weitenkampf, "John Hill and American Landscapes in Aquatint," *American Collector*, XVII (July, 1948), 6–8; Richard J. Koke, "John Hill (1770–1850), Master of Aquatint," *New-York Historical Society Quarterly*, XLIII (January, 1959), 51–117; and Koke, *A Checklist of the American Engravings of John Hill (1770–1850)*. The twenty-four views comprising the *Hudson River Portfolio* were offered to subscribers for $16.00. Stokes and Haskell, 62–63 gives the text of the prospectus appearing in the first issue of the *Portfolio* containing four views. Only twenty of the projected total were issued. An earlier projected series of aquatint city views was not as successful. These were by George Isham Parkyns, whose intentions were announced on March 3 and 10, 1795, in the *American Minerva*, a New York City publication. The series was to consist of twenty-four views of cities and such places as Mount Vernon, each print to "be 24 by 17 inches, executed in aquatinta, and published upon paper of a superior quality." Uncolored impressions were to sell for $3.00, and, if colored, for $5.00 each. Only two views of the new city of Washington and those of Annapolis, Georgetown, and Mount Vernon were published. The text of the announcement and other information on the published views can be found in Stokes and Haskell, 39–40. See also Eleanor M. McPeck, "George Isham Parkyns: Artist and Landscape Architect, 1749–1820," *Quarterly Journal of the Library of Congress*, XXX (July, 1973), 171–82. Other artists whose views of American cities were issued in aquatint were George Cooke, William James Bennett, and Robert Havell, Jr. The latter, while still in London, engraved the plates for Audubon's *Birds of America*. In addition to references to him in the usual biographical dictionaries of artists, there is a brief article on him titled "The Complete Work of Robert Havell, Jr." by Helen Comstock in *The Connoisseur*, CXXVI (November, 1950), 127. Both Cooke and Bennett were artists, the latter also serving as the aquatint engraver for many of the former's superbly rendered urban views. The publisher of many of the Cooke-Bennett views was Lewis P. Clover. He sold them for $4.00 and $5.00 each. See the text of Clover's price list in Stokes and Haskell, 72. For a note on Clover with a small view of his New York City shop, see "New-York Artists Fifty Years Ago," *Appletons' Journal*, VII (May 18, 1872), 572–75.

[8] The definitive study on the invention, development, and spread of lithographic printing in western Europe is Michael Twyman, *Lithography, 1800–1850: The Techniques of Drawing on Stone in England and France and their Application in Works of Topography*. Senefelder's own fascinat-

appeared as a small illustration in *The Analectic Magazine* accompanied by a long technical description of the novel process.[9]

During the 1820s lithography rapidly gained popularity in America. Isaac Doolittle and William Barnet studied the process in France and started a printing house in New York in 1821.[10] The appropriately named Henry Stone set up a lithograph press in Washington late in 1822.[11] Anthony Imbert, a Frenchman, established his business in New York in 1825. Among his earliest lithographs are several small views of Buffalo and Lockport used to illustrate an elaborate publication of 1825 celebrating the opening and dedication of the Erie Canal.[12] These would appear to be the earliest views of American cities printed in this country by lithography.[13]

William Lucas began publishing lithographs in Philadelphia in 1828, and a year later found himself in competition with the new firm of Pendleton, Kearny & Childs. J. B. Martin and George Endicott in Baltimore and Daniel Kellogg in Hartford were also in business by 1830, and there must have been several others as well.[14] Among them was the important Boston firm founded by John Pendleton in 1825. Several of the artists employed by Pendleton and his brother, William, were to produce some of the earliest single-sheet lithographic views of American cities. They included Andrew Jackson Davis, whose view of Harvard College and Cambridge was produced by the Pendletons in 1828; E. A. Farrar, the artist of a view of Lowell, Massachusetts issued in 1834; FitzHugh Lane, who drew the Pendletons' view of Gloucester, Massachusetts, published c. 1835; and Henry Walton, whose first three views of Ithaca, New York appeared in 1836.[15]

It was shortly after the Pendleton firm opened for business that a Boston journal, noting this new enter-

ing treatise was published in German in 1819. An English translation is now available: Alois Senefelder, *A Complete Course in Lithography*. With an Introduction by A. Hyatt Mayor. See also Wilhelm Weber, *A History of Lithography*.

[9] *The Analectic Magazine*, XIV (July, 1819), 66–72. Otis had produced a slightly earlier print using a lithographic stone. See Joseph Jackson, "Bass Otis, America's First Lithographer," *Pennsylvania Magazine of History and Biography*, XXXVII (1913), 385–94. This print was a portrait of the Reverend Abner Kneeland published as the frontispiece to a printed collection of the clergyman's sermons. It is generally thought to be an example of stone engraving, with the image produced by cutting away the stone except where lines were to print. Otis may have used the same technique for his view of an unidentified building illustrating the *Analectic Magazine* article. Senefelder had begun his own experiments in printing from stones in much the same manner. As will be described in the text of this essay, true lithographic printing is from a flat, not an incised or raised, surface and depends on a chemical and not a mechanical separation of the portion of the stone charged with ink. For a note on Otis and his significance in American lithography, see Harry T. Peters, *America on Stone*, 303–04.

[10] *American Journal of Science and Arts*, IV (October, 1821), 159–71.

[11] Edith A. Wright and Josephine A. McDevitt, "Henry Stone, Lithographer," *Antiques*, XXXIV (July, 1938), 16–19; and Charles Henry Taylor, "Some Notes on Early American Lithography," *Proceedings of the American Antiquarian Society*, New Series, XXXII (April, 1922), 68–80.

[12] Cadwallader David Colden, *Memoir . . . at the Celebration of the Completion of the New York Canals*. For brief notes on Imbert see Taylor, "Early American Lithography" and Peters, *America on Stone*, 234–35.

[13] There is at least one earlier lithograph view of an American settlement, that of the presidio at San Francisco in 1816, published in Paris in 1822 by Louis Choris, *Voyage Pittoresque autour du Monde*. Shortly after the Imbert views appeared, several views of American cities were lithographed and published in Paris from drawings by the author in J[acques] Milbert, *Itinéraire Pittoresque du Fleuve Hudson*, Paris, 1828–29. Apparently other Milbert views were also published in Paris in 1825 under the title, *A Series of Picturesque Views in North America*. Stokes and Haskell, 60–61. One of these has the title, "View of the City of New-York, taken from Brooklyn Hills."

[14] Thomas Carey, "The American Lithograph from its Inception to 1865 . . ," (unpublished Ph.D. dissertation, Ohio State University, 1954); George H. Eckhardt, "Early Lithography in Philadelphia," *Antiques*, XXXVII (December, 1935), 249–52; Nicholas Wainwright, *Philadelphia in the Romantic Age of Lithography*; Taylor, "Early American Lithography;" Rhea Mansfield Knittle, "The Kelloggs, Hartford Lithographers," *Antiques*, X (July, 1926), 42–46; Peters, *America on Stone*. A helpful list of major

prise, described for its readers the way in which lithographs were produced. Although this treatment of the process is oversimplified, it is still a useful summary of the basic procedure:

> The drawing is made on a polished stone, with an ink or chalk composed of greasy materials in the same way as drawings are executed on paper with common ink or chalk. The stone is then given to the lithographic printer, that he may obtain impressions from it. In order to do this, he wets its whole surface, but as the greasy materials, which constitute the drawing, will not receive water, only the uncovered part imbibes it. A thick greasy ink is then passed over the stone, and received by the lines of the drawing, while the remainder of the surface being wet refuses to take it. A sheet of paper is then pressed strongly on the stone, and a reversed impression of the drawing obtained. The stone is again wetted, again charged with ink, and thus a series of impressions are procured. The result is the same as in copperplate printing, but the means are different. The process of engraving is mechanical, that of lithography chemical.[16]

In a later passage, the article described the important transfer process which, among other advantages, did not require the artist to draw a reversed image on the stone but permitted him to draw in the normal way on special paper whose image could then be transferred to a lithographic stone. It also made possible certain printing economies and allowed the publisher to set aside the original stone as insurance against possible breakage from the substantial pressure on it required to obtain good impressions.[17]

This article also identified the source of the best stone for lithographs as that quarried "at Solenhofen, near Pappenheim, in Bavaria," referring to it as "a nearly pure carbonate of lime." Omitted, however, was any treatment of how cut slabs of the stone were finished by polishing the surfaces of two stones, placed with their faces together, and using abrasives of progressive fineness with water to obtain the desired texture on the printing surface by moving the top stone laterally under pressure. Later in the century special machines would be developed to polish the stone surfaces.[18]

Nor did the anonymous author discuss, perhaps because it had not been revealed to him as a jealously guarded trade secret, the treatment of the stone after the lithographic artist had drawn on its surface with the greasy ink or crayon to which black pigment was added

American lithographic firms with brief notes on their work can also be found in John and Katherine Ebert, *Old American Prints for Collectors*, 90–119.

[15] The views mentioned are listed and briefly described in Stokes and Haskell. The founding and operation of the Pendleton firm and its successor, Thomas Moore, is ably treated in David Tatham, "The Pendleton-Moore Shop: Lithographic Artists in Boston, 1825–1840," *Old-Time New England*, LXII (October-December, 1971), 29–46. For the work of Henry Walton see Leigh Rehner, *Henry Walton: 19th Century American Artist*. Additional material can be found in Carey, "The American Lithograph," 374–91.

[16] *United States Literary Gazette*, IV (June 15, 1826), 224–27.

[17] *Ibid*. The full text of this portion of the article reads as follows: "The power of transferring the copies, is another singular advantage attending the art of lithography. Whenever it is of importance that the impression should be a perfect *fac-simile*, and not a reversed picture of the original, the drawing may be made on prepared paper, and then, by an easy process, be transferred from the paper to the stone. This process is not confined to drawings originally made on paper, but is applicable to impressions already taken from the stone. In this manner, an indefinite number of impressions may be obtained by transferring the copy to several stones, or, when the prints are small, several copies to one large stone, which will greatly diminish the expense of printing; or if a large number of impressions of any important paper were suddenly wanted, several might be thrown off in a few moments, on several stones, and given to be printed in different presses."

[18] For illustrations of one such machine and others of presses and related equipment near the end of the era of stone lithography see Alfred Seymour, *Practical Lithography*.

so that the design could be seen. This involved the use of gum arabic and a weak acid solution which fixed the design to prevent it from spreading and gave the balance of the stone a greater affinity to water.[19] Other and later descriptions of lithographic printing analyzed this and other techniques in far more detail, although the precise chemical reactions that took place between the stone, the ink or crayon used for the design, the solutions used to treat the stone, and the ink used in printing remained obscure.[20]

This new, inexpensive, and versatile method of printing was used to produce a wide variety of graphic images. Americans in the nineteenth century seemed to have an insatiable yearning for pictures of all kinds: portraits, patriotic scenes, pioneer and Indian views, sporting prints, political cartoons and caricatures, views of farm and rural life, depictions of natural disasters, military and naval engagements, Biblical scenes, copies of works of art, objects of natural history, images of important buildings, theatre and tavern views, and many other categories. Nothing failed to attract the interest of the public, escaped the eye of the artist, or lacked one or more lithographic publishers.

The earlier engravings and aquatints of city views having already proved their popularity, it was only to be expected that this subject would also be pursued by artists and lithographers working in the new medium. Among the earliest of the single-sheet city views to be lithographed were those of Bethlehem, Pennsylvania in 1830; Lowell, Massachusetts, Glens Falls, New York, and Paterson, New Jersey in 1834; Lancaster, Pennsylvania, Gloucester, Massachusetts, and Natchez, Mississippi in 1835; Ithaca, New York and Reading, Pennsylvania in 1836; Washington, D.C. and Worcester, Massachusetts in 1838; and Cincinnati in 1839, to list but

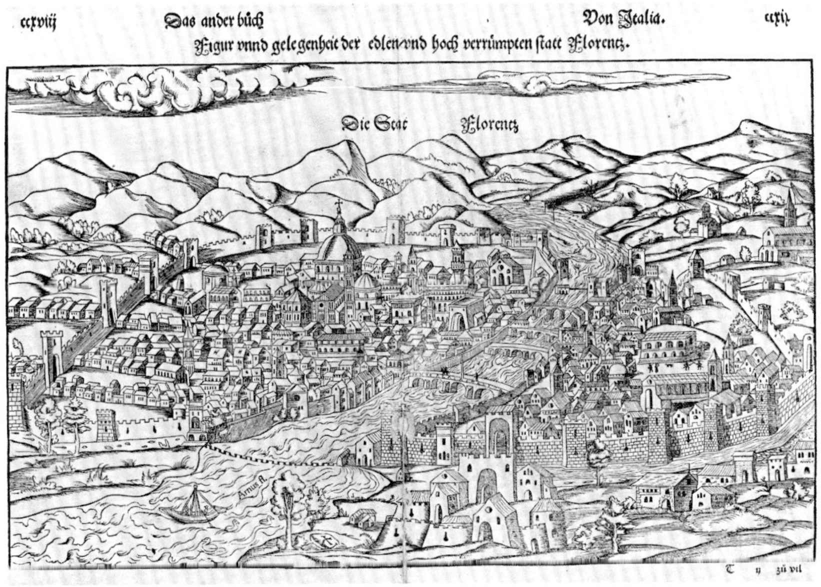

FIGURE 2. *Die Stat Florenz*. Sebastian Münster. 1550, in *Cosmographiae Universalis*. Woodcut. 8-7/8 x 14-1/4 in. (22.5 x 36.2 cm.) Courtesy Collection of Professor John W. Reps.

[19] The effect of this treatment has been described by a modern authority as follows: "It has been established, empirically, that a properly compounded solution of gum arabic and nitric acid will, when rubbed thin and dried, provide a hydrophilic coating around the image. It attracts, not repels, water." Review of Michael Knigin and Murray Zimiles, *The Technique of Fine Art Lithography*, by Robert Gardner, in *The Print Collector's Newsletter*, I (September-October, 1970), 93.

[20] For those who wish to pursue this seemingly simple but complicated and fascinating subject, the following references may be helpful: *Journal of the Franklin Institute*, IV (1827), 57–62, 135–40, 164–65, 168, 264–68, 334–39, 393–96, 415; V (1828), 267–70, 341–44, 403–07; III, New Series (1829), 279–83, 302–05; V, New Series (1830), 142; VI, New Series (1831), 138–39; Edward Hazen, *The Panorama of Professions and Trades*, 175–76; "Lithography," *Appleton's Dictionary of Machines, Mechanics, Engine-work & Engraving*, II, 212; "Lithography," J. Luther Ringwalt, ed., *American Encyclopaedia of Printing*, 276–86; "Lithographic Crayon," "Lithographic Ink," "Lithographic Paper," "Lithographic Pen," "Lithographic Press," "Lithographic Roller," "Lithographic Stone," "Lithographic Varnish," and "Lithography," in Edward H. Knight (ed.) *Knight's American Mechanical Dictionary*, II, 1329–36; Edward Young, "Lithography," in *Leading Pursuits*

a few of those in one major collection which appeared prior to 1840.[21]

During the two decades prior to the Civil War views increased in popularity. It was in the early years of this period that Edwin Whitefield began an extensive series of lithographic city views for which he was both artist and publisher. He also prepared the stones for several of his views, although the printing in all cases was done by others. Beginning in 1845 with Albany and Troy, New York, he published large folio lithographs of such cities as New York, Brooklyn, Boston, Baltimore, Providence, and Cincinnati, in addition to many smaller American towns and several major cities of Canada, including Montreal, Toronto, Quebec, Ottawa, and Kingston. In all, his series contained forty views issued before 1860. At a later period in his life he settled in Massachusetts where he produced several bird's-eye views of towns in the Boston area.[22]

Another series of city views was produced at this same time by August Köllner under the title, *Views of American Cities*. His fifty-four small lithographs included many non-urban scenes, and those of cities are mainly of monuments, public buildings, and partial street scenes, rather than views of entire cities. Köllner was a German who came to America as early as 1839. He settled in Philadelphia and did work for, among other firms, Huddy & Duval. All fifty-four views were apparently put on stone in Paris by Deroy and published by Goupil & Co. of Paris and New York. These views have copyright dates from 1848 to 1851.[23]

Although all of Whitefield's views prior to the Civil War continued the tradition of showing the cities from a slightly elevated position, other artists began to produce views that depicted cities as if seen from a point high overhead. One early example was drawn and printed by John Bachmann of New York in 1851. It showed the then separate cities of New York and Brooklyn as seen from the south and high enough in the sky so that one can see details of buildings throughout the two cities in addition to those in the foreground.[24]

---

and Leading Men; and "Lithography," *History of American Manufacturers, I: 1800–1860*, 252. Modern treatments of the development of lithographic techniques include Peter C. Marzio, "American Lithographic Technology before the Civil War," in John D. Morse, ed., *Prints in and of America*, 215–256 and Carey, "The American Lithograph." The most detailed discussion of contemporary lithographic methods can be found in Garo Z. Antreasian and Clinton Adams, *The Tamarind Book of Lithography: Art and Techniques*.

[21] Views mentioned are all in the Stokes Collection and are listed and described under the appropriate date in Stokes and Haskell. I have not made an effort to list additional lithographic city views prior to 1840, but there were many others.

[22] A partial list of Whitefield's views appears in Stokes and Haskell, 94–96. Material on his life and work, together with a checklist of his known views is provided in Bettina A. Norton, "Edwin Whitefield, 1816–1892," *Antiques*, CII (August, 1972), 232–43. A forthcoming book on Whitefield by Mrs. Norton will contain additional information on this pioneering artist and publisher of American lithographic views. See also Carey, "The American Lithograph," 392–404.

[23] Wainwright, *Philadelphia*, 81; Stokes and Haskell, 87, 99–100. The last page cited has a list of the Köllner views. For a biographical sketch, a treatment of his work and a partial checklist of his lithographs, see Carey, "The American Lithograph," 303–14.

[24] If any biographical material on Bachmann exists, I have not been able to locate it. On his prints the final letter of his name is occasionally omitted. I suspect that he was German and came to this country with some training and experience as a lithographer during the great wave of German migration to America in 1848. He had ties with European lithographers. His view of New Orleans in 1850 was printed in Paris by Aug. Bry. Another view of New York of c. 1850 was printed by the Lemercier firm in Paris. Old Print Shop, *Portfolio*, I (June, 1942), 20. C. Bachman is identified as having drawn from nature and on stone a splendid view of New York looking south from a point above Union Square. This print lists John Bachmann as publisher in New York, with the date of 1849. I have not found a lithograph with any earlier date bearing Bachmann's name. The 1849 view is in the Prints and Photographs Division of the Library of Congress. It was

Bachmann did other views of New York in the same style, as well as similar large folio views of Philadelphia, Hoboken, and Boston before the Civil War.[25] Doubtless a more complete list of his early views in this country would be far more impressive, but in terms of their quality, attention to detail, fine color, and attractive composition they are unsurpassed in their field.

Rivaling Bachmann's work in appearance and, perhaps, even more numerous, were the views published from 1848 to 1857 by the Smith Brothers. Most of these were from drawings by John William Hill, the son of the aquatint engraver, or by one of the four Smith Brothers, Benjamin Franklin Smith, Jr. At least one, that of Bangor, Maine in 1854, was drawn by Charles Parsons who was later to do many of the large folio city views published by Currier and Ives, including those of Chicago (Plate 46), St. Louis (Plate 45), and San Francisco. The Smith Brothers firm was responsible for at least twenty handsome views, and possibly as many as thirty. Appearing in their series were prints of Albany, Buffalo, Cincinnati, Portsmouth, New Hampshire, Oswego, New York, Philadelphia, Bangor, Milwaukee, Richmond, New Haven, Cleveland, Newark, New York, Utica, Rochester, and Salem, Massachusetts.[26]

During the period when the Smith Brothers were publishing their large and handsome views, John B. Bachelder of Boston was working on a series of views of towns in New England, and the much smaller but quite delightful views of Mississippi Valley towns drawn by Henry Lewis a decade earlier were published in Germany during the years 1854–57.[27] The seventy-eight Lewis views and the thirty-four views of many of the same towns drawn in 1841–42 by John Caspar Wild provide an excellent pictorial record of early urban development along the great river transportation corridor of

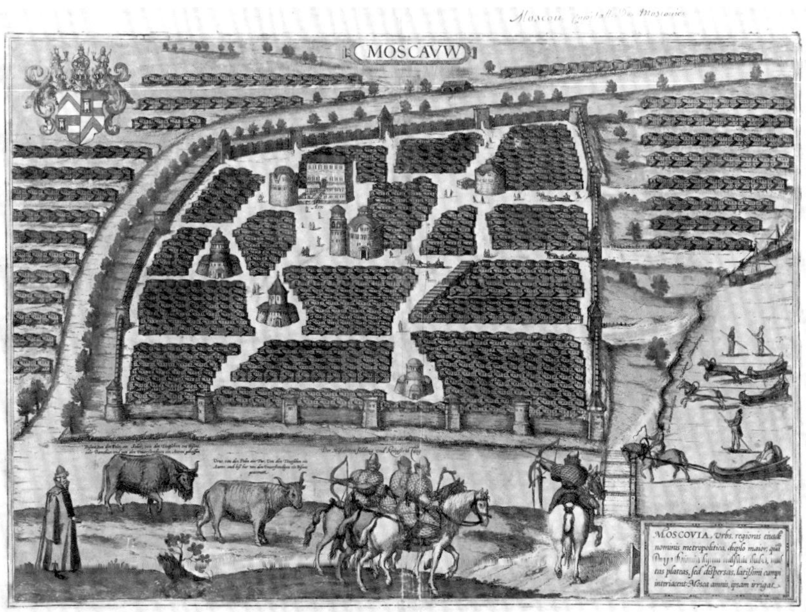

FIGURE 3. *Moscow*. Georg Braun and Franz Hogenberg. 1575, in *Civitas Orbis Terrarum*. Copper engraving (hand colored). 13-3/4 x 19-1/4 in. (34.9 x 48.9 cm.) Courtesy Collection of Professor John W. Reps.

printed by Sarony & Major. Stokes and Haskell list what is apparently the same view but with a slightly different imprint listing Williams & Stevens as publishers, and with J. Bachman as having entered it for copyright. Stokes and Haskell state that this is the second state of the view, and that there was a third state with the copyright date changed to 1850. Stokes and Haskell, 102.

[25] The Philadelphia view was published by John Weik and printed by P. S. Duval & Son, both of Philadelphia, in 1857. It was printed in colors and measures 26-1/2 x 35-3/4 inches. One of the few recorded impressions is in the collection of the Historical Society of Pennsylvania. The original colored drawing on which the lithograph was based is in the Free Library of Philadelphia. This view is Number 28 of the checklist of Philadelphia lithographs in Wainwright, *Philadelphia*.

[26] The estimate of twenty to thirty views is from a statement by Harry Shaw Newman in The Old Print Shop, *Portfolio*, XIII (January, 1954), 99. My own partial list is compiled from issues of the *Portfolio* and from those listed in Stokes and Haskell. The Smith Brothers were from Maine and were involved in their print business only from 1848 to 1857. The business panic in 1857 forced them to abandon this enterprise and seek their fortunes in

the Mississippi.[28] Wild was also responsible for many earlier views of Philadelphia, including a four-sheet panorama of the city in 1838.[29]

One additional artist and publisher of eastern city views who flourished in this period was Edward Sachse of Baltimore. In addition to publishing, apparently from his own drawings, several fine views of Baltimore, Sachse executed many splendid views of Washington, D.C. In his 1852 view of that city is a note that it was printed in colors, one of the early city views to be so published. His superb view of Georgetown, c. 1855, was also a fine example of multi-stone color printing. Sachse published other views of such cities as Harrisburg and York, Pennsylvania before the Civil War.[30]

Thus, when the rapid settlement of the American West began in the middle of the nineteenth century there were many artists and publishers producing city views in ever-increasing numbers. Most began to include western town and city views among their publications, but they soon faced competition from newly-organized western publishing firms, notably those established in San Francisco shortly after the Gold Rush. Other publishers in such cities as Cincinnati, St. Louis, Milwaukee, Chicago, and Madison also entered the market before and after the Civil War.[31]

The first urban views showing the effect of the California Gold Rush came from the presses of established eastern publishers. Possibly the earliest was the long panorama of San Francisco by Henry Firks that Thomas Sinclair issued in Philadelphia in 1849. This print was copied by others and re-issued in later years, a practice not uncommon in the world of nineteenth-century American publishing. A year later Nathaniel Currier, always on the lookout for a dramatic event as the subject for a lithograph, published William McMurtrie's

the West. Brief notice of their publishing venture and a fuller account of their highly successful later careers can be found in William J. Hartford, *Benjamin Franklin Smith: A Biography of One of Maine's Successful Americans*; and John Paul Heffernan, "A Maine Family of Smiths," *Down East: The Magazine of Maine*, XXI (April, 1975), 36–41, 66–70. A note on B. F. Smith, Jr.'s view of Philadelphia after a drawing by Smith and J. W. Hill appears in Stefanie A. Munsing, *Made in America: Printmaking 1760–1860: An Exhibition of Original Prints from the Collections of The Library Company of Philadelphia and The Historical Society of Pennsylvania, April-June, 1973*, 69. Ms. Munsing's exhibition catalog is a helpful supplement to Wainwright, *Philadelphia*.

[27] The Batchelder view of Brattleboro, Vermont, in 1856 is in the Stokes Collection. Stokes and Haskell, 119. The brief note on him in Peters, *America on Stone*, 82, does not mention any of his city views. I do not know of a checklist of his work. The views of Lewis are most readily available in modern reproduction. See Henry Lewis, *The Valley of the Mississippi Illustrated*, translated by A. Hermina Poatgieter and edited with an introduction and notes by Bertha L. Heilbron. Many of the views are listed by Stokes and Haskell, 98–99, and two copies of the complete series are in the New York Public Library. The Lewis sketch books are in the collection of the Missouri Historical Society.

[28] Wild's views have also been reproduced. See J. C. Wild, *The Valley of the Mississippi Illustrated in a Series of Views*. Lewis Foulk Thomas, ed. Material on his life and work in the West can also be found in Carey, "The American Lithograph," 405–17; John Francis McDermott, "J. C. Wild, Western Painter and Lithographer," *Ohio State Archaeological and Historical Quarterly*, LX (April, 1951), 111–25; and McDermott, "John Caspar Wild: Some New Facts and a Query," *Pennsylvania Magazine of History and Biography, LXXXIII (October,* 1959), 452–55. A complete set of the original Wild lithographs are in the collection of the State Historical Society of Missouri, Columbia.

[29] Wild's career in Philadelphia is the subject of Martin P. Snyder's "J. C. Wild and his Philadelphia Views," *Pennsylvania Magazine of History and Biography*, LXXVII (January, 1953), 32–75. Reproductions of the north, east, south, and west views comprising the panorama can be found in Wainwright, *Philadelphia*.

[30] The Library of Congress and the Peale Museum and Maryland Historical Society in Baltimore have significant numbers of Sachse views. Those of Baltimore and elsewhere in Maryland are listed, described, and illustrated in Lois B. McCauley, *Maryland Historical Prints, 1752 to 1889*. For a note on Sachse and the firm's work see McCauley, 232–34 and Peters, *America on Stone*, 348–49. No complete checklist of the Sachse city views exists. In addition to views of Baltimore, Annapolis, Hagerstown, Frederick, Ellicotts Mills, Georgetown, and Washington, Sachse also issued views of

lively scene of San Francisco in 1850 showing the crowded harbor, the sandy streets, the hastily-constructed buildings, and the incomparable physical setting as the artist sketched it from atop Telegraph Hill.[32]

George Cooper's fascinating panorama of the Sacramento waterfront in 1849 (Plate 3) also appeared in 1850, the work of the Endicott firm in New York. It was from this bustling supply center that miners were fanning out into the stream valleys cutting the western slopes of the Sierras where new gold strikes were reported almost daily. While Monterey (Plate 4) lay well south of the gold area, Thomas Larkin rushed two views of the town in 1842 to the firm of Francis D'Avignon in New York to be printed in 1850. Copies of all of these early views were doubtless eagerly purchased by Easterners curious about the look of the new Eldorado on the Pacific Coast.

It was not only Americans who clamored for news about and pictures of the gold region and its towns. S. F. (Frank) Marryat's superb scene of the streets of San Francisco (Plate 5) must have found a ready market in England when the London firm of Henry Squire and Company put copies up for sale on July 1, 1851 at their Cockspur Street shop. French and German versions of the Cooper view of Sacramento were also issued, among others, to satisfy residents of the continent.

Illustrations of many of the mining camps, some of them destined to have but a brief life, others to develop into permanent communities, seem to have appeared first on letter sheets used by the forty-niners to describe and show friends and relatives in the east the appearance of their crude surroundings.[33] Soon, however, artists and publishers who had followed the Gold Rush to California began issuing larger, more detailed, and better executed single-sheet lithographic views of the camps, the supply centers, and San Francisco.

George Goddard, an English architect and engineer, failed to strike it rich as a miner and turned his artistic talents to drawing lettersheet views. At least two of them, Sonora and Columbia, were also issued in a larger

---

St. Louis. Impressions of the latter can be found in the Missouri Historical Society.

[31] Prior to the Gold Rush new urban settlements in the West could be found in Texas, Oregon, and Utah. Following the Mexican War, American settlers began to filter into such communities of Hispanic origins as San Antonio, Santa Fe, Los Angeles, San Diego, San Jose, Santa Barbara, and Sonoma. At such places as Monterey and Yerba Buena, later to be renamed San Francisco, there had been some Anglo settlers previously, as there doubtless had been in several other Spanish or Mexican borderland towns. Apparently no large views of these communities were published at this time in America. Small illustrations of Santa Fe and San Diego in 1846 appear in W. H. Emory's *Notes of a Military Reconnaissance from Fort Leavenworth in Missouri, to San Diego in California*. Two views in etching and aquatint of an abortive settlement in Texas by a group of French military officers were published in France in 1830. They are reproduced in Fannie Elizabeth Ratchford, ed., *The Story of Champ d'Asile as told by Two of the Colonists*. Two different views are in the collection of the Amon Carter Museum. Sir Henry James Warre included an 1846 view of Oregon City (Plate 2) in his Sketches in *North America and the Oregon Territory*. This lithograph, also in the Amon Carter Museum collection, bears the title, "The American Village." For a reproduction of the original watercolor sketch, titled "American Settlement, Willametta River, called Oregon City," see the 1970 Imprint Society reprint of Warre's sketchbook: *Sketches in North America and the Oregon Territory, by Captain H. Warre, A. D. C. to the Late Commander of the Forces*, with an Introduction by Archibald Hanna, Jr., Plate 59. A lithograph view of the Russian settlement in California at Fort Ross was published in Auguste Bernard Duhaut-Cilly, *Voyage autour de Monde*, Paris, 1833.

[32] The Firks view is identified as "the earliest . . . of the early printed views of San Francisco after the discovery of gold," in Stokes and Haskell, 104. For their note on two lithographs of San Francisco published before the Gold Rush, see 146–47. For William B. McMurtrie and several other artists whose paintings or drawings were issued in lithographic form see Paul Mills, ed., *Early Paintings of California in the Robert B. Honeyman, Jr. Collection*.

[33] An authoritative study of these sources of pictorial information is Joseph Armstrong Baird, Jr., *California's Pictorial Letter Sheets, 1849–1869*

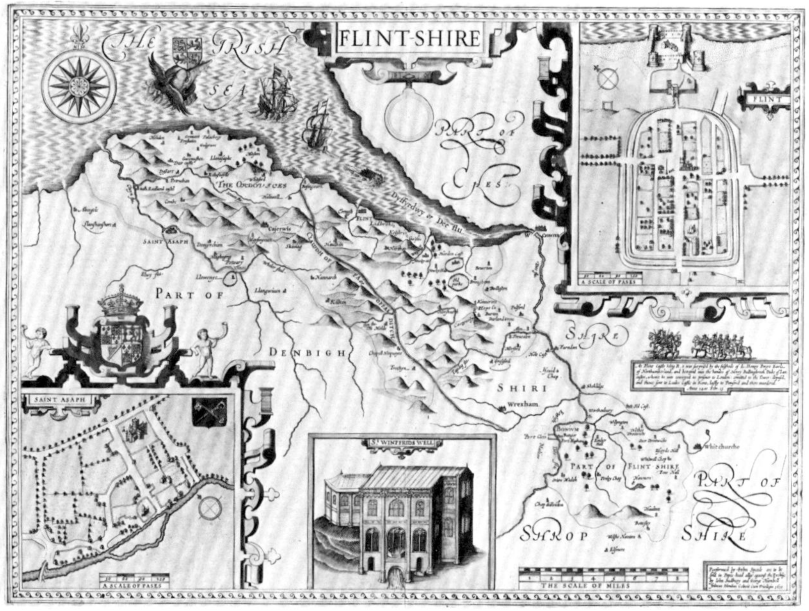

FIGURE 4. *Flint-Shire.* John Speed. 1611, in *The Theatre of the Empire of Great Britain.* Copper engraving (hand colored). 15-1/4 x 20-3/16 in. (38.7 x 51.3 cm.) Courtesy Collection of Professor John W. Reps.

format by Pollard and Britton (later Britton and Rey) of San Francisco in 1852. Goddard sketched Columbia from a hill overlooking the town not long after thousands of miners had crowded into the location following the discovery of one of the Sierra's greatest gold deposits. Among the buildings, Goddard may have included a drug and general store of which he was part owner—a fact suggesting that in frontier California an artist needed a supplementary source of income.[34]

Dozens of other mining towns were the subjects for a splendid series of lithographs published by Charles Kuchel and Emil Dresel and printed by Britton and Rey beginning in 1856. Their views of such places as Forrest Hill (Plate 6), St. Louis (Plate 7), Union (Plate 8), Todd's Valley (Plate 9), and Shasta (Plate 10), allow the modern viewer to understand, as no printed word could, what it was like to have been part of this unique episode in our history.[35]

Kuchel and Dresel included a number of older towns in their series of California views: Santa Clara, San Jose (Plate 11) and Los Angeles (Plate 12). The latter prints, like several others, appeared in two versions. One, perhaps the earlier, omitted the border vignettes of individual buildings. In 1858 they also issued large folio views of Vancouver, Washington and the principal settlements

---

[34] Goddard's career is traced in Albert Shumate, *The Life of George Henry Goddard: Artist, Architect, Surveyor, and Map Maker.* Goddard compiled a detailed and accurate map of California in 1857, did views of San Francisco in 1860 and 1868, prepared maps of portions of Los Angeles County, San Francisco, and Fresno County, painted many pictures of California scenes, helped to survey the route of the transcontinental railroad, and designed the South Park neighborhood in San Francisco among other achievements of his long and varied life. His collection of five hundred drawings and paintings and six hundred maps, in addition to an extensive library of books, notes, and journals, was destroyed in the earthquake and fire of 1906 while negotiations for their purchase by Stanford University were still in progress. Goddard died a few months later at the age of eighty-nine.

[35] A list of the Kuchel and Dresel lithographs issued together as *Kuchel & Dresel's California Views,* but also sold separately, can be found in Stokes and Haskell, 123. These were reproduced in 1936. See Douglas S. Watson, *California in the Fifties: Fifty Views of Cities and Mining Towns in California and the West.* The firm appears to have listed themselves as publishers on one edition of the prints and to have issued others bearing the imprints of local publishers. One example is the 1857 view of Auburn, California. The Amon Carter Museum impression lacks the border views and has only the name of Kuchel and Dresel as lithographers along with Britton & Rey as printers. The impression in the Society of California Pioneers has border views and the name of W. K. Parkinson of Auburn as publisher. The two versions of the Los Angeles view have similar differences in their imprints. However, the views of Santa Clara and San Jose, both with border views, include "Published by Kuchel & Dresel." A detailed study of the variant states in this firm's city views would be helpful. A note on the firm and a list of many of their lithographs, in addition to city views, can be found in Harry T. Peters, *California on Stone,* 141–51.

of Oregon: Portland, Oregon City (Plate 13), Salem, The Dalles (Plate 14), and Eugene. All of their views were drawn from a slightly elevated position rather than from a point high in the air which was soon to become the popular mode of depicting cities.

Among the many San Francisco publishers of city views, a few stand out because of the volume or quality of their work. Britton and Rey, the printers of the Kuchel and Dresel series, published George H. Baker's enormous toned lithograph of Sacramento in 1857. When compared to Cooper's view less than a decade earlier, this splendid toned print reveals the incredible speed with which this important supply and mercantile center had grown. In 1868 the firm's name appears on two views of San Francisco, one unsigned, the other by George Goddard (Plate 15), showing the now greatly expanded city from a point high in the air over the Pacific Ocean.[36]

In later years the firm published or printed for others several California and Nevada views drawn by Augustus Koch, an accomplished and prolific artist of such subjects. Of Koch, like so many of his fellows, little or nothing is known. His first recorded views date from 1870: Cheyenne and Salt Lake City, published by the artist; and Stockton (Plate 16) and Sacramento (Plate 17), issued by Britton and Rey. The latter two are represented in the Amon Carter Museum collection by a unique double impression, with one view on each of the two sides of a single sheet. The firm published Koch's California views of Vallejo, Petaluma, Woodland, Nevada City and Los Angeles in 1871, and those of the Nevada communities of Virginia City in 1875 and Carson City in 1876.[37]

Another major San Francisco printing house producing bird's-eye views was the firm of A. L. Bancroft & Co. They were responsible for the lithographic work of the West Coast views drawn by Eli S. Glover, who published most of his own views as well as a few later views of Michigan cities drawn by Albert Ruger. Glover's California, Oregon, and Washington views were all done during the years 1876–79. Those of San Diego, Santa Barbara (Plate 18), and Los Angeles are of special importance, capturing those cities at the time of the first major real estate boom in Southern California. Glover also produced clear, well-composed, and attractive depictions of Victoria, British Columbia, and of Portland, Salem, Seattle, Tacoma, and Olympia (Plate 19), among others in the Pacific Northwest. In the foreground of his Olympia view one can see a tiny figure seated before an

---

[36] The numerous views of San Francisco are described and listed, with many large facsimiles, in Joseph Armstrong Baird and Edwin Clyve Evans, *Historic Lithographs of San Francisco.*

[37] A reproduction of the City of Nevada, California, view can be found in Peters, *California on Stone*, Plate 20. The last city view to bear the name of Britton & Rey that I have been able to locate is a large folio, unsigned lithograph of Fresno, California, in 1901. It was copyrighted by L. W. Klein, who may have been its publisher. There is an impression in the Geography and Map Division of the Library of Congress. It may be helpful to provide a list of the Koch views that I have found. It is almost certainly incomplete. They were published by a variety of firms, and some do not carry a publisher's credit line. My list is presented chronologically to give some idea of the peripatetic life Koch and his fellow city view-makers lived: Cheyenne, Salt Lake City, Sacramento, and Stockton, 1870; Los Angeles and Vallejo, 1871; Austin and San Antonio, 1873; Lincoln and Columbus, Nebraska, 1874; Virginia City, 1875; Carson City, Jacksonville, Florida, and Omaha, 1876; Leadville, Colorado, 1879; Nebraska City and Lincoln, Nebraska, Topeka, and Atchison, Kansas, 1880; Brenham, Cuero and New Braunfels, Texas, 1881; Lincoln and Galveston, 1885; San Antonio and Albuquerque, 1886; Austin, 1887; Norfolk and Seattle, 1891; Atlanta, 1892; Jacksonville, Florida, 1893; Kansas City, 1895; and Pensacola, 1896. The several gaps in this record of production strongly suggest that there were many other Koch views. There is an undated view by Koch of Oakland, California, printed by Britton and Rey and published by Snow and Roos. An impression of this can be found in the collection of the Society of California Pioneers which also has Koch's views of the City of Nevada, Oakland, and Woodland, California.

easel, doubtless a self-portrait of the artist. Many of his other views have similar foreground figures which add to the interest and appeal of his prints.[38]

On his way to the West Coast, Glover prepared views of several towns and cities of Colorado, Utah, Montana, and Wyoming during the years 1873–74. He had two of these printed in Chicago, but the remainder were produced at the firm of Strobridge and Company of Cincinnati. Four, all in Colorado and dated 1873 or 1874, appeared in similar format: Central City (Plate 20), Georgetown (Plate 21), Colorado Springs (Plate 22), and Pueblo. The Denver view of 1874 and those of Ogden, Brigham City, and Salt Lake City, Utah in 1875 more closely resemble those Glover was to begin publishing on the West Coast in 1876.

Whether this represents a stylistic change on the part of Glover, or, equally likely, decisions made by the lithographer in putting Glover's drawings on stone or the printer's choice of format and appearance, cannot be determined. It is, in fact, almost impossible to discuss the "style" of a particular city view artist in this period because in almost all cases a lithographer stood between him and the finished print. Even where the artist served as his own lithographer, as was apparently true of Thaddeus Fowler, changes were made in the original drawing as it was transposed to the stone. We need to know far more than we do now about which artists, lithographers, and publishers combined to produce urban views with certain distinguishing characteristics.

Well before the time when Glover travelled from the Midwest to Colorado and the Great Basin, the swift pace of settlement had dotted the plains and mountains with hundreds of new towns. Kansas and Nebraska had been thrown open to white occupancy in the mid-1850s and there seemed to be as much interest among the settlers in the platting of towns as in breaking the stubborn prairie sod for farming. In promoting these real estate ventures the officials of many townsite companies enlisted the aid of artists and lithographers to draw and print real or fanciful views of their projected cities.

One example is the beautifully executed, unsigned view of Sumner, Kansas in 1857 (Plate 23), printed and published by Middleton, Strobridge and Company in Cincinnati. This was evidently widely displayed in the East to promote real estate sales. One young Bostonian, John J. Ingalls, lured to the place by this view of an apparently flourishing city, wrote to his father in disgust shortly after his arrival. The supposed metropolis, he complained, consisted only of a "few log huts and miserable cabins." The printed view Ingalls dismissed as a "lithographic fiction," and an "engraved romance."[39]

---

[38] The other views by Glover printed by the Bancroft firm that I have found are of Santa Rosa, San Luis Obispo, San Buenaventura (Ventura), Healdsburg and Russian River Valley, and Anaheim—all in California. In addition to those mentioned in the text, Glover also published Washington views of Port Townsend and Walla Walla. Bancroft also printed his view of Helena, Montana, in 1875, published by D. K. Wells of Helena. Biographical material on Glover has proved as elusive as that for Koch. The earliest lithographs with his name as the artist are four views of small towns in Michigan published in 1870. He also is listed as publisher in 1868 of five other Michigan views drawn by Albert Ruger. He drew two additional Michigan views in 1872 and 1873, and a view of London, Ontario, in 1872. The 1872 view of Saline, Michigan, was printed by Strobridge and Company of Cincinnati, a firm that Glover was to employ shortly to print at least eight views of Colorado and Utah in the years 1873–75. Glover's last recorded view is of Port Arthur, Texas, in 1912, an impression being in the Geography and Map Division of the Library of Congress. Information on Glover's Michigan output is from John Cumming, *19th Century Lithographs*. The Library of Congress collection also has Glover views of Anniston, Alabama, in 1888 and Muskegon, Michigan, in 1889.

[39] Letter from Ingalls, October 5, 1858, Kansas State Historical Society, *Collections*, XIV (1915–18), 100. The same firm published similar views of Leavenworth and Lawrence in 1858 and Tecumseh in 1859. The latter view

More accurate depictions of Kansas and Nebraska towns began to appear after the Civil War. It was here that Alfred Mathews, later to become better known for his sets of lithographs of Colorado and Montana, produced his earliest city views. This first work consisted of four views in 1865 of Nebraska City, an important port on the Missouri River through which passed much of the freight and many of the settlers swarming westward. Mathews drew in a rather mechanical style, and his prints are not very rewarding if looked on as works of art. They are, however, of considerable historic importance, recording as they do scenes from the first decade of settlement of Nebraska and the opening up of Colorado and Montana. First issued separately and then gathered together in his *Pencil Sketches of Colorado*, published in 1866, his views of Denver and many small Colorado mining towns show the communities as they emerged from their frontier phase.

His *Pencil Sketches of Montana*, issued in 1868, contained thirty-one views, that of Virginia City being the most important of those showing urban settings.[40] Mathews must have found it difficult to make a living as an artist, for in 1869 he purchased a large ranch near Cañon City to begin raising cattle. To promote the area, he prepared five views, one showing the town and the others the scenery of the vicinity. By the winter of 1872–73 he decided to resume his artistic endeavors and prepared at least three views of cities in Southern California: San Diego, Los Angeles, and Santa Barbara.[41] Evidently these represent his last efforts at lithography, and after his return to Colorado Mathews died in 1874.

More revealing of the patterns and the extent of growth of these new communities on the western prairies were the bird's-eye views drawn by Albert Ruger in the 1860s. Ruger began his artistic career while a mem-

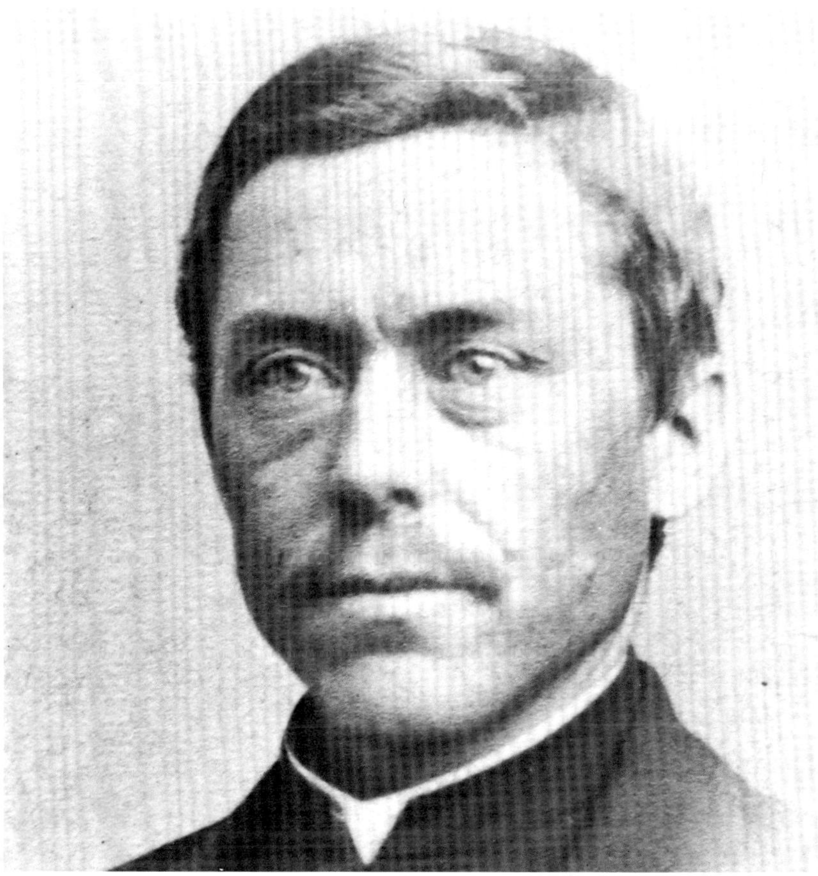

Alfred E. Mathews (1831–1874).
Courtesy Library, The State Historical Society of Colorado, Denver.

seems to have anticipated actual development in much the same manner as that of Sumner. Those of Leavenworth and Lawrence are apparently more realistic, although the Leavenworth view includes a large, domed building that was probably intended to represent the territorial capitol Leavenworth so badly wanted but did not get. Impressions of the Tecumseh and Sumner views are in the collection of the Kansas State Historical Society, Topeka, and that of Leavenworth is owned by the Leavenworth Historical Society.

[40] For the work of this artist whose energy exceeded his talents, see Robert Taft, *Artists and Illustrators of the Old West, 1850–1900*, 72–85. Taft reproduces two of the Nebraska City views and six of those of Colorado.

[41] His California views are rare. Impressions of those of San Diego and Los

ber of the Ohio Volunteers in the Civil War. In 1866, travelling extensively from his home in Battle Creek, Michigan, he started an itinerant life that would take him through most of the eastern half of the nation sketching city views. He worked with incredible speed, producing the drawings for more than sixty cities in 1869 alone and being responsible for well over two hundred of them during his lifetime.[42]

Typical of his work is the view of Omaha in 1868 (Plate 24). The city appears as a gigantic gridiron of streets extending westward from the banks of the Missouri River. Every building is shown in perspective, with the details of major structures clear and precise. As the designated eastern terminal of the Union Pacific whose transcontinental lines were to be completed the following year, Omaha was then in the midst of a building and commercial boom, and the river bank was already being pre-empted by industrial and warehouse activities that could be served both by rail and river steamboats which still remained an important element in the region's transportation system. Linked to the decorative border at the bottom is a little scene of Indian life, recalling the days before white settlement began.

In his Hannibal, Missouri view of the following year (Plate 25) Ruger provides us with many additional details of life in these river towns. In the foreground one can see the railroad station on the Illinois side of the Mississippi with its steam ferry and Concord coaches waiting for or delivering passengers at the depot. In the river is a great log raft with its steering sweeps to guide its passage to the lumber mills of Hannibal or some other river port further downstream. Beyond lies the river landing where Mark Twain a few years earlier contracted his incurable case of steamboat fever.

Every building of the town itself, from the commercial structures and churches around the public square to the smallest dwelling at the outskirts is drawn with careful detail and apparent accuracy. To the left can be seen the line of the Hannibal and St. Joe railroad providing connections with the Union Pacific and which the citizens of Hannibal confidently expected would make their town a second St. Louis or Chicago. In this, as in most of Ruger's other views, the colors are printed through the use of multiple lithographic stones, each inked with a single color and carefully registered on the paper by a system of pins as the sheets were passed through the lithographic press. This printing technique is more easily seen by examining Ruger's 1896 view of McGregor, Iowa (Plate 26), childhood home of the Ringling Brothers of circus fame. Only three stones were used for this lithograph, and each color is clearly discernible. A black-inked stone produced the shaded drawing; a second stone,

---

Angeles are in the collection of the Nevada Historical Society, Reno, and that of Santa Barbara can be found in the Bancroft Library, University of California, Berkeley.

[42] Ruger was born in Prussia in 1829 and died in Akron, Ohio at the age of seventy-one in November, 1899. Akron *Beacon Journal*, November 13, 1899, and Hudson, Ohio *Independent*, November 17, 1899 obituaries, as supplied to me by John Cumming from information furnished him by the Akron Public Library and Historical Society. I am indebted to Mr. Cumming also for providing me with his typescript paper, "Albert Ruger and His Views." Ruger's career is also briefly treated in Hébert, *Panoramic Maps*, 5, and Cumming, *19th Century Lithographs*, iii. Many of Ruger's views were published by Joseph J. Stoner of Madison, Wisconsin and by Stoner and Ruger, in partnership. As has already been noted, Glover also published a few of Ruger's early views. These lithographs were printed by many firms, including Charles Shober and Louis Kurz of Chicago, C. H. Vogt and Beck & Pauli of Milwaukee, Ehrgott & Krebs of Cincinnati, Schmidt & Trowe of Baltimore, and several others. The efforts by Cumming and Hébert to locate additional material on Ruger have been discouraging, and it is quite possible that there are no other surviving records of this prolific artist. Many of his personal copies of the views are now in the Geography and Map Division of the Library of Congress.

inked in a buff color, blocked in the areas representing land; and a third stone, almost completely covered with blue ink, provided the over-all tone of the print. In the finished lithograph, the eye is drawn to the light-colored topographical features Ruger wanted to emphasize—a few rocky outcroppings, the white-faced buildings of McGregor, and the pattern of streets and roads which gave structure to the town.[43]

Railroad building across the continent further stimulated the publication of city views. Some publishers issued lithographs of the towns that sprang up along the tracks hoping to sell them to their new residents. Others were probably subsidized by the railroads themselves in efforts to promote settlement in these towns, many of which had been planned by their subsidiary townsite companies. It is difficult to believe, for example, that prospects for sales of town views to residents would have justified publication of the numerous lithographs issued in the 1880's by Joseph J. Stoner of several tiny railroad communities in the Dakotas, Colorado, and Montana.[44]

If it was Stoner's practice to obtain publishing subsidies from railroad or real estate interests, he was probably not alone. However, most of his views were doubtless produced at his risk or after soliciting subscriptions in a manner that will presently be described. Stoner employed or had associated with him several artists, Ruger being one of the more important. Many of the prints issued by Stoner, such as those of Butte, Montana in 1884 (Plate 27) and Cheyenne, Wyoming in 1882, were unsigned, but a number have a close stylistic resemblance to those bearing the signature of Henry Wellge. Wellge's views of Fort Worth in 1891 (Plate 28), Honey Grove, Texas in 1886, Seattle and Tacoma in 1884 (Plate 29), and Billings, Montana in 1904 (Plate 30), are typical examples of his work.

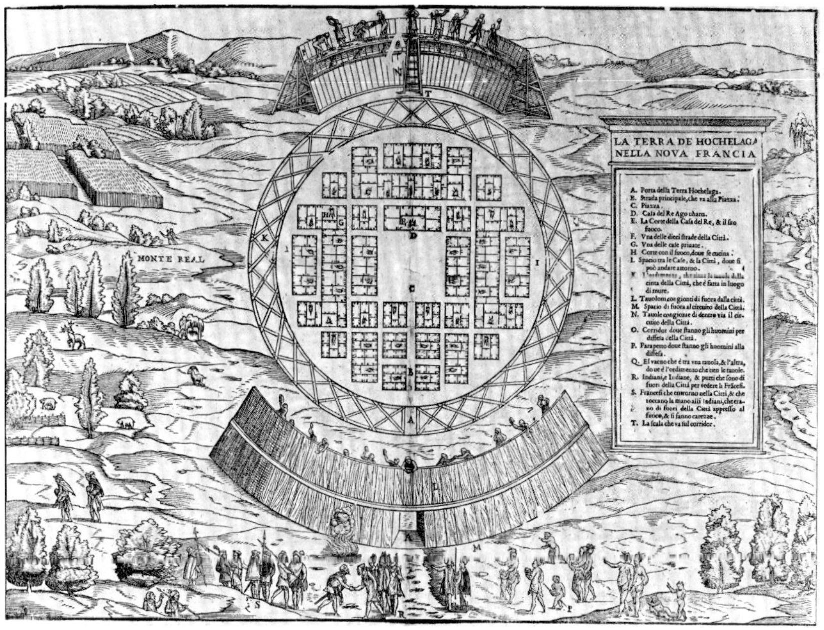

FIGURE 5. *La Terra De Hochelaga Nella Nova Francia.* Giovanni Battista Ramusio. 1556, in *Delle Navigationi e Viaggi.* Woodcut (hand colored). 10-5/8 x 14-1/2 in. (27.0 x 36.8 cm.) Courtesy Amon Carter Museum.

[43] Ruger's views are too numerous to list here. Many of them can be found in Hébert, *Panoramic Maps*, and Cumming, *19th Century Lithographs*, but a complete checklist compiled from records in other collections or states would doubtless reveal many others. The several Ruger views in the Wisconsin Historical Society collection, however, are duplicated in the Library of Congress. I am indebted to Elizabeth Singer Maule, Map Curator of the Society, for providing me with a preliminary and unpublished list of their holdings of city views.

[44] For example, Stoner published a view of Clark, South Dakota, in 1883. He used the following subtitle: "A Town of One Years Growth." The town then consisted of fewer than eighty structures, and the legend identifies the location of several "proposed" buildings, including a courthouse, two churches, and a "Flouring Mill." Stoner could not possibly have sold enough views in the town to meet his expenses, let alone a profit, and it seems highly unlikely that anyone in another location would have wanted a view of this infant settlement. A lithograph view of Frederick, South Dakota, virtually identical in size, format, and style, but not bearing

The Billings print was published in Milwaukee by Wellge himself. Earlier, he was associated with the firm of Norris, Wellge & Co., much of whose printing was done by Beck & Pauli of Milwaukee who also printed many of the views published by Stoner. The American Publishing Company of Milwaukee, which issued Wellge's Fort Worth view, published several similar lithographs in the years 1888–92, and this short-lived but productive enterprise probably was an outgrowth of the several earlier lithographic printing and publishing companies active in Milwaukee, whose presses Stoner in Madison and artists throughout the West kept busy with a constant flow of manuscript town sketches to be put on stone.[45]

Wellge, Koch, and such other city-view artists as Herman Brosius, D. D. Morse, and Thaddeus M. Fowler did not overlook Texas as a potential market for their talents. Working during the period after 1870, they produced drawings to be published by others or, like Fowler, issued their own lithographs from stones prepared by them or under their direction.

This region had been largely ignored by American publishers of views prior to the Civil War, but because of the extensive German population in Texas resulting from the activities of colonization societies from that country, there was some demand in Germany for scenes of Texas towns. In 1855, C. O. Bähr sketched a largely fictitious view of Galveston which was lithographed in Dresden. Five years later Helmuth Holtz did drawings of two other Gulf Coast ports, Indianola and Matagorda, both of which were published in Hamburg.[46]

The finest of these German lithographs of pre-Civil War Texas, however, were the work of Hermann Lungkwitz. Born in Halle, Lungkwitz studied painting in Dresden under Ludwig Richter before fleeing to America in 1849. First settling in New Braunfels in 1851, he moved to a farm near Fredericksburg where he continued to paint. At least two of his paintings of c. 1852 were published in lithographic form in Dresden, probably being issued after 1860. One is an attractive distant view of Fredericksburg, perhaps as Lungkwitz saw it from his home.

Stoner's name, was also issued in 1883. The name of C. F. Campau is given as copyright holder, and his signature also appears at the end of a long paragraph of text extolling the virtues of this tiny settlement which was said to have a population "now numbering about 700 . . . ." Including outbuildings, stores, and the railroad watertower, there are less than 75 structures shown in the view. Campau doubtless contracted with Stoner to print the view for him as an advertising device for use in real estate sales promotion. Both views are in the Geography and Map Division of the Library of Congress. The view of De Smet, South Dakota, in 1883, published by Stoner is also of a very small settlement as is the view of Gary, South Dakota, in the same year. The latter view does not have Stoner's name, but it closely resembles the other views from his firm. It was published by P. A. Catchell, Editor and Proprietor of the Deuel County Advocate. Both of these views are in the collection of the South Dakota State Historical Society, Pierre.

[45] In the Geography and Map Division of the Library of Congress is a view of Fort Worth in 1886, signed by Henry Wellge, published by Norris, Wellge & Co., and printed by Beck & Pauli of Milwaukee. It closely resembles the Fort Worth view of 1891 which also has Wellge's signature. Possibly Wellge's drawing of 1886, owned by Norris, Wellge & Co., was one of the assets transferred to the new company if, as I surmise, it was a successor to the older firm. Among the handsome folio views published by the American Publishing Company, the following are in the Geography and Map Division of the Library of Congress: Davenport, Iowa, and Evansville, Indiana, in 1888; Kearney, Lincoln, and Norfolk, Nebraska; Moline and Rock Island, Illinois; Dubuque, Fort Madison, and Burlington, Iowa; and Denver, Colorado, in 1889; Colorado Springs and Pueblo, Colorado; Helena, Montana, Beloit, Wisconsin, and Ogden, Utah, in 1890; Missoula and Great Falls, Montana; Fort Worth, Texas, Salt Lake City, Utah, and Roanoke, Staunton, Waynesboro, and Buena Vista, Virginia, in 1891; and Laredo, Texas, and Norfolk, Virginia, in 1892. Twelve of these are signed by Wellge: two dated 1888, seven in 1889, two in 1891, and one in 1892.

[46] For a discussion of the Galveston view see Stokes and Haskell, 119–20. It is reproduced in that study as Plate 91-b. The Matagorda view is in the

The other is a superbly executed view of San Antonio as seen from the edge of the city, with the Alamo at the extreme right (Plate 31). Embellishing the print are attractive border vignettes of the several missions in the area and other local scenes. Printed in colors from several stones and with some additional hand coloring, it is a splendid example of lithographic craftsmanship.[47]

When artists of bird's-eye views began their work in Texas in the decade of the 1870s, therefore, they were introducing to that region a type of pictorial representation almost completely novel to its residents. Perhaps Texans were not ready for this new art form. Certainly the fact that few impressions of Texas city views are known suggests that small editions were sufficient to satisfy the demand.

The Herman Brosius view of Dallas in 1872 (Plate 32) is apparently the earliest large and detailed bird's-eye lithograph of a Texas city. Others of that decade—Austin and San Antonio in 1873 by Koch, and Fort Worth in 1876 as drawn by D. D. Morse (Plate 33)—are similar in character and provide valuable information about the appearance of these cities of the southern Great Plains as they began a period of rapid expansion during the last quarter of the nineteenth century.[48]

The material changes that a decade of growth brought to these cities can be appreciated by comparing the earlier views with those drawn by Koch of San Antonio in 1886 and Austin in 1887. San Antonio had grown substantially, and the capital city of the Republic of Texas, planned by Edwin Waller in 1839 under the direction of President Mirabeau Buonoparte Lamar was beginning to fill the generous grid of streets established by its found ers and to use the numerous civic squares and public building sites set aside with such admirable foresight in Austin's original plat.

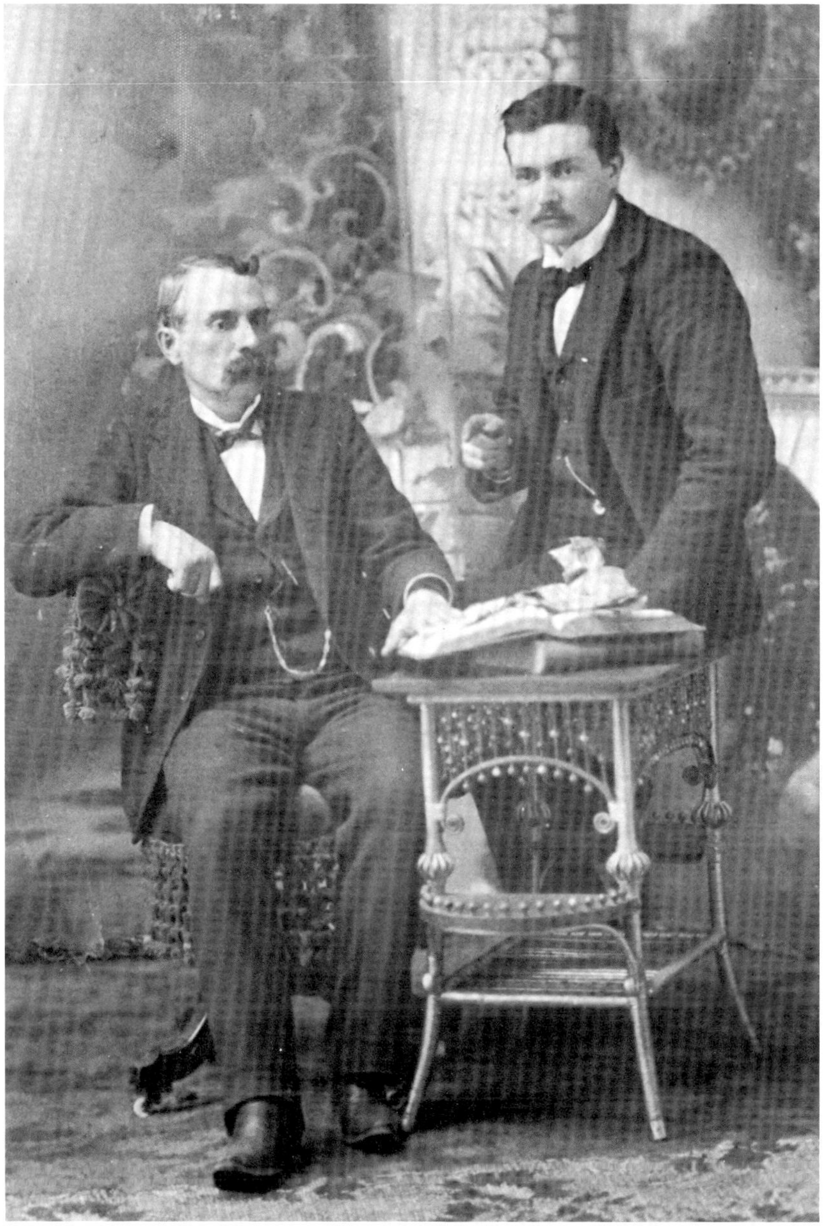

Thaddeus M. Fowler (1842–1922) and photographer J. G. Nestor. Courtesy James Raymond Warren, Sr., Wheaton, Maryland.

Koch also sketched such smaller towns as Brenham, Cuero and New Braunfels in 1881 (Plate 34), adding one of much larger Galveston in 1885 (Plate 35). Henry Wellge must have learned of the growing demand for city views, for he came to Texas to prepare drawings for Paris in 1885 and Waco, Honey Grove, Greenville, Denison, and Fort Worth in 1886, the latter view to be revised to reflect additional changes in 1891 (Plate 28).[49] Several other Texas city views were published in the final decade of the century, including those of Houston (Plate 36), Laredo (Plate 48), Dallas, Waco, Wichita Falls, Denison, Clarendon, Childress, and Quanah (Plate 50). The last five were the work of Thaddeus Fowler, once an artist employed by Stoner who in 1880 established his own company to produce scores of views chiefly in Pennsylvania, West Virginia, and Maryland, but who also was active in Texas, Oklahoma, Virginia, North Carolina and Georgia.[50]

It is to Fowler that we owe much of our knowledge of the appearance of the early towns in Oklahoma. Many had been founded by townsite companies participating in the great land rush of 1889 and had grown in a matter of hours from a few shacks near railroad depots to communities of several thousand persons. The tents and hastily-erected wooden shelters thrown up in the first frantic days of the rush soon were replaced by more substantial buildings of frame, brick, and stone. When Fowler visited Oklahoma City to record its appearance the town was only six months old, but even then it differed little in appearance from communities of greater age and more conventional origins. Many years later Fowler was to return to Oklahoma to draw Tulsa (Plate 37) and Bartlesville, towns that were founded at a later time and under other circumstances.[51]

As the rail lines in the Southwest were extended

Geography and Map Division of the Library of Congress and that of Indianola in the Prints and Photographs Division of the Library of Congress. The Amon Carter Museum collection includes an impression of the Indianola view and a letter sheet view of the hotel at Matagorda by Holtz. *Meyer's Universum*, a multi-volume work published by Hermann J. Meyer in Germany between 1835 and 1860, included views of Galveston, New Braunfels and Salt Lake City. Impressions of these are also in the Amon Carter Museum collection.

[47] The painting from which the lithograph was made is in the Texas Collection, University of Texas Library, Austin. It is reproduced in Kent Keeth, "Sankt Antonius: Germans in the Alamo City in the 1850's." *Southwestern Historical Quarterly*, LXXVI (October, 1972), 183–202. On the cover of that issue is a reproduction in color of another Lungkwitz painting of San Antonio from the collection of Mrs. Ernst Schuchard. In addition to the information on the artist supplied by Keeth, other material on Lungkwitz may be found in Martha Utterback, comp., *Early Texas Art in the Witte Museum*; "Texas in Pictures," *Antiques*, LIII (June, 1948), 486; Samuel E. Gideon, "Two Pioneer Artists in Texas," *American Magazine of Art*, IX (September, 1918), 452–56; and Pauline A. Pinckney, *Painting in Texas: The Nineteenth Century*.

[48] Concerning Brosius and Morse I can provide no information except for what surely is a partial listing of their other views, for they, too, have left no recorded biographical records. Of the fourteen Brosius views in the Geography and Map Division of the Library of Congress, eight were published by Stoner and printed by Beck and Pauli of Milwaukee. He drew views of Shreveport, Louisiana and Jefferson, Texas in 1872, along with that of Dallas. His latest view is dated 1895 and is of St. Thomas, Ontario. All other views are dated 1873–76 or 1881–84. In addition to those mentioned, his views are of Aurora and Mount Vernon, Illinois; Luverne, Minnesota; Jamestown, Olean, and Utica, New York, Flandreau, South Dakota; Waco, Victoria and New Braunfels, Texas; Madison and Delavan, Wisconsin; and Brantford and Ottawa, Ontario. Brosius' 1873 view of Victoria is reproduced in Leopold Morris, *Pictorial History of Victoria and Victoria County*. Views by Morse seem to be less numerous. Other than the Fort Worth lithograph of 1876, I have seen only his views of Golden, Colorado, in 1873 and San Gabriel, California, c. 1893. The former is in the Department of Western History, Denver Public Library, and the latter is in the Geography and Map Division of the Library of Congress. There are doubtless a number of others.

[49] While the Paris and Waco views are not signed, both were published by Norris, Wellge & Co. and were doubtless drawn by Wellge.

[50] Thanks to the indefatigable energy of James Raymond Warren, Sr., of Wheaton, Maryland, a good deal is known of Fowler's career. John Hébert has added to this information and has summarized Fowler's long life as a view publisher in *Panoramic Maps*, 5–8. Hébert reproduces a photographic

through New Mexico and Arizona, new towns sprang up and older settlements experienced renewed growth. Stoner knew that where there were cities there was business, and in 1882 he published two unsigned and similar views of Santa Fe (Plate 38) and Las Vegas, New Mexico. The Santa Fe view reveals the persistence of urban patterns, for the central plaza and rectangular street system that can be seen so clearly were laid out by the Spanish in the first decade of the seventeenth century. Like San Antonio slightly more than a century later, this oldest capital city in the nation had been planned to conform to the Spanish colonial Laws of the Indies, proclaimed by Philip II in 1573, and which prescribed in minute detail every aspect of urban development. The same approach to urban design can be seen in the upper portion of Augustus Koch's rare view of Albuquerque in 1886. That shows the old town in the distance, founded in 1706. It was spared from certain and drastic change by the decision of the railroad engineers to run their tracks several miles away and to establish a completely new town around the depot.

For some reason, artists and publishers seem to have ignored the older settlement of Tucson in Arizona in favor of Prescott (Plate 39), the newly-planned territorial capital, and Phoenix (Plate 40), the city that eventually captured this cherished prize of the seat of government. Both cities were drawn by C. J. Dyer, a person probably doomed to anonymity, but whose two glowingly colored lithographs indicate either that he was an artist of considerable skill or was particularly fortunate in his choice of lithographer and printer. Only the Phoenix view is dated, but 1885 is probably correct for both, and it is equally likely that it was the Schmidt Label and Litho. Co. of San Francisco, identified on the Phoenix view, that printed the one of Prescott as well.

Both are remarkable examples of lithographic printing in multiple stones as well as being wonderfully revealing scenes of frontier towns only just emerging from the struggles of birth and the pangs of early youth. The Phoenix lithograph is particularly appealing with its rustic, elliptical border enclosing the principal view and the

---

portrait of the artist on page 6. The Geography and Map Division of the Library of Congress has over 200 Fowler views. Another significant collection is in the library of Pennsylvania State University, and the Amon Carter Museum owns most of his Texas and Oklahoma views. For a list of his twenty-six Virginia views accompanied by small reproductions, see *West Virginia Hillbilly*, January 25, 1975. Fowler was born at Lowell, Massachusetts, in 1824. Discharged from the Union Army after being wounded at the second battle of Bull Run, he became a photographer and traveled west to work for an uncle in his Madison, Wisconsin, studio. In 1870 he drew and published views of Omro, Sheboygan Falls, and Waupaca, Wisconsin, but his firm, Th. M. Fowler & Co., disbanded within two years and he found employment as an artist with J. J. Stoner's Madison firm. About 1880 he moved to New Jersey, living also in two places in Pennsylvania before settling in Morrisville, Pennsylvania, in 1885. From Morrisville he traveled constantly through Pennsylvania and other eastern states drawing the hundreds of sketches which he then transferred to stone at his studio. In the early 1890s he visited Texas and Oklahoma. In his eightieth year, while drawing Port Jervis, New York, he fell on an icy pavement and died shortly thereafter in 1922. In his later years he was associated from time to time with James B. Moyer, Albert E. Downs, and Oakley H. Bailey. Bailey had a similar career, drawing and publishing hundreds of town views, mainly in New England and New York. He, also, began to draw city views in Madison, moving to Boston in 1874. The largest collection of his work is in the Boston Public Library which has more than 200 of his lithographs. Some seventy of his views are in the Geography and Map Division of the Library of Congress. Bailey retired in 1927, but he lived to the age of 104, dying in 1947 at Alliance, Ohio. Hébert, *Panoramic Maps*, 8.

[51] The Tulsa and Bartlesville views were produced by a photogravure process rather than as lithographs. His earlier lithographic views of Oklahoma places include those of Fort Reno, Edmond, and Ardmore, all of which are in the Amon Carter Museum Collection. The Oklahoma City view is known in only two impressions, one in the Stokes Collection and the other, formerly owned by Thomas Streeter, in the collection of Mr. George Shirk of Oklahoma City.

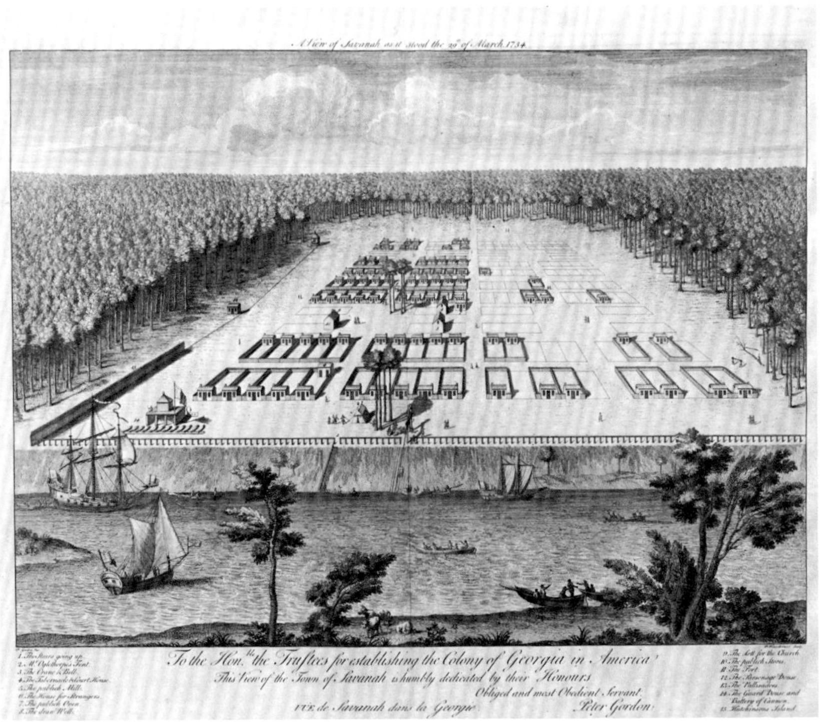

FIGURE 6. *A View of Savanah as it stood the 29th of March. 1734.* Peter Gordon. c. 1734. Engraving. 15-7/8 x 21-7/8 in. (40.3 x 55.5 cm.) Courtesy Amon Carter Museum.

several street scene vignettes around its edges. While the Prescott view is more conventional in composition, it is scarcely less attractive. Its vivid colors help to distinguish the major elements of the town's structure and to emphasize the great central square which must have provided the focus of civic life in the early territorial capital.

It is a pity that Dyer evidently did only these two city views, for he obviously possessed far greater artistic skill than such less talented men as Fowler or Brosius. Several other artists in the American West, like Dyer, are known to have prepared only single views although their work demonstrates considerable ability. G. R. Bechler's sketch of Helena, Montana in 1865 (Plate 41), lithographed by the Philadelphia firm of Herline and Hensel, has perhaps more historic importance than artistic merit, although it, too, is far from unattractive. It shows this mining town just a year after it mushroomed into existence following the gold strike at Last Chance Gulch.[52]

Equally interesting is the fine elevated panorama of Salt Lake City in 1867 (Plate 42), drawn by Christian Inger two decades after Brigham Young had founded the city as a Mormon sanctuary far from the frontier of civilization. While Inger anticipated by more than twenty years the completion of the great Mormon Temple, here shown as finished, he correctly portrayed the massive Tabernacle to the right as still under construction. Our view is down one of the many extremely wide streets surveyed under Young's direction to carry out the town planning specifications that had been proclaimed by Joseph Smith, the founder of the Mormons, as early as 1836.[53]

Who was the H. Lambach, credited as the artist for the attractive view of Omaha in 1867 as seen from Forest Hill? (Plate 43) We know only that his elevated panorama of the city was lithographed by the firm of Gast, Moeller & Co. of St. Louis, a firm that printed a few other views and many townsite plats of the speculative

[52] Bechler served, I believe, as an artist for one of the transcontinental railway exploring parties, although I cannot now locate the reference to him that I once encountered.

[53] Inger's view of Chicago in 1857 is in the Geography and Map Division of the Library of Congress. See Hébert, *Panoramic Maps*, 25. Inger is known for several other lithographs published in Philadelphia. I am indebted to Stefanie Munsing, Curator of Historical Prints, Library of Congress, for calling my attention to Inger's Philadelphia work.

communities surveyed in such astonishing numbers in Kansas and Nebraska.[54]

There are many other artists whose names appear on only a few western city views. They include Grafton T. Brown, a versatile black artist, lithographer, and publisher of San Francisco who published San Francisco views in 1868 and 1877, drew and published a splendid view of Virginia City, Nevada in 1861 and printed views of Portland and Astoria, Oregon in 1870, among other works.[55] Charles Parsons, well known for his paintings, earlier lithographs of eastern cities, and for his numerous marine scenes done for Currier and Ives, prepared the drawing of San Francisco which that firm issued as a large folio lithograph in 1878. Parsons was also responsible for a similar view of St. Louis in 1874 (Plate 45) and, in that same year, for the first state of a view of Chicago which was revised and re-issued in 1892.[56] (Plate 46)

While the Parsons views are attractive on first glance or as observed from a distance, they provide good detail only for the foreground and for major structures elsewhere. Structures in the background are drawn in a highly conventionalized manner and cannot be relied on to portray anything more than their general character.[57]

Seven views of South Dakota cities are known to have been done by W. F. Herancourt, whose work suggests that he must have had some training or experience. Like Koch and Glover, however, he remains unknown except for his views. They were done in the medium of wood engraving, but closely resemble the more numerous lithographs of the period. His view of Deadwood is typical, capturing the appearance of this lively city in the gold mining area of the Black Hills when such colorful personalities as Wild Bill Hickok, Calamity Jane, and Deadwood Dick were among its prominent residents.[58]

The majority of the frontier view-makers remain largely anonymous because at the time they flourished they were not recognized by the artistic establishment as true artists. We can take a more tolerant and understanding position, looking on their work—not as great art, which it rarely even approaches—but as a variety of popular American artistic expression that appealed originally to unsophisticated tastes and civic pride and

---

[54] In a note on an impression of this view in the Stokes Collection, Stokes and Haskell state that "a corresponding view of Kansas City exists," evidently also by Lambach. Stokes and Haskell, 130.

[55] The 1868 view of San Francisco is a re-issue of the view by Firks of the city in 1849. Peters, *California on Stone*, 120. Peters has a note on Brown, with a list of some of his lithographs, 89–90, identifying him as the artist of the Kuchel and Dresel view of Santa Rosa. Peters also reproduces the Virginia City view as Plate 71. An original impression of the view is in the collection of the Bancroft Library, University of California, Berkeley. Among the many fascinating vignettes surrounding the principal view is one of the *Territorial Enterprise*, the newspaper office where Mark Twain began his writing career as a cub reporter. Some additional material on Brown can be found in Daniel Trowbridge Mallett, *Mallett's Index of Artists*. Efforts to compile a list of his work and to assemble biographical data on Brown are being carried out in the Department of Prints, Oakland Art Museum, California.

[56] Parsons, Lungkwitz, Mathews, Whitefield, Brown, and Emil Dresel are among the very few city view artists listed in George C. Groce and David H. Wallace, *The New-York Historical Society's Dictionary of Artists in America, 1564–1860*. Only Parsons is listed in one of the major nineteenth-century compilations of biographical material on American artists, and it is his oil paintings that are discussed. There is no suggestion that he was involved in lithography or popular art. See Clara Erskine Clement, *Artists of the Nineteenth Century and Their Works: A Handbook Containing Two Thousand and Fifty Biographical Sketches*. The most recent biographical dictionary of western artists lists only George Baker, Joseph Britton, Grafton Brown, George Cooper, George Goddard, Herman Lungkwitz, William McMurtrie, S. F. Marryat, Alfred Mathews, and Charles Parsons, of the view artists discussed in this essay. See Doris Ostrander Dawdy, *Artists of the American West*.

[57] On the Currier and Ives city views bearing his name, the inscription usually reads "Sketched & Drawn on Stone by Parsons & Atwater." Of Atwater I can find no information whatsoever.

[58] Impressions of the Deadwood and Lead City views of 1884 are in the

which to us has the charm of antiquity and the virtue of simplicity.

Quite probably, the custodians of artistic high culture ignored or rejected those who produced these city views because their preparation and publication of necessity had a commercial foundation. No "art for art's sake" attitude would have resulted in the great numbers of urban views that came from the presses. Only if they could be sold—either in advance of publication or shortly thereafter—could the artist, lithographer, printer, and publisher continue their activities. It is worthwhile, therefore, to examine how these views were sold, what they cost to produce and to buy, and why they were purchased. Like the information on those who were responsible for their existence, material on the commercial aspects of their publication is fragmentary. Enough can be pieced together, however, to provide some understanding of view-making as an economic enterprise.

Publishers of city views almost always attempted to limit their financial risk by securing advance subscriptions of copies from citizens, local businessmen, or other purchasers. The usual procedure was to use the artist's preliminary or final drawing in soliciting subscribers. A favorable notice in the local newspaper made the work of the publisher or his representative easier.

When Alfred Mathews moved to Colorado in November, 1865, for example, he lost no time in calling on the editor of a local newspaper. The following day his arrival was called to the attention of Denver residents in these words:

> "We received a call this morning from Mr. A. E. Mathews . . . who arrived here yesterday with the purpose of making sketches of the scenery in town and country, to be lithographed and furnished to subscribers. He showed us several of his pictures of scenes of interest in and around Nebraska City . . . which . . . bear the marks of an Artist's hand . . . . We bespeak for him, a liberal patronage from our business men, and the lovers of the beautiful, upon whom he may call. He commences his labors in this city this morning.[59]

In the early 1870's Joseph J. Stoner and one of his artists, Augustus Koch, used these sales techniques in several cities of Texas. On January 9, 1873, the *Austin Daily Democratic Statesman* carried the following announcement in its "Local Matters" column:

> We have been shown the drawing of a bird's-eye view of the city of Austin, made by Mr. A. Koch, which for accuracy and beauty is remarkable. The supposed elevation from which the view is taken is two thousand feet, a height in which the beholder has the view of the topographical inequalities and enables him to see and recognize many individual houses in the city.
>
> Mr. Stoner, who has already furnished admirable views of this kind for Galveston and Houston, will call upon our citizens and take subscriptions to enable him to have the work lithographed at once. Unless a sufficient number of subscribers are obtained to justify the expense of lithographing, of course the work will fall through.[60]

Two weeks later the San Antonio *Daily Herald* provided its readers with a similar but much longer description of the Stoner and Koch view of their city. Stoner must have been elated with the favorable publicity:

> Mr. J. J. Stoner called at our office yesterday morning, and submitted a very accurate pen and ink sketch of our beautiful city.

Amon Carter Museum collection. Views of Aberdeen, 1883; Deadwood, 1884; Spearfish, 1884; Pierre, 1883; and a photograph of the view of Rapid City in 1883 are in the collection of the South Dakota State Historical Society. A reproduction of his view of Huron, identified as "in the early 1880s" appears in Mildred McEwen Jones, *Early Beadle County, 1879–1900*.

[59] Denver *Rocky Mountain News*, November 13, 1865, [4], col. 2.

[60] Austin *Daily Democratic Statesman*, January 9, 1873.

> Upon it were faithfully represented, the location of our various plazas, streets and alleys, of all our churches and public and *private buildings*. Having been subjected to the inspection of several gentlemen, they failed to discover wherein a single house had been omitted from the drawing. The courses of the San Antonio River, the San Pedro Creek, and of our various irrigation ditches, with all our bridges, are accurately delineated. This has been laid down by Mr. A. Koch, a capable artist, who has drawn the picture after having actually gone through the labor of personally visiting the location of every house in our city to ensure its accuracy.

The account continued with a statement that the view would be "handsomely lithographed in colors" if Stoner could secure subscriptions for two hundred and fifty copies. The newspaper called attention to Stoner's previous views of such cities as Chattanooga and Galveston and stated that he then had under preparation views of Austin, Waco, Houston, Dallas, and Sherman, among others. These were all said to be "characterized by great beauty and accuracy."

The announcement concluded with the information that Stoner would be shortly calling on businessmen of San Antonio to obtain subscriptions. In this endeavor, the paper wished "him every success and feel satisfied that most of our business men, after having seen the drawing and the style upon which it is proposed to complete it will be happy in having an opportunity to subscript for a copy." Payment, it was noted, was not necessary until the complete lithographs were delivered.[61]

By February 12 Stoner had obtained the necessary number of subscribers to the projected view and departed for his place of business in Madison, Wisconsin. This was announced in the *Daily Herald* the following day in a brief statement that the views would be available in about two months and that Stoner wished the editor to convey his thanks to "our citizens for the uniform courtesy with which he has been received."[62]

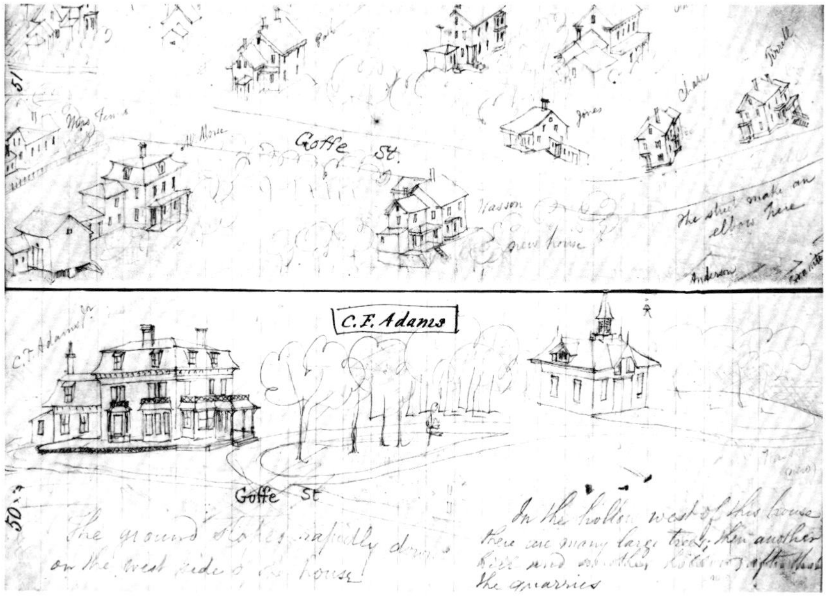

FIGURE 7. *Untitled* (Quincy, Massachusetts). Edwin Whitefield. c. 1878, in Whitefield sketchbook. Pencil on paper. Courtesy Collection of William Osgood.

Almost two months to the day later Stoner returned to San Antonio with the completed lithographs. The *Daily Herald* noted the event with a long and highly complimentary story:

> Mr. J. J. Stoner has returned to San Antonio, and is prepared to deliver his beautiful pictures of our city. . . . The picture comes fully up to the promises made in reference to it, and the drawing exhibited was but a feeble foreshadowing of the striking lithograph now to be furnished. In point of accuracy, we have only to say, that we have yet to hear of the first resident who has not been able to find his domicil accurately located upon it. The bird's eye view of our city is highly ornamental and would make a handsome and useful decoration for an office.

---

[61] San Antonio *Daily Herald*, January 28, 1873.
[62] San Antonio *Daily Herald*, February 13, 1873.

The paper stated that Stoner "will have a few copies left after subscribers have been furnished," and those "who may wish extra copies to send to friends at a distance, can be accommodated."[63] While the paper did not mention the retail price of the view, it doubtless sold for $5.00, the charge established by Stoner for his view of Austin by the same artist, approximately the same size, and published the same month.[64]

Some additional information is available on the prices for which these views were sold, but it is far from complete. Size and color were important considerations, as was potential competition from other publishers. The population of the city may also have been a factor. If any catalogs or price lists were issued by one or more of the major nineteenth century city view publishers, they do not seem to have survived. Since the demand for any single view must have been highly localized, their publishers relied heavily on subscription sales, supplemented by additional sales in local art, book, and stationery shops when the lithographs were published.

Prices seem to have risen throughout the period with which we are concerned, reflecting both increased interest in such prints and changes in the value of money. In January, 1838, John Caspar Wild announced a forthcoming series of twenty views of Philadelphia which subscribers could obtain for only $2.50, and the first four were offered for sale at only fifty cents. While these were quite small, five by seven inches, they were incredibly cheap. Wild's four-sheet panorama of the city was offered for sale that same year for only $1.00. Each of those prints measured 6 by 12 inches.[65]

In 1842 a large folio view of Wilmington, Delaware, colored, could be purchased for only seventy-five cents.[66] Edwin Whitefield's view of Harrisburg in 1845 sold for $1.00, colored.[67] Large folio views by the same artist of Albany in 1845 and Troy in 1848 were priced at $2.00, colored. The prices for his Buffalo and Newark views, both published in 1846, were $3.00, while the equally large colored view of Baltimore in 1847 sold for $5.00. In 1848, however, Whitefield priced his large folio view of Troy at only $2.00, possibly a reflection of the small demand for such a print in that industrial city.[68]

Most of the western views were sold for prices in this range. H. H. Bailey's 26 by 40-inch view of Milwaukee in 1872 could be obtained for $3.00. For an additional fifty cents the customer could have it mounted and varnished in a plain frame. Or, it could also be purchased in a "2-1/2 inch polished Black Walnut Frame (also mounted and varnished)" for an extra charge of $2.50.[69] Whitefield's view of Galena in 1856 was selling in the shops of that Illinois town for $4.00 and $5.00.[70] At

[63] San Antonio *Daily Herald*, April 15, 1873, 3, col. 2.

[64] The price of the Austin view is given in that city's *Daily Democratic Statesman* for April 9, 1873. Both the San Antonio and Austin newspaper accounts mention that Stoner was prepared to furnish rollers for those copies to be sent through the mails. The postage for shipment to any United States address was six cents. Postage to foreign countries was then twenty-four cents.

[65] Snyder, "Wild," 35–36, 42–43.

[66] Stokes and Haskell, 91. This view was drawn by B. Gluck, lithographed by Thomas Sinclair of Philadelphia and measured 15 x 27-7/16 inches, excluding the title. The Stokes Catalog information is from the January 18, 1842, issue of the Wilmington *Delaware State Journal*.

[67] Edwin Whitefield Scrapbook, Print Department, Boston Public Library, undated and unidentified newspaper account. I am indebted to Sinclair Hitchings, Keeper of Prints, for calling to my attention this valuable source of information.

[68] All of the Whitefield prices mentioned are from newspaper accounts in his scrapbook. Only that in the Newark *Eagle* for August 21, 1846 is fully identified.

[69] See the notice appended to the impression of the view in the Geography and Map Division, Library of Congress, as quoted in Hébert, *Panoramic Maps*, 4.

least one view carried a substantially higher price. The toned lithograph of Portland, Oregon in 1879, drawn and published by Eli S. Glover and printed by the A. L. Bancroft firm of San Francisco, included a printed price of $10.00 below the title of the 25 by 40-1/2-inch print.[71]

While such fragmentary information is far from definitive, it at least provides enough evidence to conclude that most city views could be purchased for from $3.00 to $10.00, with $5.00 as perhaps an average price. Smaller views doubtless sold for less, and many must have been given away for promotional purposes or sold at nominal figures. It would not be unreasonable to surmise—although there is no evidence to support such a belief—that publishers may have disposed of any remaining copies of a view a year or two after publication at lower prices in order to reduce their inventories and realize some slight additional profit from the undertaking.

Profits depended on other factors: costs of production, selling expenses, promotion and advertising, overhead, and sales volume. Concerning such matters we have little data on which to draw. The most important is the bill sent to Thomas O. Larkin in February 1851 for the cost of lithographing and printing the handsome pair of toned views showing Monterey, California from the land (Plate 4) and from the harbor in 1842. Larkin, the American consul in what was then Mexican California, had commissioned an unknown artist to prepare the two views. In 1843 he sent both watercolors to a Boston relative to be printed, but for some reason this project was not carried out until 1850 when Larkin visited the East.

At that time he commissioned the New York firm of Francis D'Avignon to have them published. Charles Gildemeister transferred the views to stone, for which Larkin was billed the sum of $300.00. One hundred copies of each were printed on heavy paper at a cost of twenty-five cents each. An additional printing at the same unit price was made of twenty-five copies of each view on thin paper, to be sold folded in cases.[72]

Larkin's Monterey views are quite scarce, and it is likely that no other copies were printed after this initial run. Larkin's costs, not including the cases for the thin paper edition, would therefore have been $1.75 each. We can only guess at their retail price, but it was doubtless in the $3.00 to $5.00 range. What Larkin paid the artist is not known—nor, indeed, do we know artist's fees for any other city view. While Larkin may not have published these views primarily for commercial purposes, his costs were doubtless representative of those faced by other publishers who made their living mainly from painting and selling such views.

Quite clearly, the business of view publishing could not yield substantial profits unless large editions of the prints were sold. This seems to have happened only rarely. Whitefield's view of Providence, Rhode Island, published in 1849, must have been one such exception. It was issued in an edition of at least 1,300 copies, since in the previous year the artist's agent reported that he had received that many subscriptions. That orders of this magnitude were unusual is suggested by Whitefield's diary entry that this was "a much larger number than I anticipated for such a place as Providence."[73]

---

[70] Letter from J. P. Dezoya to Edwin Whitefield, December 16, 1856, as quoted in Betty I. Madden, *Art, Crafts, and Architecture in Early Illinois*, 216.

[71] This price appears on impressions of the lithograph in the Library of Congress; the Honeyman Collection of the Bancroft Library, University of California, Berkeley; and the Oregon Historical Society.

[72] Jeanne Van Nostrand, *A Pictorial and Narrative History of Monterey: Adobe Capital of California, 1770–1847*, 90–91.

[73] Whitefield, *Diary*, entry for Thursday, January 12, 1848. Manuscript in Boston Public Library, Print Department.

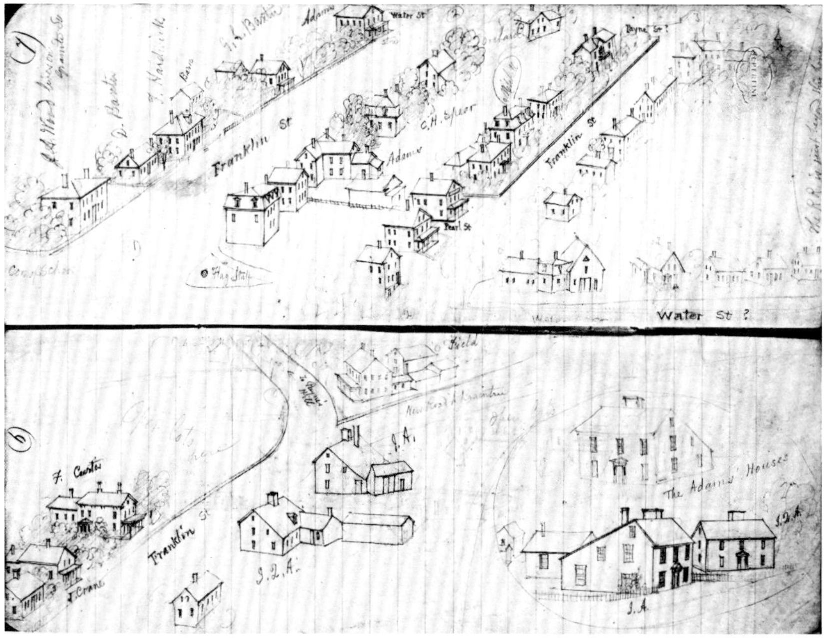

FIGURE 8. *Untitled* (Quincy, Massachusetts). Edwin Whitefield. c. 1878, in Whitefield sketchbook. Pencil on paper. Courtesy Collection of William Osgood.

There could be disappointments as well. Whitefield visited Louisville to solicit subscriptions for a view of that city. Perhaps he spent several days or weeks in sketching the town. He did succeed in obtaining the usual newspaper notices, but the warning in one of them that "the project will be abandoned and the artist go to some other city" unless he received "sufficient encouragement . . . by the citizens" apparently went unheeded. In other cities Whitefield had established a minimum subscription list of only two hundred purchasers before proceeding to finish his drawings and complete the lithographs; in Louisville he failed to attract sufficient interest, the project was dropped, and Whitefield's expenses must have been substantial.[74]

Stoner seems to have required two hundred and fifty subscribers for the Koch view of San Antonio before he would undertake to print the lithograph. Extra copies were surely made to be used for sales to non-subscribers, but, as has been suggested by one writer, the average edition of each view was probably around five hundred.[75] In the larger cities the number of copies printed might have been significantly larger than this, and there must have been many views of small towns where three hundred or less would have satisfied the restricted market. It seems doubtful that a view would have been in demand more than a few months after it first appeared. Most of the cities were undergoing rapid changes, and a print would be badly out of date before long. It is unlikely, therefore, that more copies were ever printed than the publisher believed would be purchased within a short time after they were first offered for sale.

Although the number of surviving impressions is not an entirely reliable index of the size of editions, such information does suggest that many of them were published in very small numbers. Only two copies of Thaddeus Fowler's view of Oklahoma City are known to exist.[76] Many others, such as Augustus Koch's views of Albuquerque in 1886 and Los Angeles in 1871, the Hermann Lungkwitz view of San Antonio in 1852 (Plate 31), the view of Helena in 1865 by G. R. Bechler (Plate 41),

[74] The undated newspaper notice is in the Whitefield Scrapbook. No Louisville view is listed in Norton, "Whitefield," nor is one reproduced or mentioned in the elaborate pictorial history of Louisville. See Samuel W. Thomas, ed., *Views of Louisville Since 1766*. For his Newark, New Jersey view of 1847 Whitefield established the minimum number of subscribers as 200. Newark *Eagle*, August 21, 1846, clipping in Whitefield Scrapbook.

[75] Hébert, *Panoramic Maps*, 4.

[76] One is in the Stokes Collection of the New York Public Library, and the other is owned by Mr. George Shirk of Oklahoma City.

and the Brosius view of Dallas in 1872 (Plate 32), to name but a few, are also extremely rare.

Some additional income may have been obtained by charging local businessmen for the privilege of having their place of business included among the small border views that frequently appeared surrounding the main body of the print. Examples of such views are the 1857 lithograph of Los Angeles by Kuchel and Dresel (Plate 12), and Grafton T. Brown's view of Portland (Plate 44), issued c. 1861 by Charles Kuchel. Unfortunately, the lack of business accounts for this and other firms makes it impossible to document the probable collection of such charges or to even guess at what amount may have been established for this form of advertising.

Alfred Mathews, in his street scenes of Nebraska City and Denver, used a variation of this technique. A number of the business signs shown in his lithographs are blank, while others prominently feature the name of the store. The conclusion seems inescapable that Mathews required either subscriptions to copies of the views or direct cash payments on the part of business proprietors if they wished to have their place of business identified in the prints.[77]

One additional source of income may have been important. Many of the views include prominently displayed imprints indicating that a local real estate firm was either the publisher or had purchased a quantity for distribution. The Laredo view of c. 1890 (Plate 48), unsigned, but possibly by Wellge, has its sky overprinted in large letters with the inscription, "Presented with the Compliments of The Laredo Real Estate & Abstract Co." Augustus Koch's view of Seattle in 1891 also carries the address of a real estate and mortgage lending firm. A brewery in Helena appears as the sponsor of the large view of that city in 1890 (Plate 49). Perhaps some copies of these views were published and sold in the normal way through subscriptions and sales in local shops, while other copies were overprinted with such advertising copy and made available to the sponsor at a previously agreed quantity price. This practice seems to have developed toward the end of the nineteenth century and is not often found on the earlier views.

Small firms or individual artists who specialized in city views and produced few if any other types of prints do not seem to have made much money at the business. George Henry Goddard, whose California views have already been noted, complained to his brother in 1852 that "my views have done me little good. You are aware that in publishing them the stones remained security to the lithographers for the bill of expenses and . . . they are sold very slowly."[78]

Payments were not always in cash. Although the city council of Galena, Illinois had agreed to pay Edwin Whitefield $80 for ten of his views of their city, he was offered the sum in paper scrip rather than in currency. In complaining to the council, the artist pointed out that the scrip had a cash value of little more than $50.00. He suggested that the city either pay him the original sum in cash or increase the amount in scrip in exchange for several extra copies of the lithograph, but both proposals were refused.[79] Thaddeus Fowler reportedly accepted farm produce, such as flour and beans, for copies of his city views.[80]

---

[77] This feature of the Mathews lithographs is noted in Taft, *Artists and Illustrators*, 78.

[78] As quoted in Albert Shumate, *Goddard*, 3.

[79] See the exchange of correspondence in Betty I. Madden, *Early Illinois*, 215–16.

[80] Interview with Mrs. T. B. Fowler, November, 1971, as reported in Hébert, *Panoramic Maps*, 4.

City views were purchased for a variety of uses. Certainly they were used as wall decorations, and it is because many were framed and protected by glass that they have survived to the present. Printed on pulp paper with a high acid content, they became brittle with age and whether kept flat or rolled they were easily torn if handled. While framing usually prevented this from occurring, it often resulted in other damage. Nineteenth century framers rarely used mats, and condensation on the inside of the glass could create waterspots or stains on the face of the print. Exposure to sunlight often caused fading, and nitric oxides penetrating through the cracks of the wooden backing boards of the framed view often created vertical, yellow-brown stain lines. These tell-tale signs of framing on so many of the city views in public and private collections indicate the extent to which the views were used as wall hangings.[81]

Where were the views hung? Business and professional offices must have been one important source of sales. Urban views surely could be found also at banks, in hotel lobbies, and some retail shops. Thus, Koch's view of San Antonio in 1873 was described by the local newspaper as a "highly ornamental and . . . handsome and useful decoration for an office."[82] Not quite a decade later a Denver newspaper referred to the view of that city drawn by J. H. Flett and printed by the Strobidge Lithograph Company of Cincinnati in 1882 as being "worth a place in every office or place of business."[83]

City views must have appealed to many persons as wall decorations for the home as well as for the office. Albert Ruger's fine view of Savannah, Georgia in 1871, published by Stoner, was described by a newspaper in that city as "an admirable and interesting ornament for parlor, library or office, and would prove a most acceptable present to a friend."[84] A quarter of a century earlier many of the city views drawn and published by Edwin Whitefield were also recommended by local newspapers as suitable for either home or office display. A Rochester newspaper, for example, referred to Whitefield's view of that city in 1847 as "an ornament peculiarly worthy of

[81] Views continue to turn up in their original frames. Many of the views in major collections have been restored by removal of stains and spots through bleaching or washing, often followed by hand coloring. Depending on the condition of the print before such treatment, all or part of the age-toning, discoloration, foxing, and other staining can be removed or made far less noticeable. While restoration may make prints more attractive, it also makes it more difficult to determine whether or not the original color was printed, added by hand, or was some combination of the two.

[82] San Antonio *Daily Herald*, April 15, 1873.

[83] Denver *Rocky Mountain News*, May 9, 1882. This newspaper notice could scarcely have been more complimentary. Perhaps it, and others of similar character, were the result of payment to the editor either in cash or in one or more complimentary copies of the views. Under the heading, "Beautiful Bird's Eye View of Denver," the story reads as follows: "Denver, in all the magnificence of its extended development, finds nowhere so just and extended an elucidation as in the magnificent bird's eye view that has just been completed by J. H. Flett. To see it is to admire, praise and commend it, for it is thoroughly accurate in all its details; in fact, it is an elaborate encyclopedia of the beauteous Queen City of the Plains. It is on exhibition and sale at No. 323 Sixteen Street, the Art Gallery, where so many fine pictures grace the easel and wall to entrance the vision of the casual observer of the works of art. The chart in question is perfect in detail. Nothing has escaped the pencil of the artist who faithfully framed it. We would suggest that every one who takes any interest in our local history to avail himself of a copy ere the edition is exhausted, the same being limited in point of number. It is worthy a place in every office or place of business, and the Denverite can with pride mail it to friends in the older States. It is a handsomely colored sheet 30 x 42, and may be had of the publishers, Flett, Bischel & Ilgenfritz, 323 Sixteenth Street." The view was probably published in anticipation of the National Mining and Industrial Exposition which opened in Denver on August 1, 1882. Letter from Mrs. Alys Freeze, Head, Western History Department, Denver Public Library, to Mrs. Paul M. Rhymer, Curator of Prints, Chicago Historical Society, January 15, 1965. The original drawing had been exhibited earlier at what was then called the California Art Gallery, 323 Sixteenth Street. Denver *Rocky Mountain News*, October 2, 1881. Doubtless subscriptions were solicited at that time.

[84] Savannah *Morning News*, February 19, 1872, 3, col. 4.

a place in the offices and houses of Rochester men."[85] The artist's four views of Philadelphia were also greeted in 1850 as "admirably suited for parlor ornaments," while they were also described as of "marked interest for public institutions."[86]

Bird's-eye views were surely used to publicize and promote the cities they depicted. In the advance publicity about the view of Denison, Texas in 1891 drawn by Thaddeus Fowler and published by Fowler and James B. Moyer, the local newspaper observed that "every person who owns a home in Denison should have at least one copy, and our real estate and business men would find it profitable, as an advertisement, to purchase many copies for circulating abroad."[87] This was an echo of the proposal made by a Pittsburgh newspaper writer who had examined the view of that city in 1849 drawn by Edwin Whitefield: "If it is properly got up, and placed in hotels, and public places of resort, throughout the country, it will do much to give a proper conception of the site and size of this city and environs. Every Pittsburgher would feel proud of it."[88]

Public officials in some cities doubtless subscribed to the views in advance or purchased copies of the completed lithographs to advertise their city in other parts of the country or to use them as wall hangings in official buildings. The Galena, Illinois Common Council's agreement with Edwin Whitefield to buy ten copies of his lithograph has already been noted.[89] Probably many other municipalities subscribed to the views of their cities in similar fashion.

As has previously been mentioned, there is every reason to believe that the western railroads or their townsite subsidiary companies also purchased city views. It would have been a logical form of townsite promotion for them to have commissioned publishers to produce

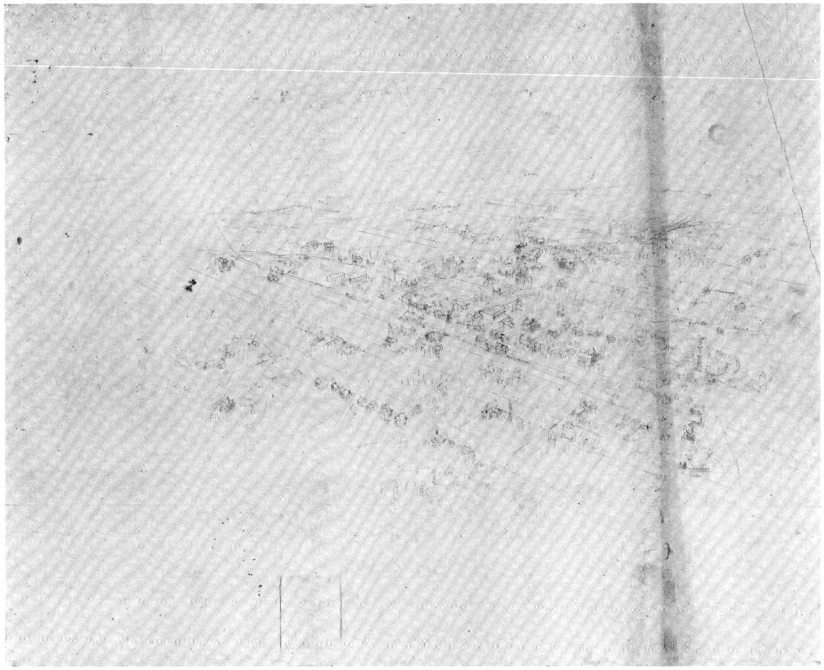

FIGURE 9. *Untitled* (Sunset, Texas). Thaddeus M. Fowler. c. 1890. Pencil on paper. 20 x 32-5/8 in. (50.8 x 82.8 cm.) Courtesy Amon Carter Museum.

[85] Rochester *Daily American*, November 24, 1847.

[86] Philadelphia *Enquirer and Courier*, June 10, 1850. Other newspaper notices of Whitefield's work can be found in his scrapbook.

[87] Denison *Sunday Gazetteer*, January 11, 1891. The newspaper account called attention to the drawing prepared by Fowler which Moyer was using to solicit subscriptions for the contemplated lithograph. It mentioned that Fowler "has been in the city several weeks making sketches for the work." This is one of the few known indications of the time required by such artists to prepare the basic drawing needed before the design could be transferred to the lithographic stone used in printing.

[88] Pittsburgh *Gazette*, October, 1849. This clipping appears in the Whitefield Scrapbook previously mentioned, but the artist neglected to note the day of the month.

[89] Letter from J. P. Dezoya to Whitefield, December 16, 1856, as quoted in Madden, *Early Illinois*, 216. Morris notes in *Pictorial History of Victoria* that Herman Brosius made a similar arrangement with the Victoria City Council, selling them 100 copies of his Victoria view for $1.00 each.

such lithographs as an aid in speeding settlement of the towns along their routes. Railroad depots, eastern company offices, and European travel and emigration centers might have been used for their display. An examination of the surviving nineteenth century business records of the transcontinental railroads may yet reveal direct evidence that this took place.[90]

Finally, it is useful to explore the methods by which the artists of these nineteenth century city views went about preparing their drawings before they were drawn on stone for printing. No artist has left an account of his method of procedure, so again we must piece together scattered bits of information and evidence to reconstruct how this was done. Nor does a full set of the various drawings required at various stages exist for any single lithograph, and we are forced to draw on the work of several persons for suitable examples.

Probably the first step was to select the approximate position from which the city would be depicted. The artist then began to sketch individual buildings or groups of structures facing one side of a city block. Rare examples are those found in a small notebook used by Edwin Whitefield in preparing his view of Quincy, Massachusetts in 1878 (Figs. 7, 8).[91] Each house, public building, and commercial structure of Quincy was drawn in pencil as Whitefield moved through the city. Notes on some of the sketches record the type of vegetation, the nature of the topography, and other information that would be needed when the detailed sketches were redrawn at smaller size with a consistent perspective, and with the buildings placed in their proper locations.[92] Thaddeus Fowler also used this sketching method, but was more economical. Examples of his preliminary sketches can be found on the verso of several of his unsold views, now housed in the Library of Congress.

Using an existing city map where available or sketching one where it was not or lacked the most recently platted streets, the artist then drew the thoroughfare pattern as if seen from the air. Since virtually all of the western cities had been platted in a gridiron street system, this was not difficult.[93] The artist then used his ground-level sketches to prepare a rough draft of the view.

What is evidently a still incomplete draft of the view of Sunset, Texas (Figs. 9, 10), drawn by Thaddeus Fowler in the 1890s shows the street grid perspective with vanishing points to left and right and with preliminary re-

[90] The extent to which townsite promotion and urban land sales provided revenues in the early days of the western railroads has never been adequately investigated. There is some reason to believe that returns on real estate may have been greater than passenger and freight charges in the first years of operation. The role of the western railroads as town planners and urban promoters will be the subject of three chapters in my forthcoming book on city planning in the American West, but the subject is far from exhausted as an area for research.

[91] The sketchbook is in the collection of William Osgood of Boston, Massachusetts who was kind enough to allow me to borrow it for examination and photoduplication.

[92] In the Whitefield sketchbook some of the buildings are drawn as if seen at street level while others are shown as if viewed from a slightly elevated position. The horizontal angles of view seem to vary as well, although all of the buildings were sketched within a range of perhaps fifteen to twenty degrees of the final horizontal angle of view adopted for the finished bird's-eye.

[93] When he was eighty-eight Oakley H. Bailey was interviewed by a reporter for the Sebring, Ohio, *Times*. His description of the process as filtered through the words of the reporter is a model of clarity: "Each job required a layout or projection in perspective of all the streets, and then the going along every street and sketching in the buildings, trees, and other objects so as to make a complete and accurate view as from an elevation of 2,000 or 3,000 feet." This is from an issue after June 14, 1931, and before June 14, 1932. The newspaper clipping was loaned to the Library of Congress by Roxana Fowler, but the exact date was not available. I am grateful to John Hébert for making a copy of the clipping available to me.

duced sketches of many of the buildings in their proper position. Perhaps this was checked on the ground and needed changes noted. The Sunset sketch has a few notes here and there to guide the artist in preparing the next revision or in making the final drawing.

Two final drawings by Fowler of Texas towns, one of Honey Grove in 1891 and the other of Quanah a year earlier (Fig. 11), illustrate what the lithographer was given to work from in drawing on the stone with lithographic ink. Or, one additional step might have been taken: tracing or redrawing the artist's design on transfer paper, whose image might then be transferred to the stone by running it through the press with the transfer paper placed face down on the stone's surface. A proof impression would then be made from the inked stone, and necessary changes made on the image. The required number of copies could then be printed.[94]

In the case of Quanah (Plate 50), the view was slightly modified from Fowler's final drawing when he, or some unnamed lithographer, put the drawing on stone. Both the vertical and horizontal angles of the print differ slightly from those of the drawing, the title has been redesigned, the portrait of Chief Quanah has been omitted, and parts of the left, bottom, and right edges have been cropped. Why this was done and with what effect on the accuracy of the view would seem impossible to determine.

Probably other changes in the interests of either clarity or composition would have been made as the artist transposed his initial ground-level sketches to the perspective grid of the rough draft. The need to fit the view within a pre-established format or on a stone of standard size might have caused other modifications. Further departures from a completely accurate representation of the city as observed by the artist may have resulted

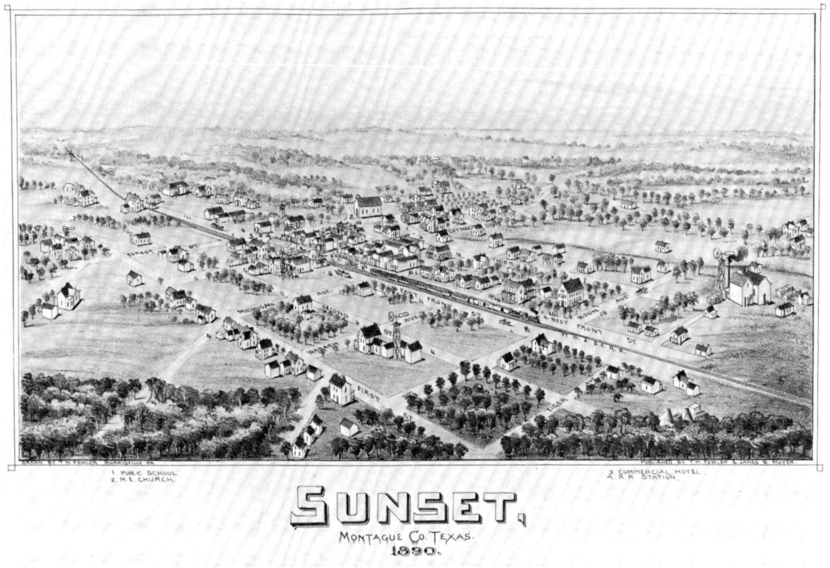

FIGURE 10. *Sunset, Montague Co. Texas. 1890.* Thaddeus M. Fowler. 1890. Toned lithograph. 8-1/16 x 14-3/8 in. (20.4 x 36.5 cm.) Courtesy Amon Carter Museum.

[94] For a lithograph to be printed with a single additional tone stone or with other stones carrying inks of various colors, further work would have been required. A clear description of the process appears in a treatise on printing techniques published in 1871. "The artist proceeds in the following manner. First he designs on a stone an outline of his subject, and gets as many impressions printed of this outline as he intends to introduce colors in his chromo. The impressions, as soon as printed, and before the ink dries, are powdered with red chalk, so as to have the lines only coated with the chalk, and in that condition are transferred or set off on the stone intended for each color. These chalk lines serve as a guide to work the drawing for each color in its proper place. Then the artist proceeds with his work, commencing with the lightest color, and using a separate stone for each color, until the picture is brought to the proper tone and finish. To aid him in judging of the tone required for each additional color, proofs are taken of his drawing as he proceeds, the printing following in the same order." Ringwalt, ed., *American Encyclopaedia of Printing*, 282. The techniques of color lithography are also described in Peter C. Marzio, *Mr. Audubon and Mr. Bien: An Early Phase in the History of American Chromolithography*. In this exhibition catalogue Marzio identifies the author of the 1871 essay on color printing quoted above as Peter Duval. Duval was one of the

from omissions, intentional or otherwise, and the errors inevitable in a work of such detail. All this raises the general question of the extent to which one can rely on these views in dating buildings, locating major activities, and judging the appearance and character of the cities as they really were.

Complete misrepresentations, such as the view of Sumner, Kansas (Plate 23) were rare, but by no means unknown.[95] More common were such bits of anticipatory detail as Inger's representation of the Mormon Temple in Salt Lake City previously mentioned (Plate 42). There are fictional railroads in some of the city views, although usually the railroad did, in fact, arrive within a year or so after the publication of the lithograph.

The circumstances under which the view was prepared should always be considered. As two authorities of pictorial Americana have put it, "a town view printed for a local urban booster will have a different value from a town view produced for an official government survey. In the former one can expect to find idealized settings and gross exaggerations. The second view may not necessarily be completely faithful to every detail, but such a study has much more of an obligation to depict a real and accurate view."[96]

This may be too strong a warning. The great bulk of the city views issued were subject to careful scrutiny by local residents, both before and after the lithograph was published. For most citizens, accurate representation of their own property, those of their neighbors, friends, and business acquaintances, and such public buildings as the city hall and courthouse, would have been more important than an "artistic" composition sacrificing truth to beauty. Civic pride and boosterism, while a strong characteristic of the frontier West, could scarcely be carried too far in graphic exaggerations without attracting damaging criticism from rival towns or irate newcomers who, like young John Ingalls at Sumner, could have spread the word of such lithographic deception.

Equally important was the integrity of the artists and their knowledge that they would be judged by potential subscribers to their views in one town by what they had accomplished earlier in other cities. Occasional artistic license in turning ahead the clock of history by a year or two, darkening the sky with a bit more industrial smoke than local factories were producing, depicting the streets as if swept and watered, or the buildings as if freshly painted should not mislead us into thinking that these views present a completely romanticized version of Western cities.

---

pioneers of color lithography in America. A number of the city view lithographs done in the early 1850s by Sachse in Baltimore were also printed in colors from multiple stones.

[95] An equally fictitious city view as that of Cairo, Illinois, prepared in 1838 by William Strickland for Darius Holbrook. Strickland was commissioned by Holbrook, a land speculator and townsite promoter then vigorously engaged in booming his land at the confluence of the Ohio and Mississippi Rivers as a great future rail center and commercial metropolis. Strickland apparently was not to blame for the deception, for this well-known architect produced both a plan and the view in question to show how the town might be designed. Armed with Strickland's view as lithographed by Duval in Philadelphia, Holbrook succeeded in borrowing more than a million dollars in England by representing the view as showing what was already built or under construction, rather than what he hoped to accomplish. Holbrook pocketed most of the money, spending only a small part of the proceeds on his town, and Cairo remained for many years the forlorn sight pictured in one of Henry Lewis's views of the 1840s. Both views are reproduced in John W. Reps, "Great Expectations and Hard Times: The Planning of Cairo, Illinois," *Journal of the Society of Architectural Historians*, XVI (December, 1957), 14–21.

[96] Peter C. Marzio and Milton Kaplan, "Lithographs as Historical Documents, *Antiques*, CII (October, 1972), 674.

What is astonishing is that, despite occasional gross errors and misrepresentations, they provide an incredible amount of reliable detail. Comparisons with photographs of the time can be made to show that even in the tiny buildings on the prints such matters as fenestration, roof types, porches, signs, chimneys, and dozens of similar architectural minutiae are rendered with faithful accuracy. They truly convey the look of the urban West when the region was young and every town could dream of a glorious future.

These city views can thus be enjoyed and studied in many ways and for a variety of purposes. Their decorative charm and special artistic quality, however primitive in many cases, are obvious. They also provide useful clues to nineteenth century lithographic techniques. Their utility as valuable sources of information for urban and architectural history is less well appreciated but is equally important. Their advertising and promotional aspects no longer have any but antiquarian interest, but the identification of leading business and industrial establishments helps us to understand better the shape and structure of our cities a century or so ago. Finally, while a typical view of this type would not prove very satisfactory as a street guide to the modern city it depicts, its limited usefulness in this respect serves as a reminder of the constant process of urban growth, change, and renewal. Decoration, printing technology, history, business, and geography are thus uniquely combined in this endlessly fascinating form of American popular art.[97]

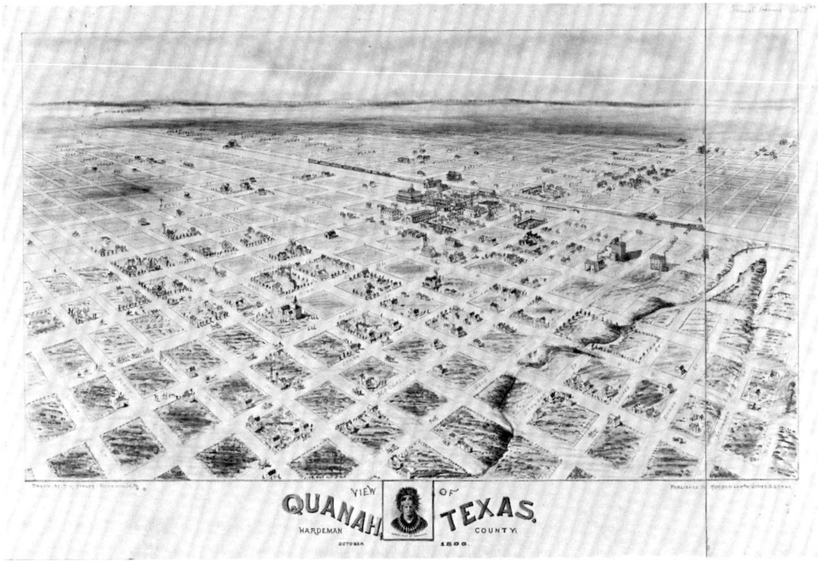

FIGURE 11. *View of Quanah, Texas. Hardeman County: October 1890.* Thaddeus M. Fowler. 1890. Pencil on paper. 20 x 32-5/8 in. (50.8 x 82.8 cm.) Courtesy Amon Carter Museum.

[97] This final paragraph is virtually identical to that in my much briefer gallery guide, *Western City Views*, written some years ago for the Amon Carter Museum. I have learned a great deal about these views since writing that earlier essay, but I am under no illusion that this newer and longer statement is either complete or without errors. I would welcome corrections, comments, and additional information.

BIBLIOGRAPHY

PRIMARY SOURCES

MANUSCRIPTS

Whitefield, Edwin. Diary. Boston Public Library, Print Department.
———. Scrapbook. Boston Public Library, Print Department.
———. Sketchbook. Collection of William Osgood, Boston.

PUBLISHED WORKS

Choris, Louis. *Voyage Pittoresque autour du Monde*. Paris, 1822.
Colden, Cadwallader David. *Memoir . . . at the Celebration of the Completion of the New York Canals*. New York, 1825.
Duhaut-Cilly, Auguste Bernard. *Voyage autour de Monde*. Paris, 1833.
Emory, W. H. *Notes of a Military Reconnaissance from Fort Leavenworth in Missouri, to San Diego in California*. Washington, D.C., 1848.
Warre, Sir Henry James. *Sketches in North America and the Oregon Territory*. London, 1848.

NEWSPAPERS

American Minerva. (New York City), March 3, 10, 1795.
Beacon Journal (Akron, Ohio), November 13, 1899.
Daily American (Rochester, New York), November 24, 1847.
Daily Democratic Statesman (Austin, Texas) January 9, April 9, 1873.
Daily Herald (San Antonio, Texas), January 28, February 13, April 15, 1873.
Delaware State Journal (Wilmington), January 18, 1842.
Eagle (Newark, New Jersey), August 21, 1846.
Enquirer and Courier (Philadelphia), June 10, 1850.
Gazette (Pittsburgh), October, 1849.
Independent (Hudson, Ohio), November 17, 1899.
Morning News (Savannah, Georgia), February 19, 1872.
Rocky Mountain News (Denver), November 13, 1865; October 2, 1881; May 9, 1882.
Sunday Gazetteer (Denison, Texas), January 11, 1891.
Times (Sebring, Ohio), June 14, 1931–June 14, 1932.

SECONDARY SOURCES

BOOKS

Antreasian, Garo Z., and Adams, Clinton. *The Tamarind Book of Lithography: Art and Techniques*. New York, 1971.
Baird, Joseph Armstrong, Jr. *California's Pictorial Letter Sheets, 1849–1869*. San Francisco, 1967.
———, and Evans, Edwin Clyve. *Historic Lithographs of San Francisco*. San Francisco, 1972.
Clement, Clara Erskine. *Artists of the Nineteenth Century and Their Works: A Handbook Containing Two Thousand and Fifty Biographical Sketches*. 2 vols. Boston, 1883.
Cumming, John, comp. *A Preliminary Checklist of 19th Century Lithographs of Michigan Cities and Towns*. Mount Pleasant, Michigan, 1969.
Dawdy, Doris Ostrander. *Artists of the American West*. Chicago, 1974.
Ebert, John, and Ebert, Katherine. *Old American Prints for Collectors*. New York, 1974.
Groce, George C., and Wallace, David H. *The New-York Historical Society's Dictionary of Artists in America, 1564–1860*. New Haven, 1957.
Hartford, William J. *Benjamin Franklin Smith: A Biography of One of Maine's Successful Americans*. New York, 1925.
Hazen, Edward. *The Panorama of Professions and Trades*. Philadelphia, 1836.
Hébert, John. *Panoramic Maps of Anglo-American Cities*. Washington, D.C., 1974.
Jones, Mildred McEwen. *Early Beadle County, 1879–1900*. Huron, South Dakota, 1961.
Knight, Edward H., ed. *Knight's American Mechanical Dictionary*, Vol. II. Boston, 1872.
Koke, Richard J. *A Checklist of the American Engravings of John Hill (1770–1850)*. New York, 1961.
Lewis, Henry. *The Valley of the Mississippi Illustrated*. Translated by A. Hermina Poatgieter. Edited by Bertha L. Heilbron. St. Paul Minnesota, 1967.
"Lithography." *Appleton's Dictionary of Machines, Mechanics, Engine-Work & Engraving*, Vol. II. New York, 1851.
"Lithography." *History of American Manufacturers*, Vol. I: *1800–1860*. Philadelphia, 1860.

McCauley, Lois B. *Maryland Historical Prints, 1752 to 1889*. Baltimore, 1975.
Madden, Betty I. *Art, Crafts, and Architecture in Early Illinois*. Urbana, Illinois, 1974.
Mallett, Daniel Trowbridge. *Mallett's Index of Artists*. New York, 1948.
Marzio, Peter C. "American Lithographic Technology before the Civil War." *Prints in and of America to 1850*. Edited by John D. Morse. Charlottesville, Virginia, 1970.
———. *Mr. Audubon and Mr. Bien: An Early Phase in the History of American Chromolithography*. Washington, D.C., 1975.
Mills, Paul, ed. *Early Paintings of California in the Robert B. Honeyman, Jr. Collection*. Oakland, California, 1956.
Morris, Leopold. *Pictorial History of Victoria and Victoria County*. San Antonio, Texas, 1953.
Munsing, Stefanie A. *Made in America: Printmaking 1760–1860 . . .* Philadelphia, 1973.
Peters, Harry T. *America on Stone*. New York, 1931.
———. *California on Stone*. Garden City, New York, 1935.
Pinckney, Pauline A. *Painting in Texas: The Nineteenth Century*. Austin, Texas, 1967.
Ratchford, Fannie Elizabeth, ed. *The Story of Champ d'Asile as Told by Two of the Colonists*. Translated by Donald Joseph. Dallas, Texas [1937].
Rees, Abraham. *The Cyclopaedia; or Universal Dictionary of Arts, Sciences, and Literature*, Vol. 2. Philadelphia, [c. 1817].
Rehner, Leigh. *Henry Walton: 19th Century American Artist*. Ithaca, New York, 1968.
Reps, John W. "Boston by Bostonians: The Printed Plans and Views of the Colonial City by its Artists, Cartographers, Engravers, and Publishers." *Boston Prints and Printmakers, 1670–1775*. Edited by Walter Whitehill and Sinclair Hitchings. Boston, 1973.
———. *Western City Views*. Fort Worth, Texas, 1972.
Ringwalt, J. Luther, ed. "Lithography." *American Encyclopaedia of Printing*. Philadelphia, 1871.
Senefelder, Alois. *A Complete Course in Lithography*. Introduction by A. Hyatt Mayor. New York, 1968.
Seymour, Alfred. *Practical Lithography*. London, 1903.
Shumate, Albert. *The Life of George Henry Goddard: Artist, Architect, Surveyor, and Map Maker*. Berkeley, California, 1969.
Snyder, Martin P. *City of Independence: Views of Philadelphia Before 1800*. New York, 1975.
Stokes, I. N. Phelps. *Iconography of Manhattan Island, 1498–1909*. 6 vols. New York, 1915–28.
———, and Haskell, Daniel C. *American Historical Prints*. New York, 1932.
Taft, Robert. *Artists and Illustrators of the Old West, 1850–1900*. New York, 1953.
Thomas, Samuel W., ed. *Views of Louisville Since 1766*. Louisville, Kentucky, 1971.
Twyman, Michael. *Lithography, 1800–1850: The Techniques of Drawing on Stone in England and France and their Application in Works of Topography*. London, 1970.
Utterback, Martha, comp. *Early Texas Art in the Witte Museum*. San Antonio, Texas, 1968.
Van Nostrand, Jean. *A Pictorial and Narrative History of Monterey: Adobe Capital of California 1770–1847*. San Francisco, 1968.
Wainwright, Nicholas. *Philadelphia in the Romantic Age of Lithography*. Philadelphia, 1958.
Warre, Henry J. *Sketches in North America and the Oregon Territory, by Captain H. Warre, A. D. C. to the Late Commander of the Forces*. With an introduction by Archibald Hanna, Jr. Barre, Massachusetts, 1970.
Watson, Douglas S. *California in the Fifties: Fifty Views of Cities and Mining Towns in California and the West*. San Francisco, 1936.
Weber, Wilhelm. *A History of Lithography*. London, 1966.
Wild, J. C. *The Valley of the Mississippi Illustrated in a Series of Views*. Edited by Lewis Foulk Thomas. St. Louis, 1948.
Young, Edward. "Lithography." *Leading Pursuits and Leading Men*. Philadelphia, 1856.

PERIODICALS

American Journal of Science and Arts, IV (October, 1821), 159–71.
The Analectic Magazine, XIV (July, 1819), 66–72.
Comstock, Helen. "The Complete Work of Robert Havell, Jr." *Connoisseur*, CXXVI (November, 1950), 127.
Eckhardt, George H. "Early Lithography in Philadelphia." *Antiques*, XXXVIII (December, 1935), 249–52.
Gardner, Robert. Review of *The Technique of Fine Lithography* by

Michael Knigin and Murray Zimiles. *The Print Collector's Newsletter*, I (September–October, 1970), 93.
Gideon, Samuel E. "Two Pioneer Artists in Texas." *American Magazine of Art*, IX (September, 1918), 452–56.
Heffernan, John Paul. "A Maine Family of Smiths." *Down East: The Magazine of Maine*, XXI (April, 1975), 36–41, 66–70.
Jackson, Joseph. "Bass Otis, America's First Lithographer." *Pennsylvania Magazine of History and Biography*, XXXVII (1913), 285–94.
Journal of the Franklin Institute, IV–V (1827–1828); N. S. III (1829); N. S. V–VI (1830–1831).
Kansas State Historical Society. *Collections*. XIV (1915–18).
Keith, Kent. "Sankt Antonius: Germans in the Alamo City in the 1850's." *Southwestern Historical Quarterly*, LXXVI (October, 1972), 183–202.
Knittle, Rhea Mansfield. "The Kelloggs, Hartford Lithographers." *Antiques*, X (July, 1926), 42–46.
Koke, Richard J. "John Hill (1770–1850), Master of Aquatint." *New-York Historical Society Quarterly*, XLIII (January, 1959), 51–117.
McDermott, John Francis. "J. C. Wild, Western Painter and Lithographer." *Ohio State Archaeological and Historial Quarterly*, LX (April, 1951), 111–25.
———. "John Caspar Wild: Some New Facts and a Query." *Pennsylvania Magazine of History and Biography*, LXXXIII (October, 1959), 452–55.
McPeck, Eleanor M. "George Isham Parkyns: Artist and Landscape Architect, 1749–1820." *Quarterly Journal of the Library of Congress*, XXX (July, 1973), 171–82.
Marzio, Peter C., and Kaplan, Milton. "Lithographs as Historical Documents." *Antiques*, CII (October, 1972), 669–74.
"New York Artists Fifty Years Ago." *Appleton's Journal*, VII (May 18, 1872), 572–75.
Norton, Bettina A. "Edwin Whitefield, 1816–1892." *Antiques*, CII (August, 1972), 232–43.
Reps, John W. "Great Expectations and Hard Times: The Planning of Cairo, Illinois." *Journal of the Society of Architectural Historians*, XVI (December, 1957), 14–21.
The Old Print Shop. *Portfolio*. I (June, 1942), 20–22; XIII (January, 1954), 99–102.
Shelley, Donald A. "William Guy Wall and His Watercolors for the Historic *Hudson River Portfolio*." *New-York Historical Society Quarterly*, XXXI (January, 1947), 25–45.
Snyder, Martin P. "J. C. Wild and His Philadelphia Views." *Pennsylvania Magazine of History and Biography*, LXXVII (January, 1953), 32–75.
Tatham, David. "The Pendleton-Moore Shop: Lithographic Artists in Boston, 1825–1840." *Old-Time New England*, LXII (October–December, 1971), 29–46.
Taylor, Charles Henry. "Some Notes on Early American Lithography." *Proceedings of the American Antiquarian Society*, N. S. XXXII (April, 1922), 68–80.
"Texas in Pictures." *Antiques*, LIII (June, 1948), 453–59.
United States Literary Gazette, IV (June 15, 1826), 224–27.
Weitenkampf, Frank. "John Hill and American Landscapes in Aquatint." *American Collector*, XVII (July, 1948), 6–8.
Wright, Edith A., and McDevitt, Josephine A. "Henry Stone, Lithographer." *Antiques*, XXXIV (July, 1938), 16–19.

NEWSPAPERS

West Virginia Hillbilly (Richwood), January 25, 1975.

UNPUBLISHED WORKS

Carey, Thomas. "The American Lithograph from its Inception to 1865. . . ." Unpublished Ph.D. dissertation, Ohio State University, 1954.
Cumming, John. "Albert Ruger and His Views." n.d. (Typewritten)

PLATES

All illustrations are from the collections of the Amon Carter Museum except plates 23, 32, and 40.

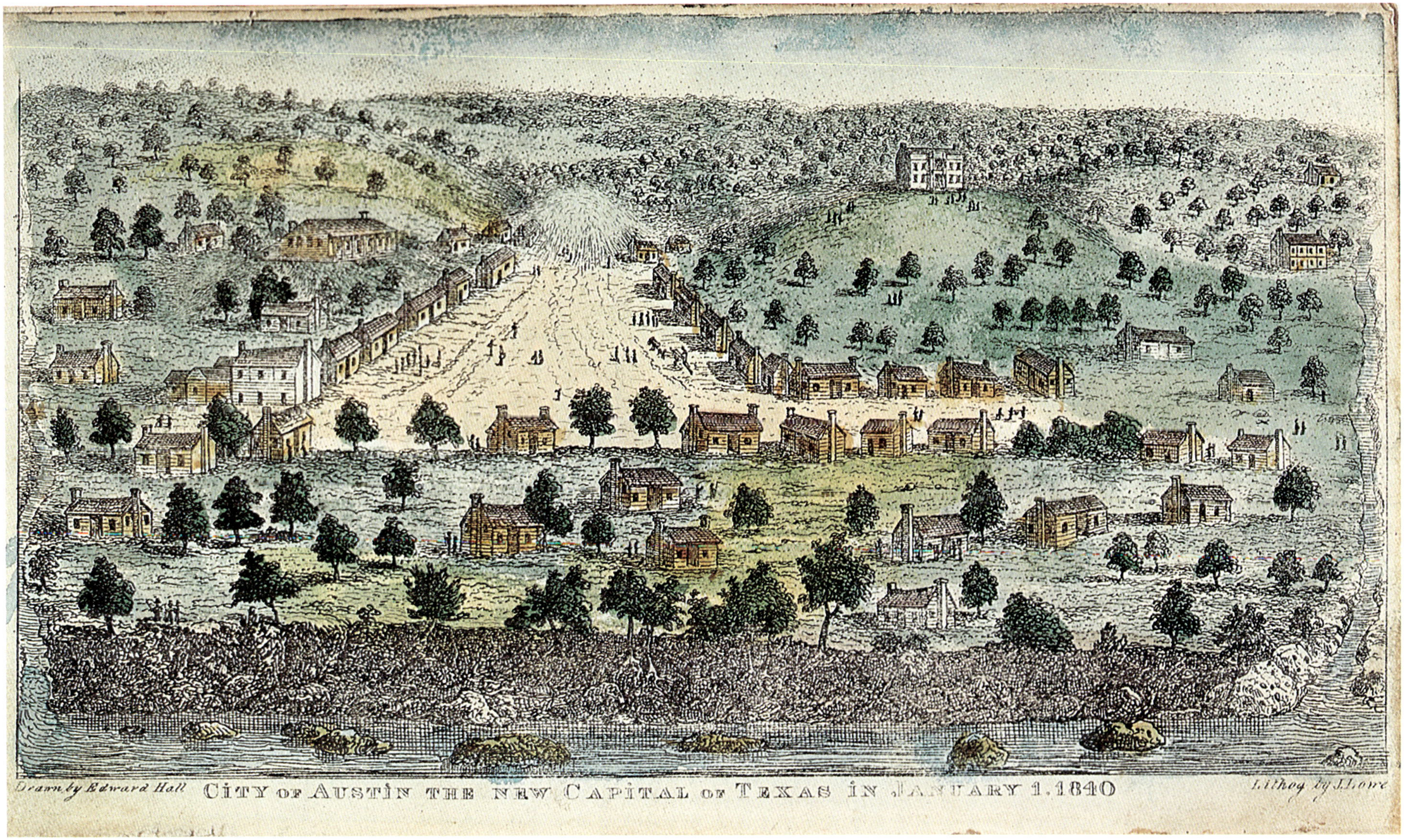

PLATE 1. *City of Austin the New Capital of Texas in January 1, 1840*. Edward Hall. 1844, in *A History of Texas, or the Emigrant's Guide to the New Republic*. Lithograph (hand colored). 4 x 7-3/16 in. (10.1 x 18.2 cm.).

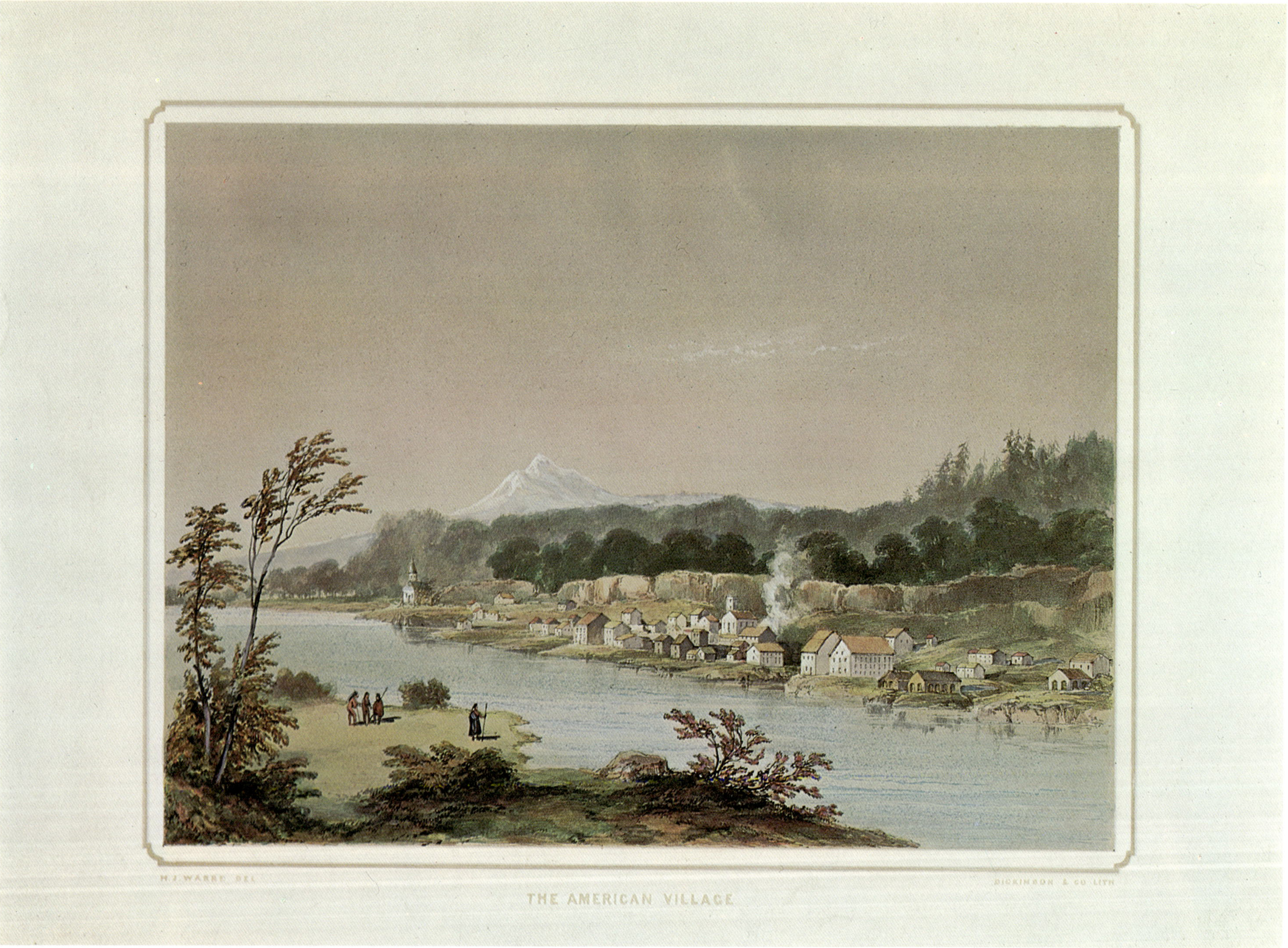

PLATE 2. *The American Village* (Oregon City, Oregon). Sir Henry James Warre. c. 1848, in *Sketches in North America and the Oregon Territory*. Toned lithograph (hand colored). 9-13/16 x 13-1/8 in. (24.8 x 33.3 cm.)

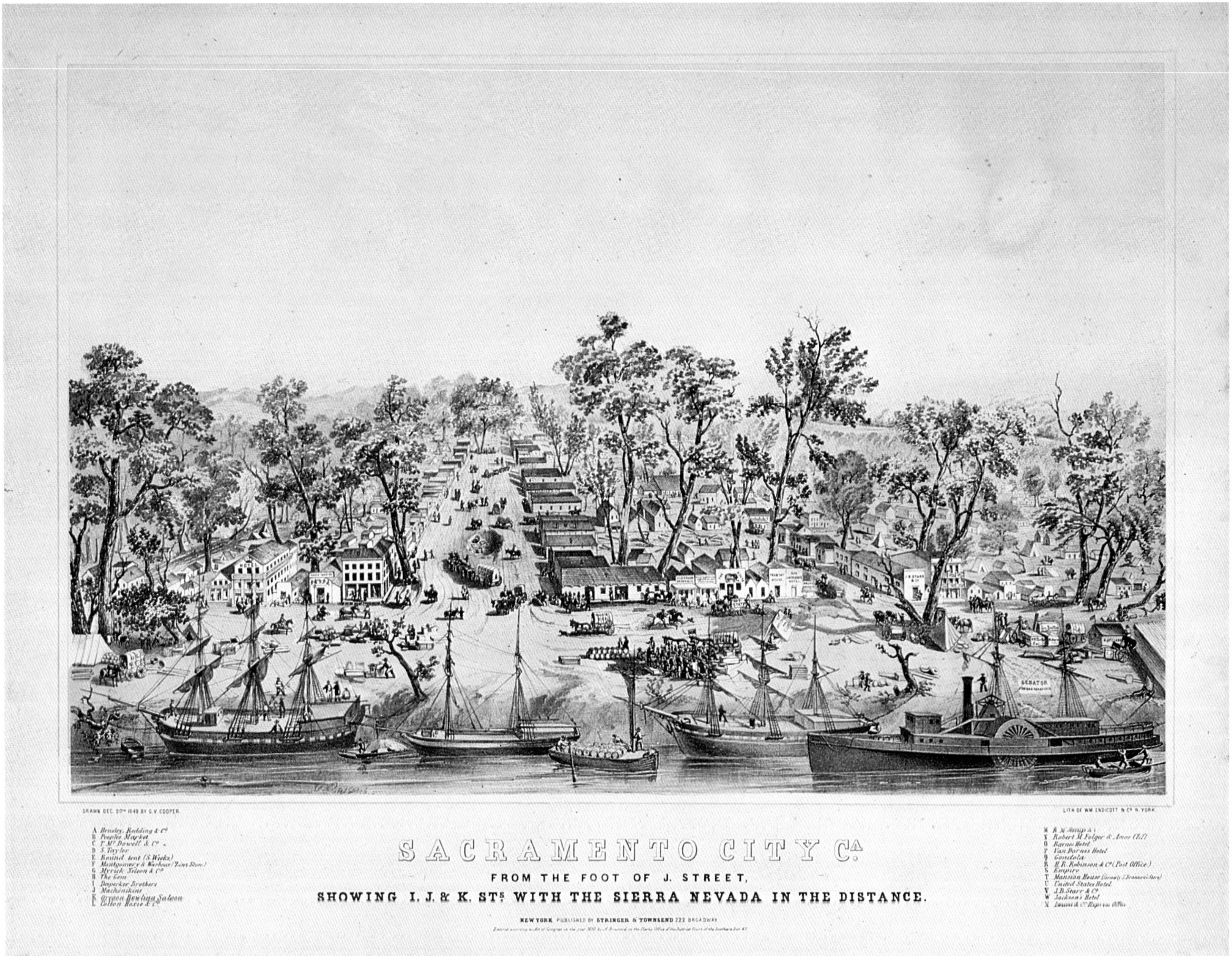

PLATE 3. *Sacramento City Ca. From the Foot of J. Street, Showing I. J. & K. Sts. With the Sierra Nevada in the Distance*. George V. Cooper. 1850. Color lithograph. 15-3/16 x 23-3/16 in. (38.5 x 58.8 cm.) Printed by Wm. Endicott & Co. Published by Stringer & Townsend.

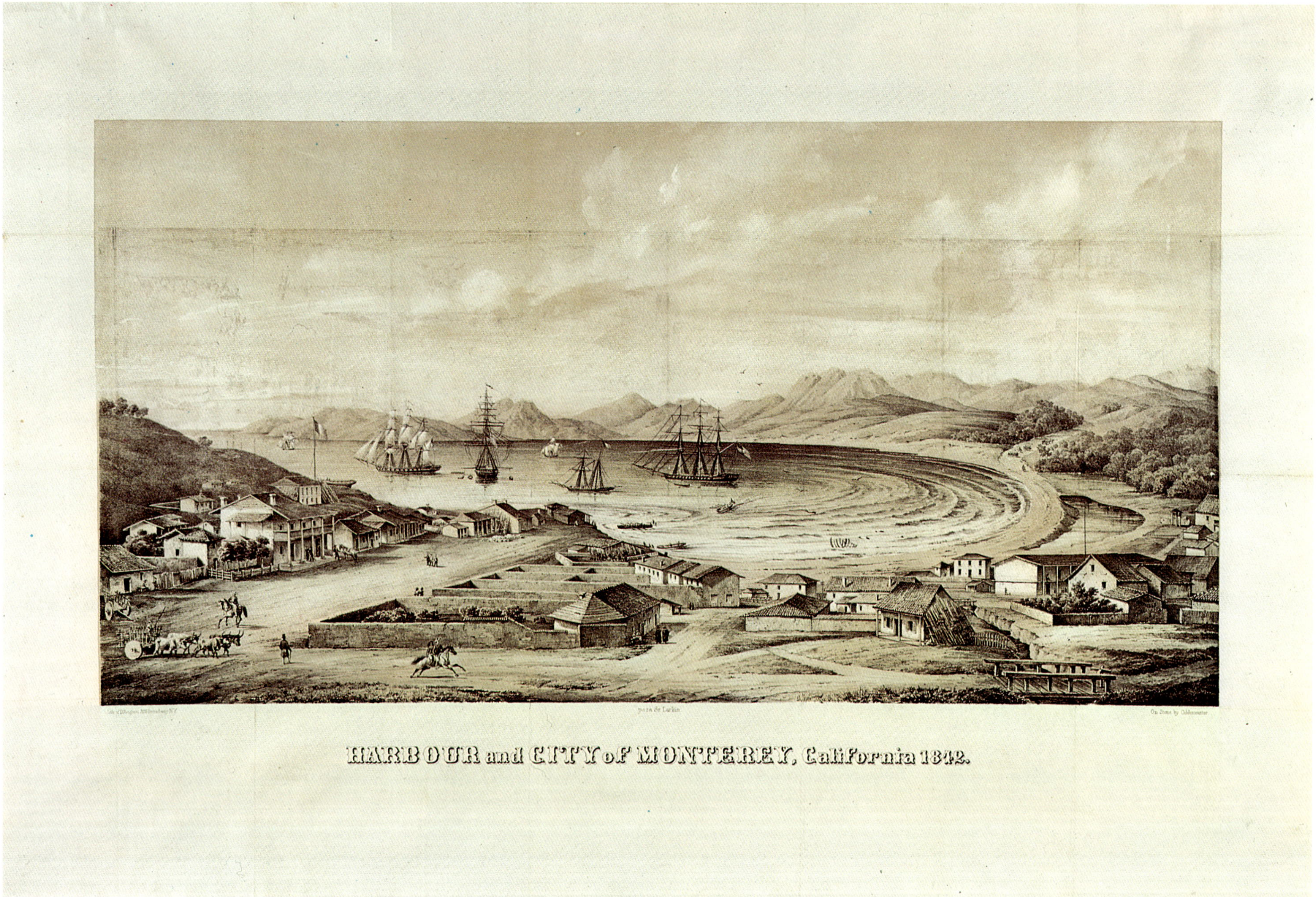

PLATE 4. *Harbour and City of Monterey, California 1842*. Unsigned. 1850. Toned lithograph. 15 x 29-3/16 in. (38.1 x 74.1 cm.) Printed by D'Avignon. Published by Thomas Larkin.

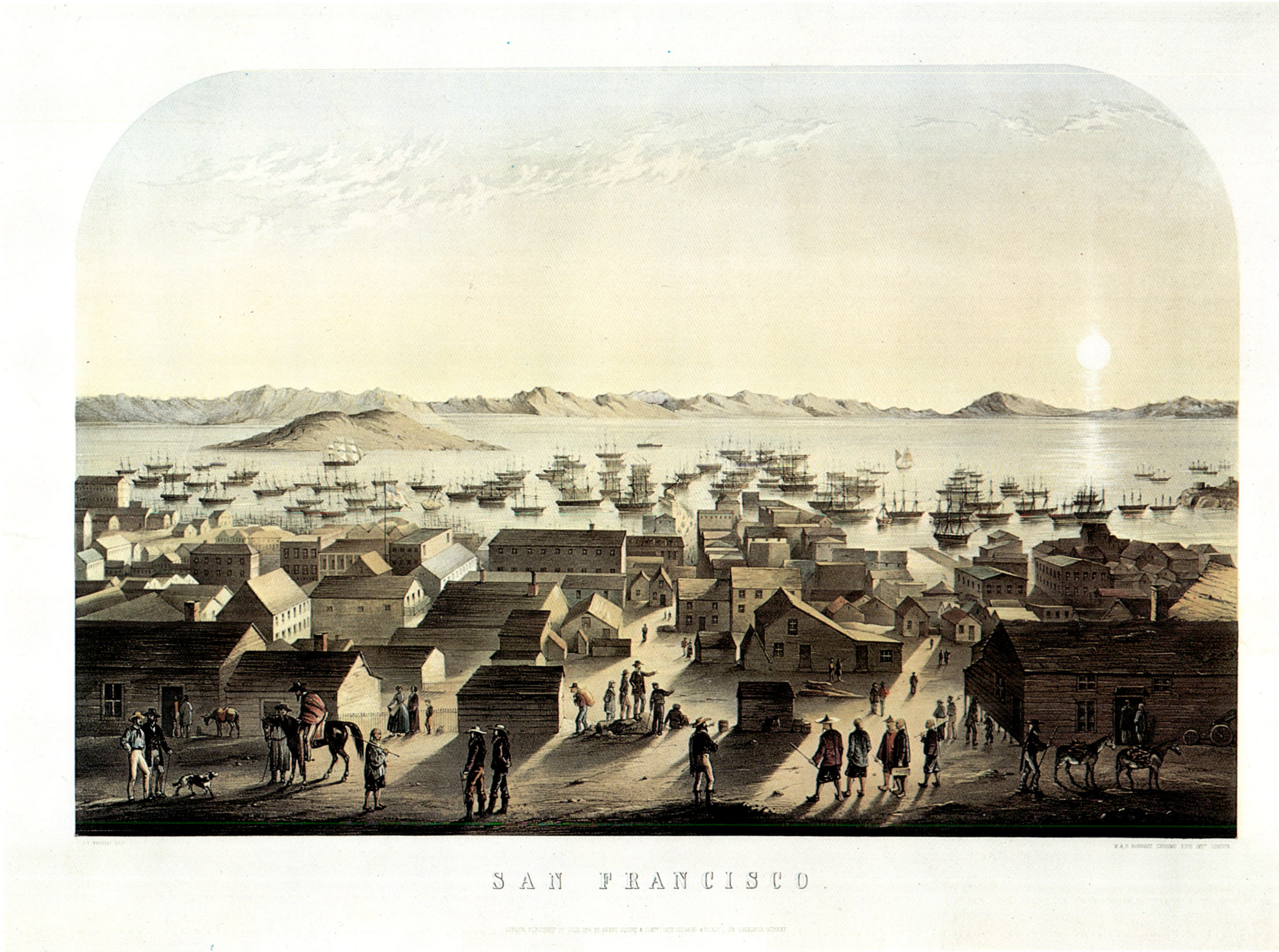

PLATE 5. *San Francisco.* S. F. Marryat. 1851. Lithograph (hand colored). 16-1/2 x 25-7/16 in. (41.9 x 64.5 cm.) Printed by M. & N. Hanhart. Published by Henry Squire & Co.

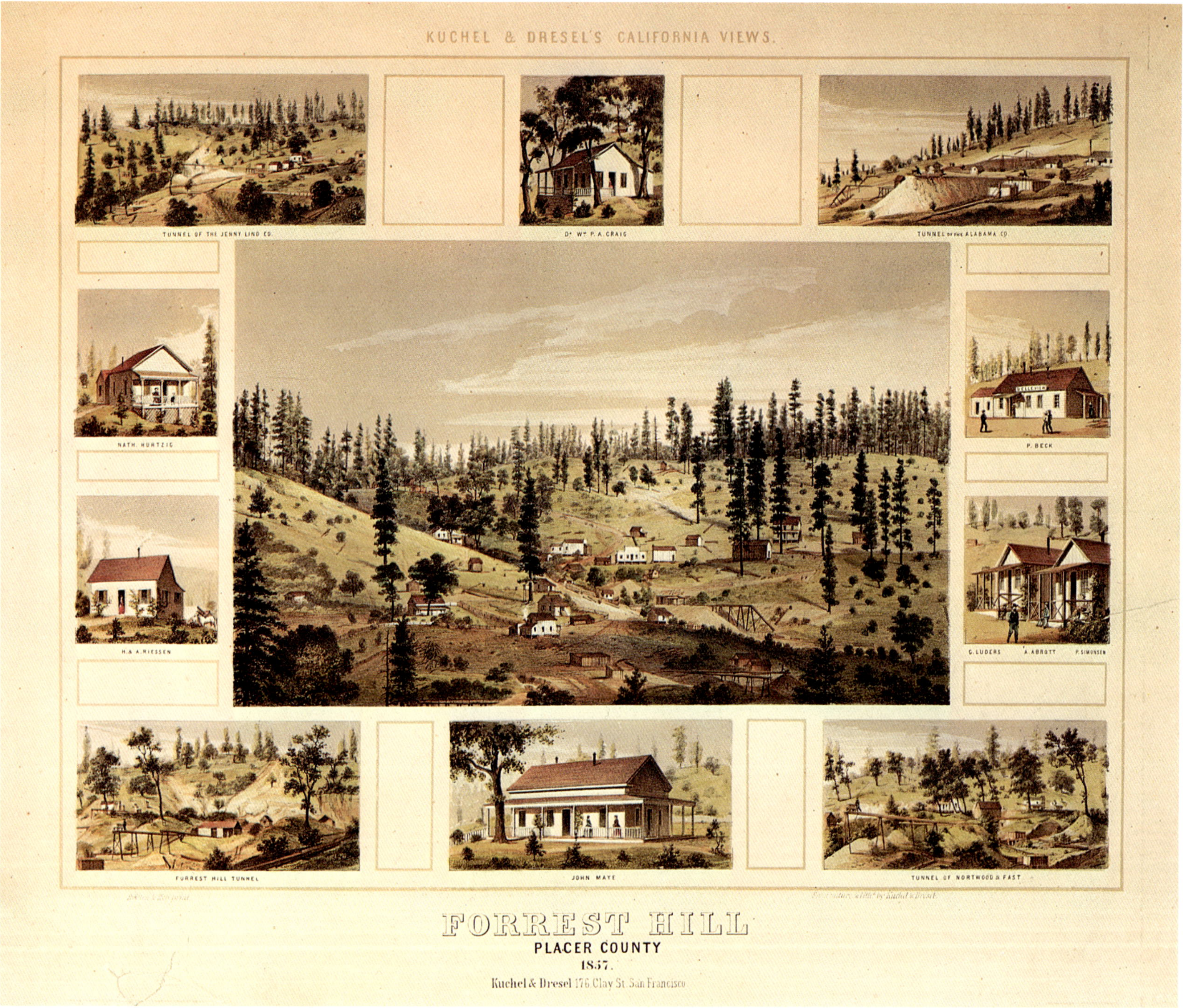

PLATE 6. *Forrest Hill Placer County 1857*. Charles C. Kuchel and Emil Dresel. 1857. Color lithograph (hand colored). 14-15/16 x 19-7/8 in. (37.9 x 50.4 cm.) Printed by Britton & Rey.

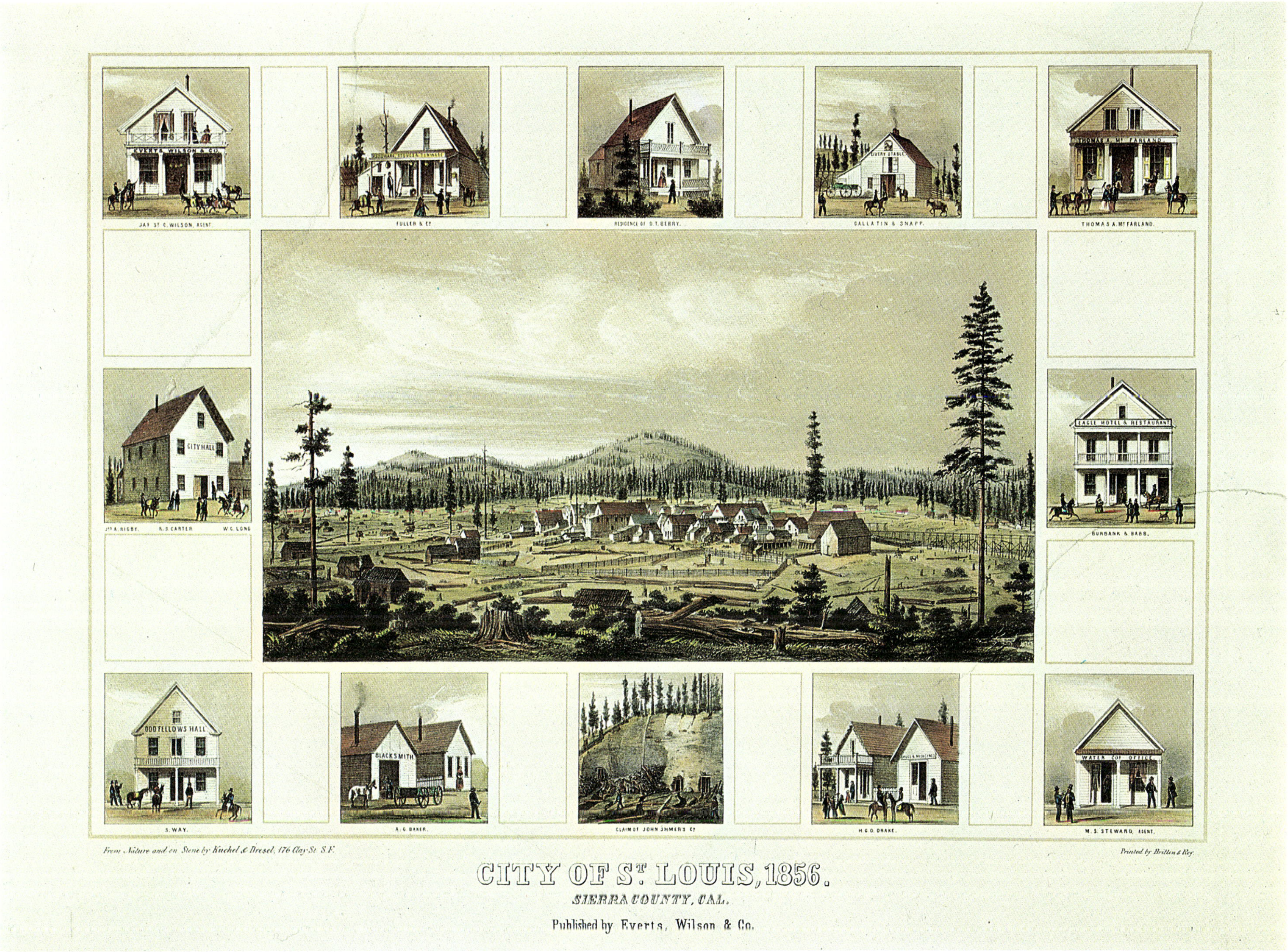

PLATE 7. *City of St. Louis, 1856. Sierra County, Cal.* Charles C. Kuchel and Emil Dresel. 1856. Color lithograph (hand colored). 14-3/16 x 20-3/4 in. (36.0 x 52.7 cm.) Printed by Britton & Rey. Published by Everts, Wilson & Co.

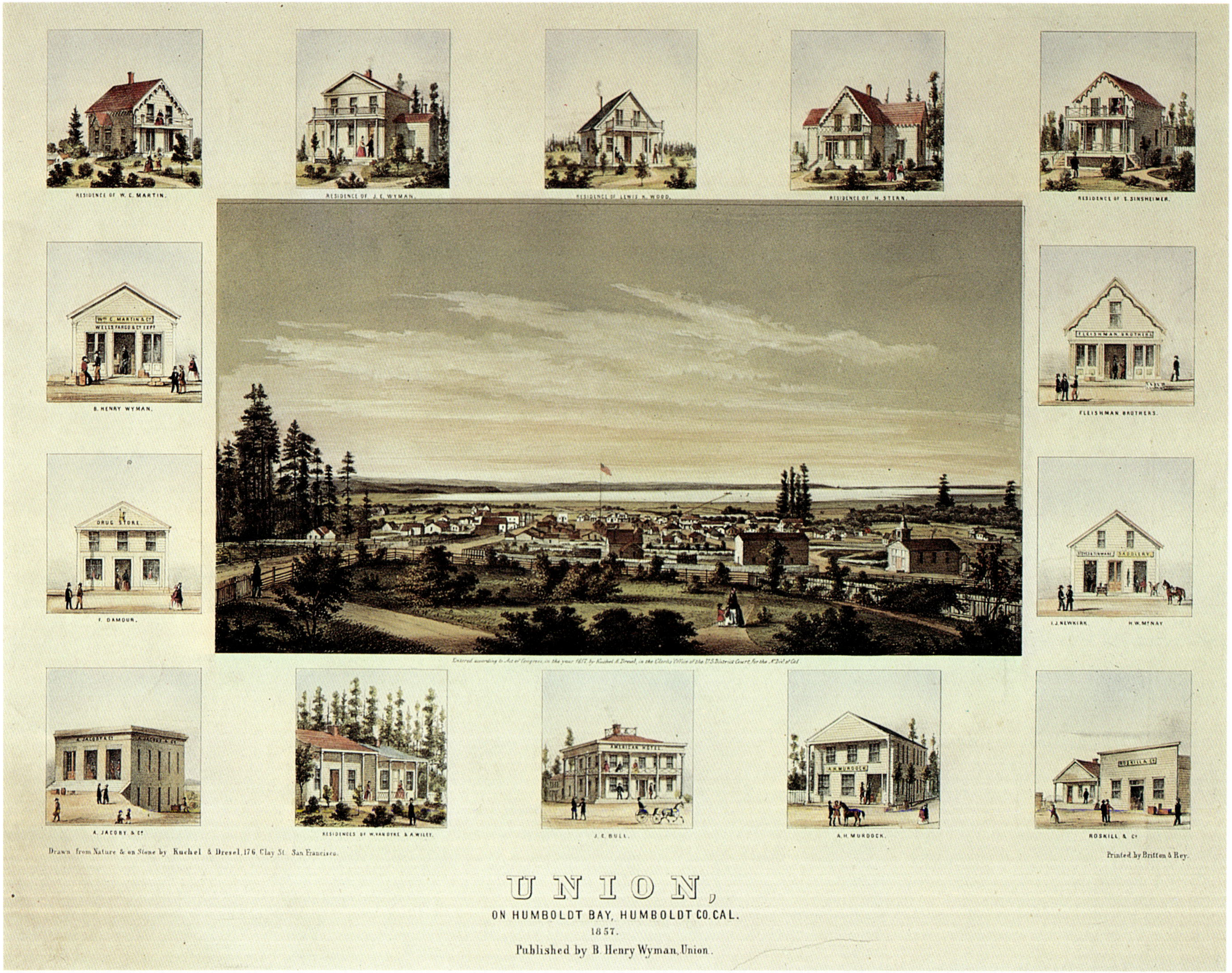

PLATE 8. *Union, On Humboldt Bay, Humboldt Co. Cal. 1857.* Charles C. Kuchel and Emil Dresel. 1857. Color lithograph (hand colored). 14-3/16 x 20-13/16 in. (36.0 x 52.8 cm.) Printed by Britton & Rey. Published by B. Henry Wyman.

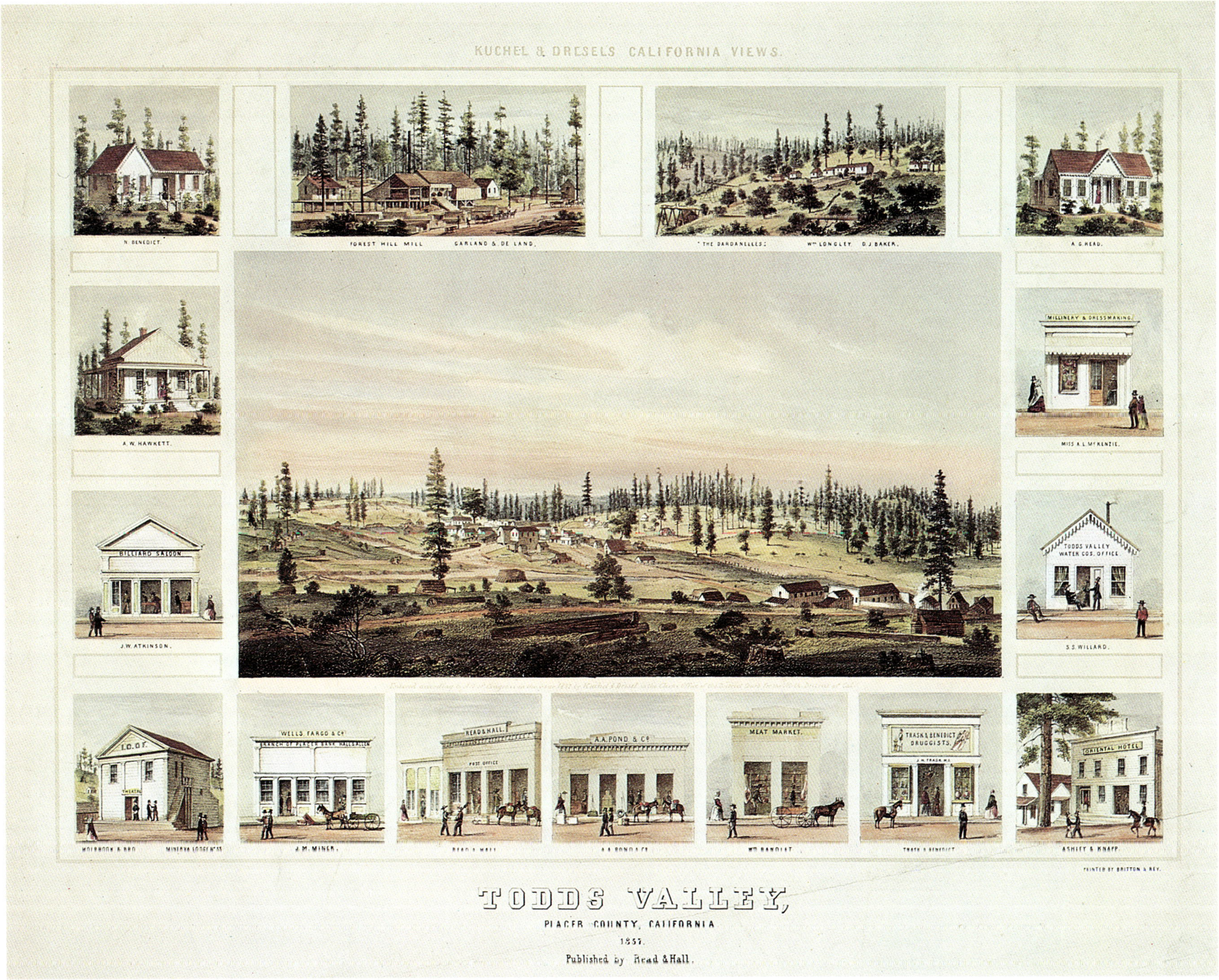

PLATE 9. *Todds Valley, Placer County, California. 1857.* Charles C. Kuchel and Emil Dresel. 1857. Color lithograph (hand colored). 14-1/4 x 20-3/4 in. (36.2 x 52.7 cm.) Printed by Britton & Rey. Published by Read & Hall.

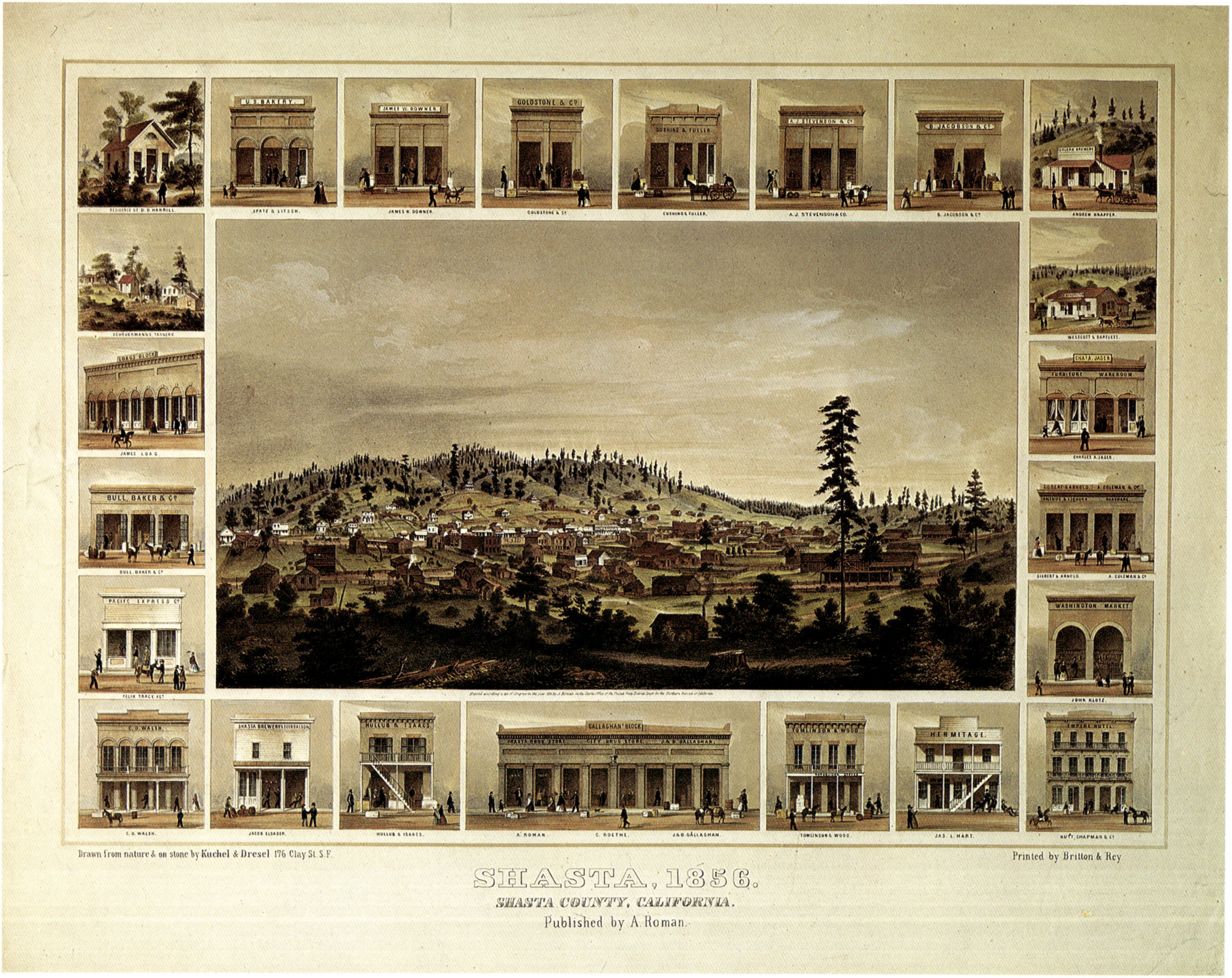

PLATE 10. *Shasta, 1856. Shasta County, California.* Charles C. Kuchel and Emil Dresel. 1856. Color lithograph (hand colored). 16-7/16 x 24 in. (41.7 x 60.8 cm.) Printed by Britton & Rey. Published by A. Roman.

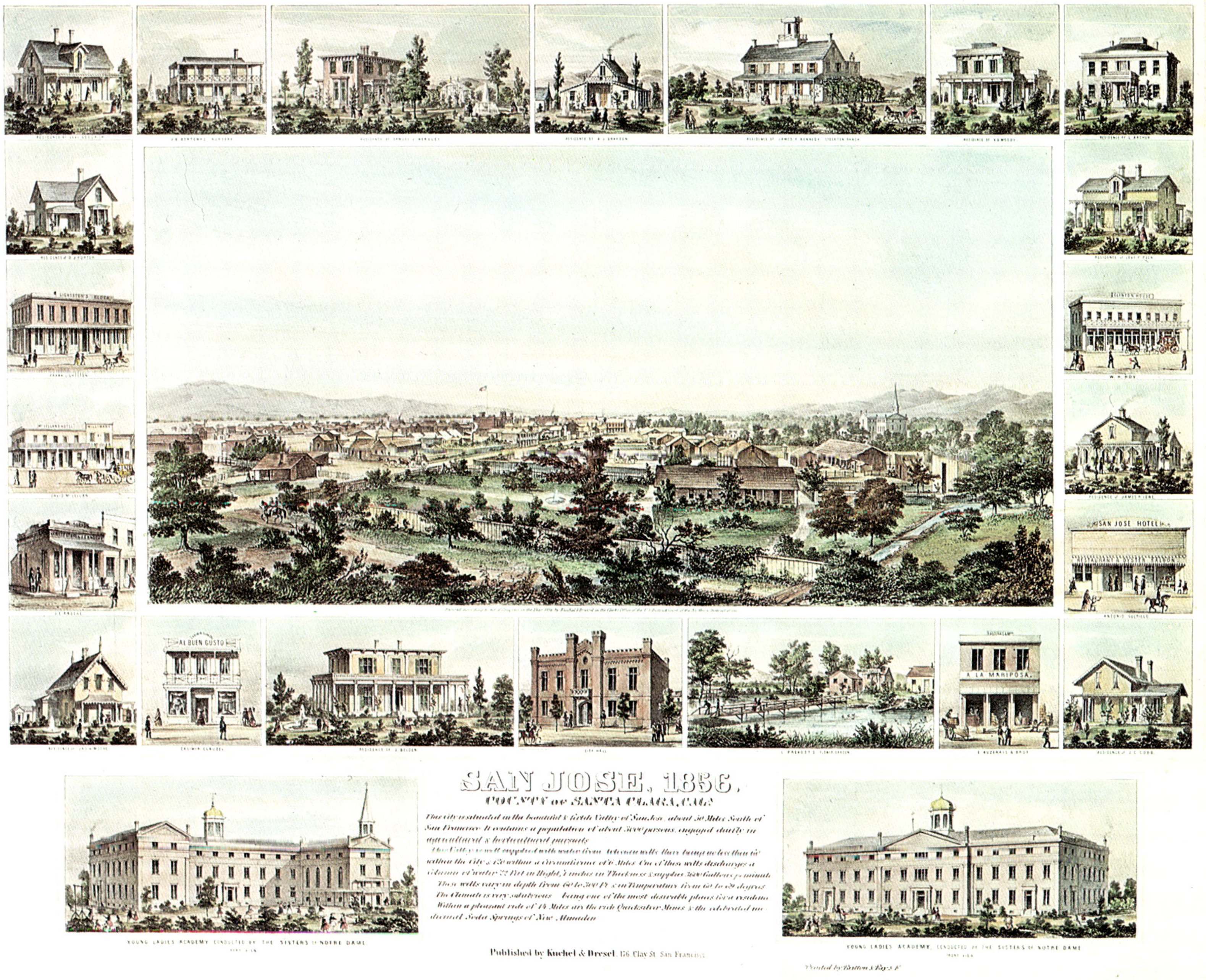

PLATE 11. *San Jose, 1856. County of Santa Clara, Cala.* Charles C. Kuchel and Emil Dresel. 1856. Color lithograph (hand colored). 19-7/8 x 25-3/4 in. (50.5 x 65.4 cm.) Printed by Britton & Rey.

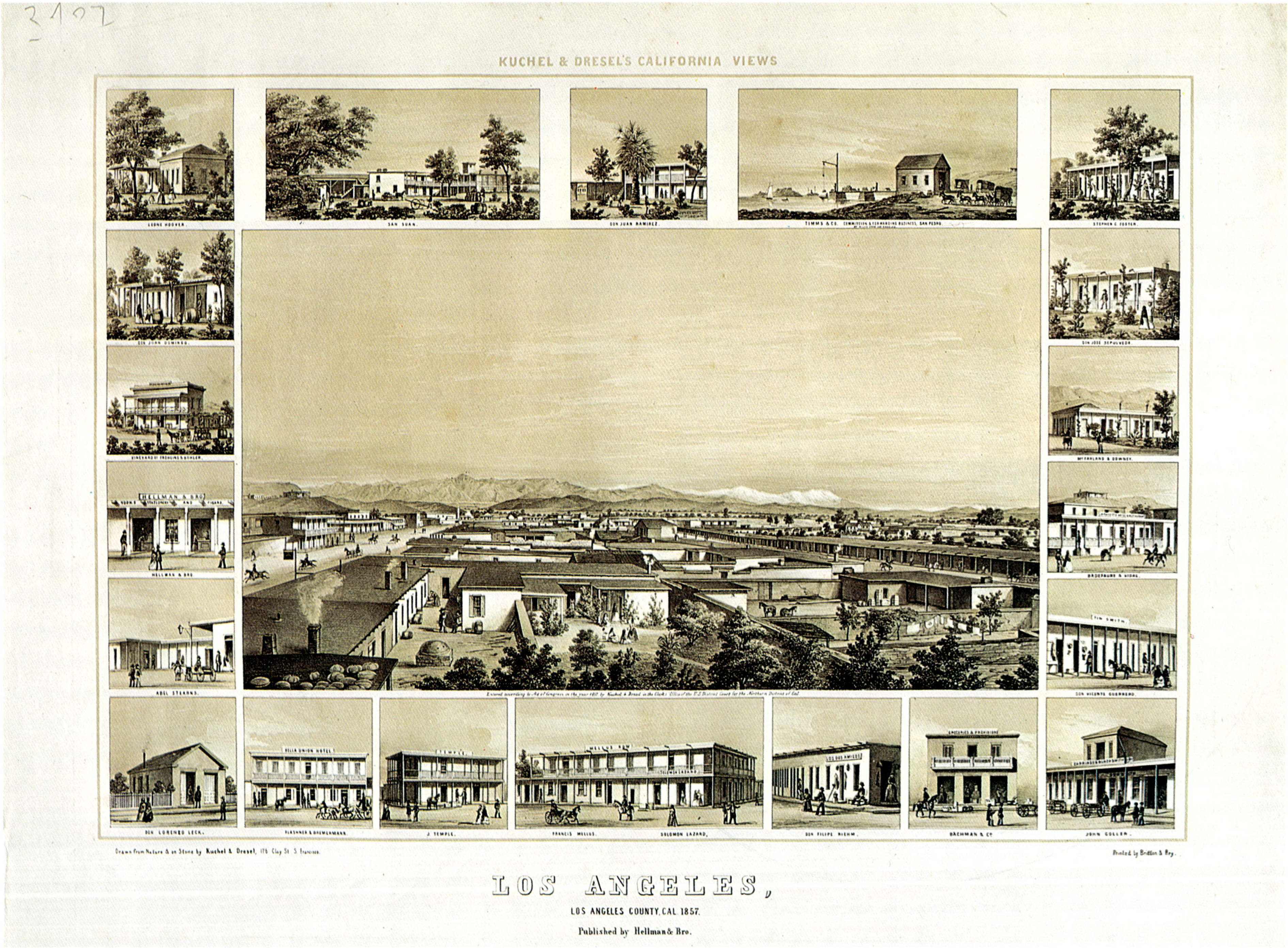

PLATE 12. *Los Angeles, Los Angeles County, Cal. 1857*. Charles C. Kuchel and Emil Dresel. 1857. Toned lithograph. 15-3/4 x 23-1/8 in. (40.0 x 58.7 cm.) Printed by Britton & Rey. Published by Hellman & Bro.

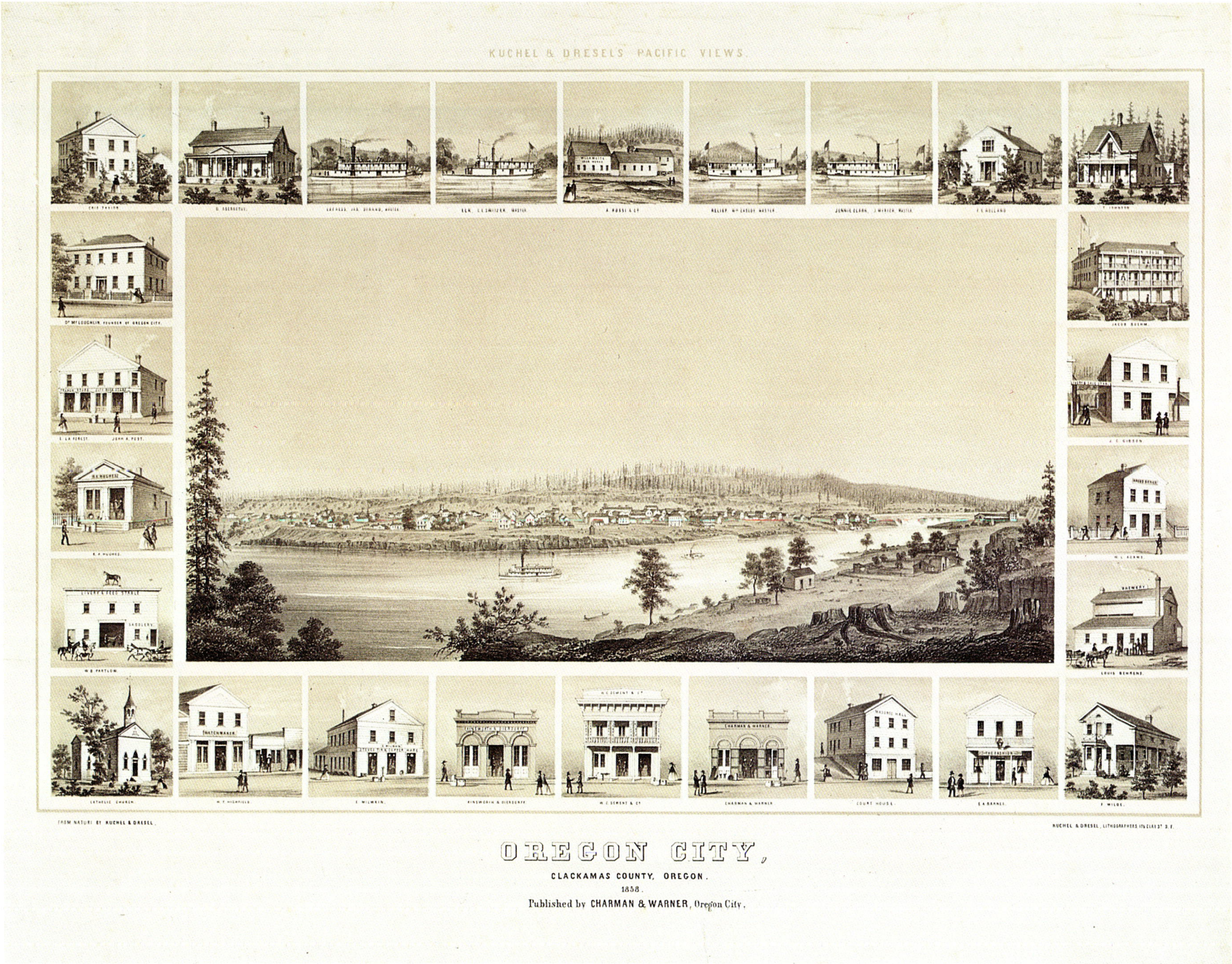

PLATE 13. *Oregon City, Clackamas County, Oregon. 1858.* Charles C. Kuchel and Emil Dresel. 1858. Toned lithograph. 15-15/16 x 25-11/16 in. (40.5 x 65.2 cm.) Published by Charman & Warner.

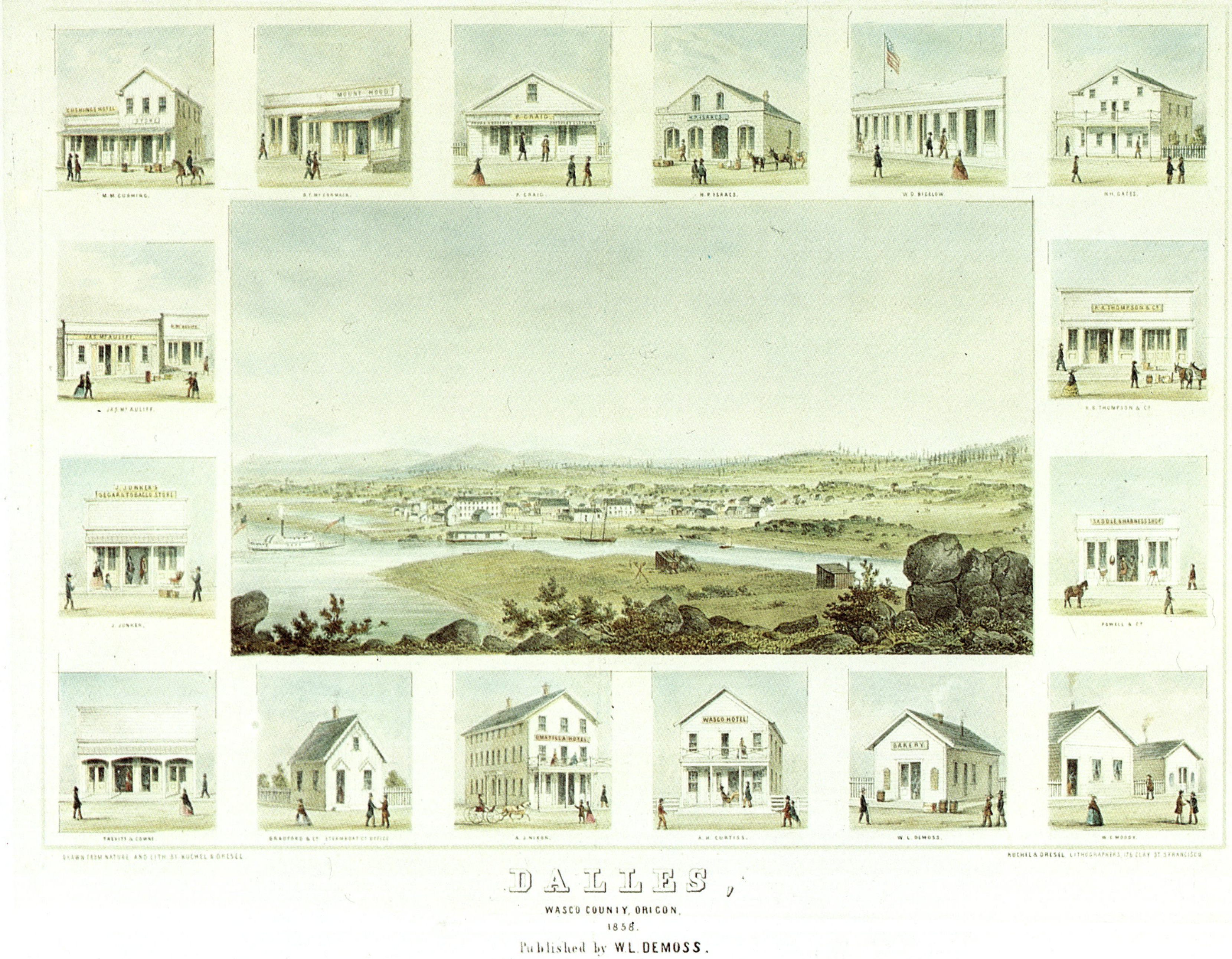

PLATE 14. *Dalles, Wasco Couniy, Oricon, 1858.* Charles C. Kuchel and Emil Dresel. 1858. Color lithograph (hand colored). 13-3/4 x 20 in. (34.8 x 50.7 cm.) Published by W. L. Demoss.

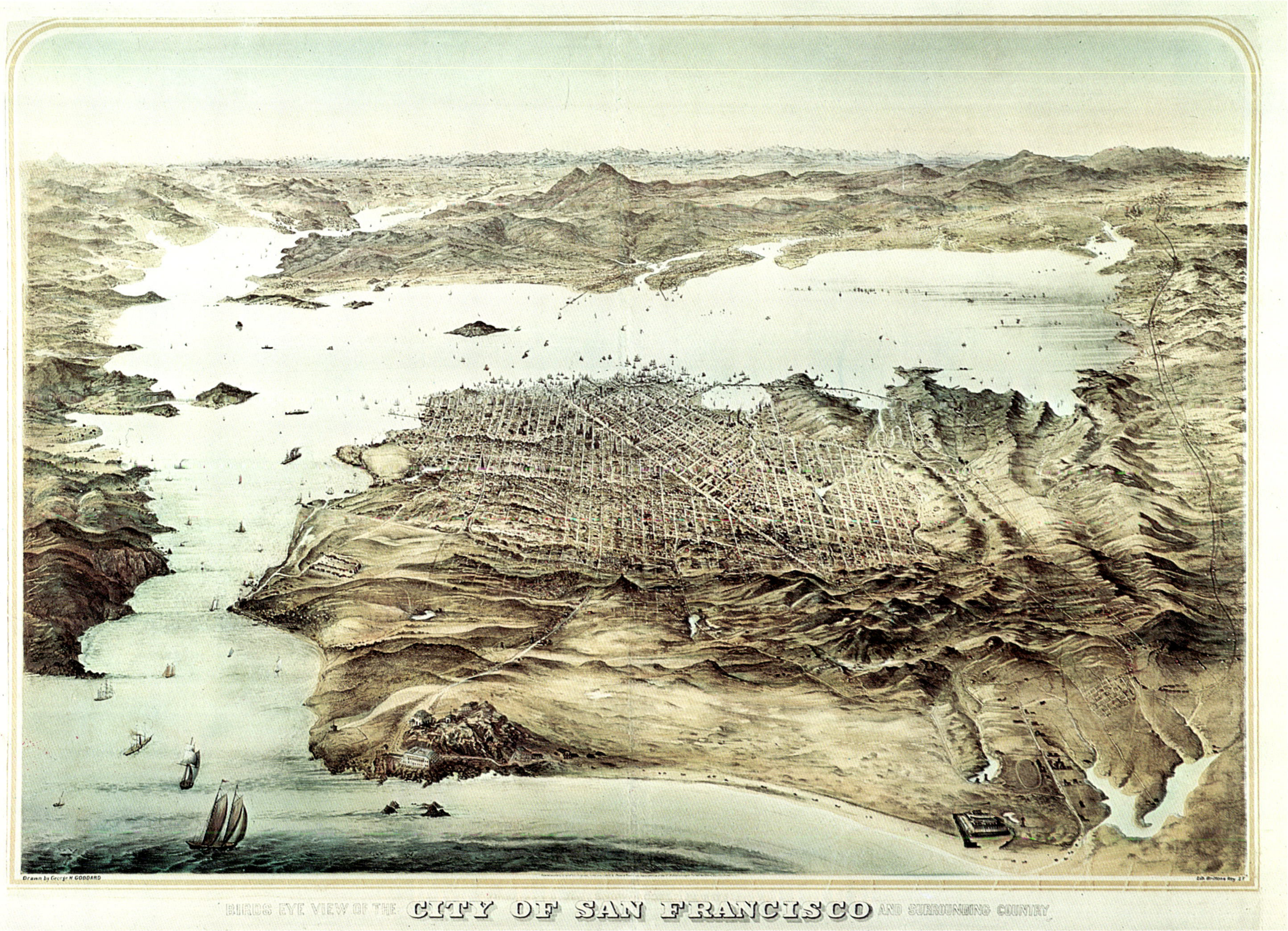

PLATE 15. *Birds Eye View of the City of San Francisco and Surrounding Country.* George Henry Goddard. 1868. Color lithograph (hand colored). 27-5/16 x 40-3/8 in. (69.3 x 102.5 cm.) Printed by Britton & Rey. Published by Snow & Roos.

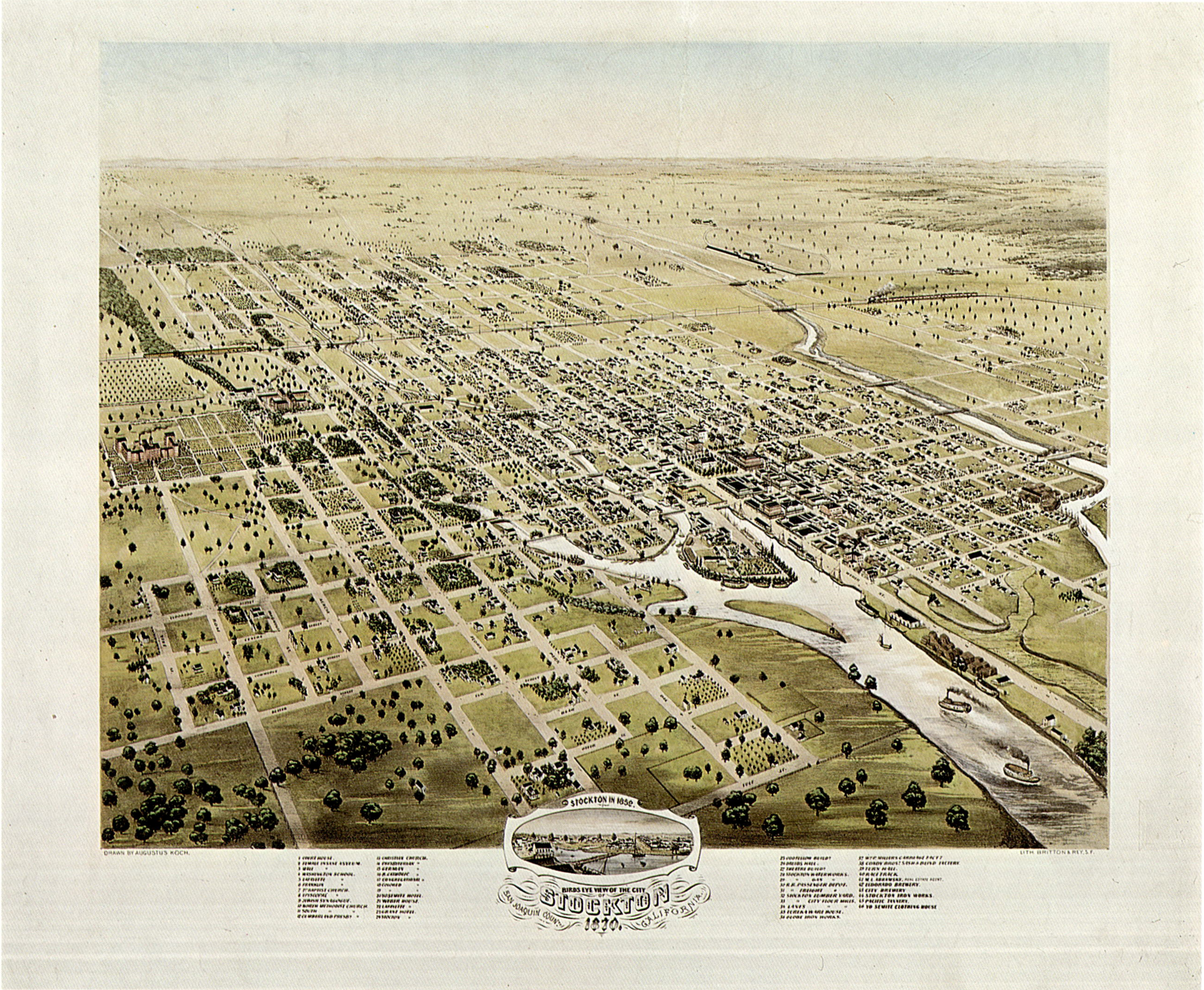

PLATE 16. *Birds Eye View of the City of Stockton San Joaquin County. California. 1870.* Augustus Koch. 1870. Color lithograph (hand colored). 22-5/8 x 28 in. (57.5 x 71.1 cm.) Printed by Britton & Rey.

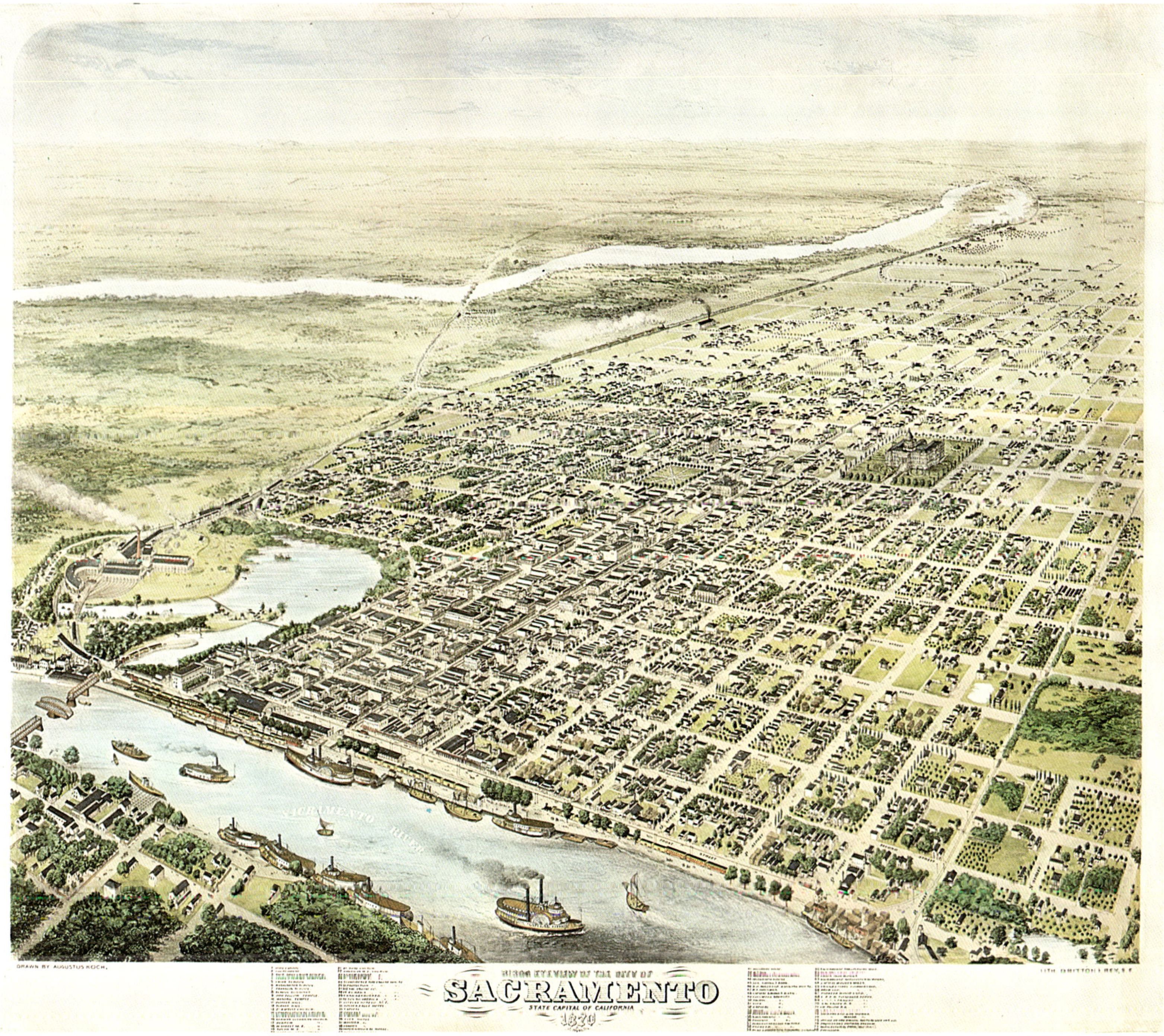

PLATE 17 *Birds Eye View of the City of Sacramento State Capital of California 1870.* Augustus Koch. 1870. Color lithograph (hand colored). 27-5/16 x 33-1/4 in. (69.3 x 84.4 cm.) Printed by Britton & Rey.

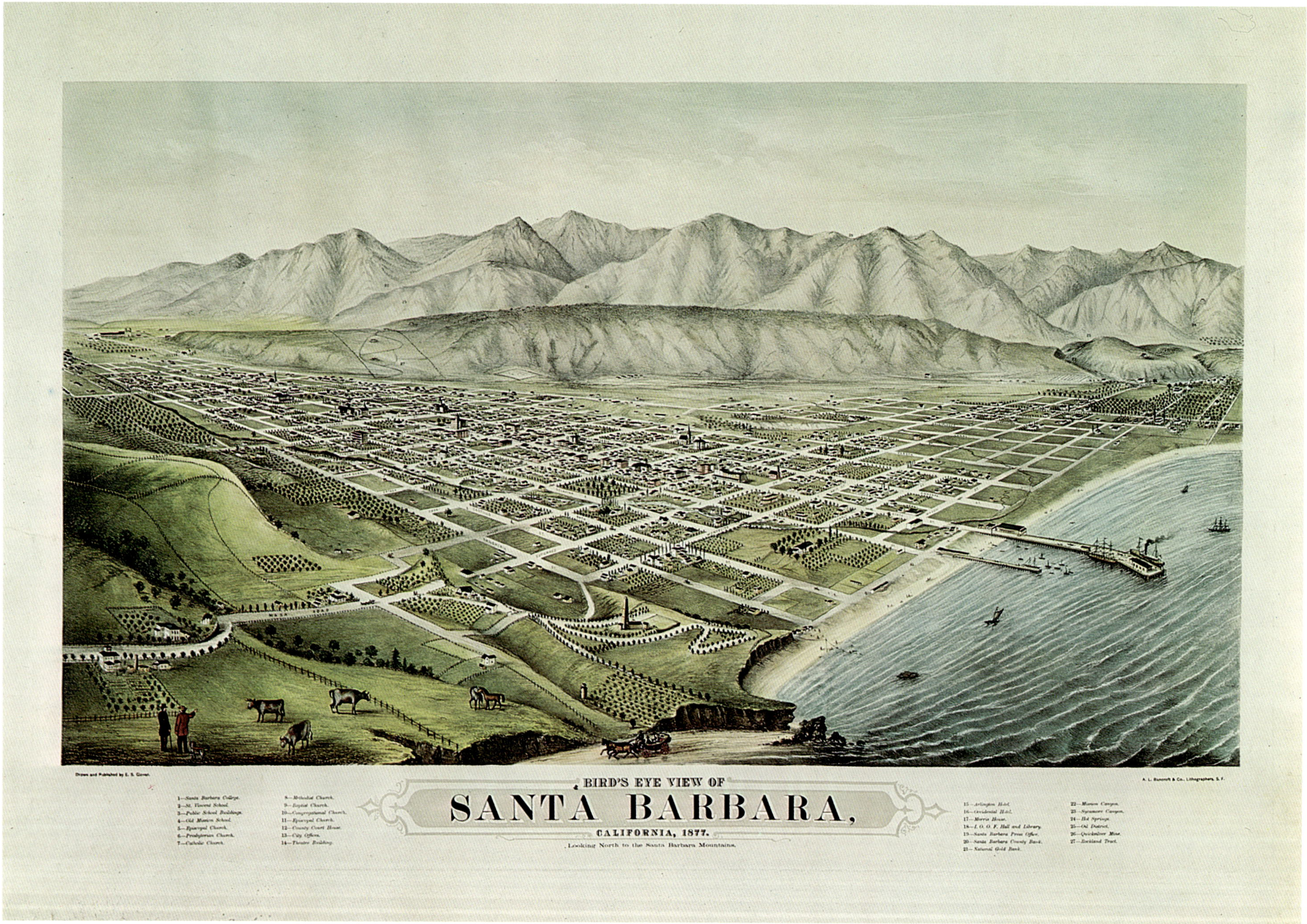

PLATE 18. *Bird's Eye View of Santa Barbara, California, 1877.* Eli S. Glover. c. 1877. Color lithograph (hand colored). 17-3/16 x 30-1/16 in. (43.7 x 74.3 cm.) Printed by A. L. Bancroft & Co.

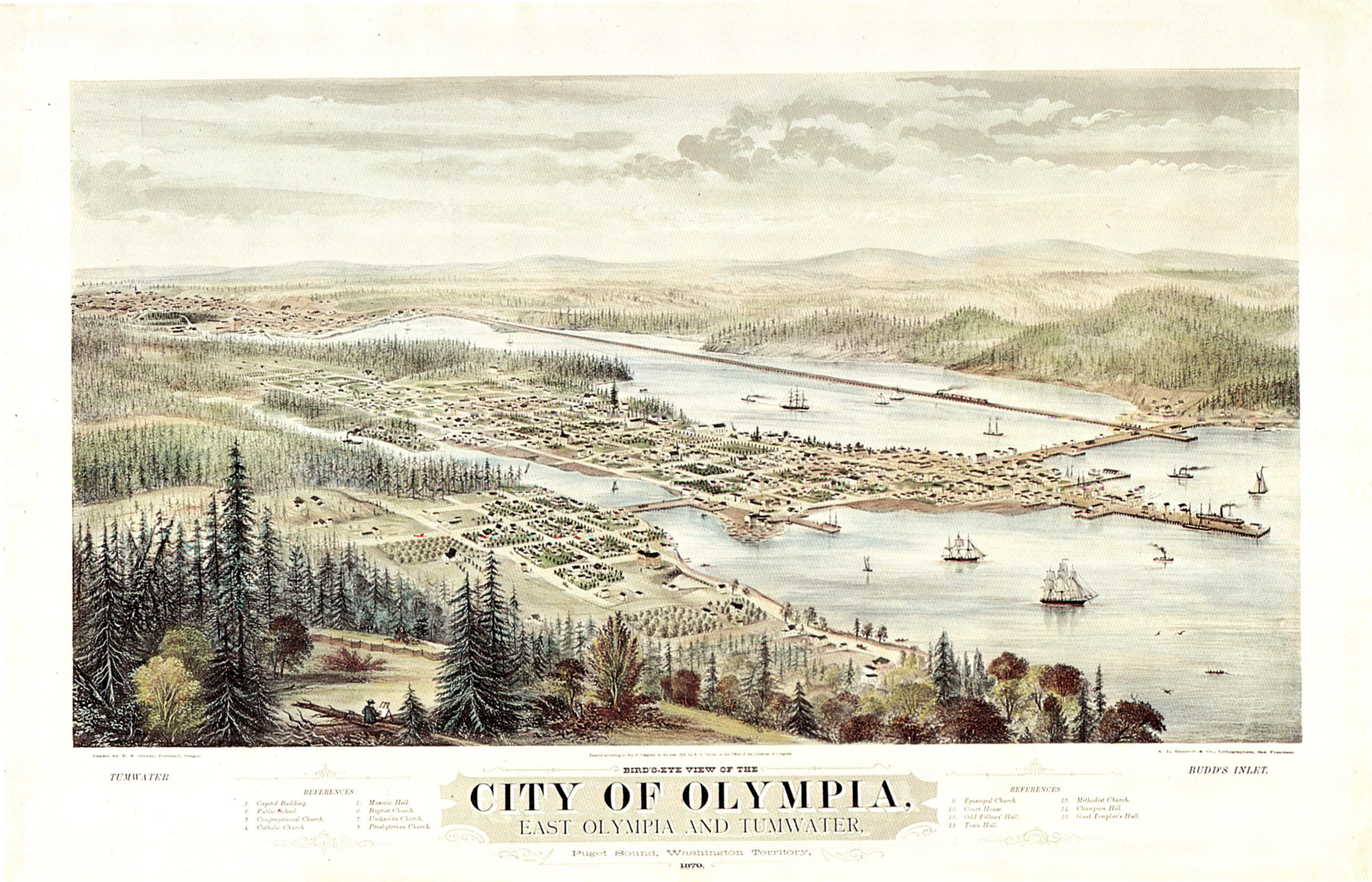

PLATE 19. *Bird's-Eye View of the City of Olympia, East Olympia and Tumwater, Puget Sound, Washington Territory, 1879.* Eli S. Glover. c. 1879. Lithograph (hand colored). 16 x 29-13/16 in. (40.5 x 75.7 cm.) Printed by A. L. Bancroft & Co.

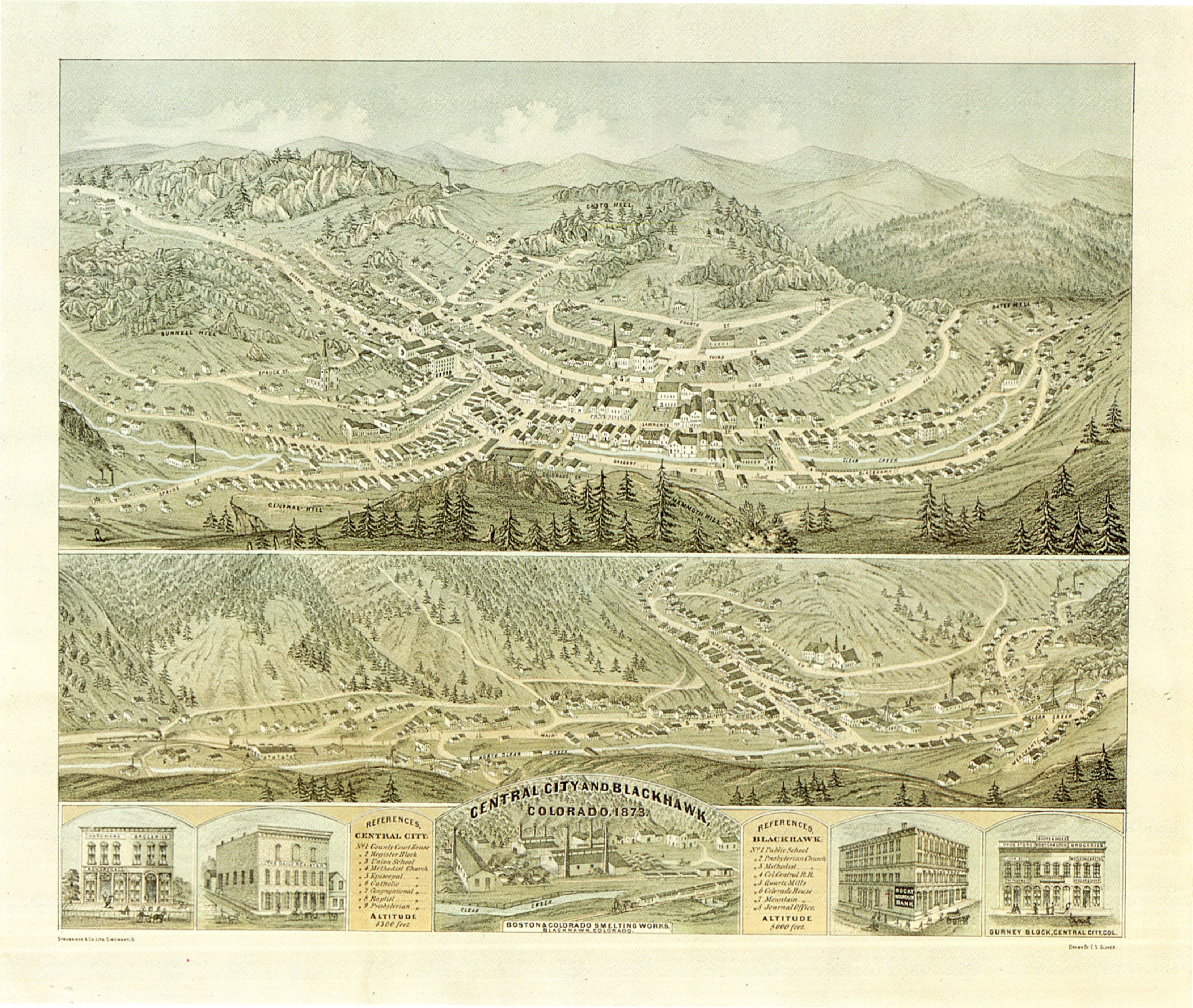

PLATE 20. *Central City and Blackhawk, Colorado 1873.* Eli S. Glover. c. 1874. Color lithograph. 16-7/8 x 22-1/4 in. (42.8 x 56.4 cm.) Printed by Strobridge & Co.

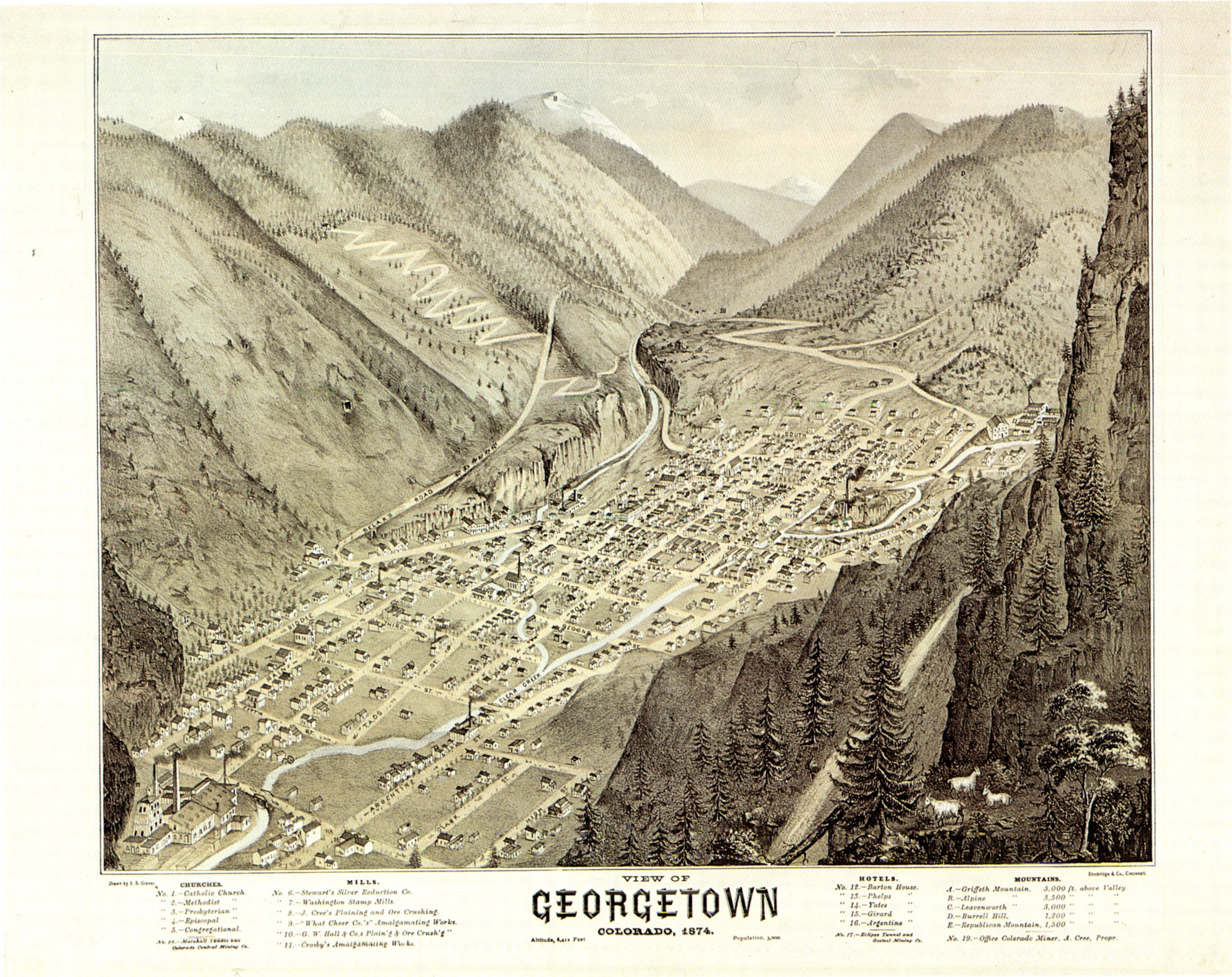

PLATE 21. *View of Georgetown Colorado, 1874.* Eli S. Glover. c. 1874. Color lithograph. 15-1/2 x 20 in. (39.3 x 50.7 cm.) Printed by Strobridge & Co.

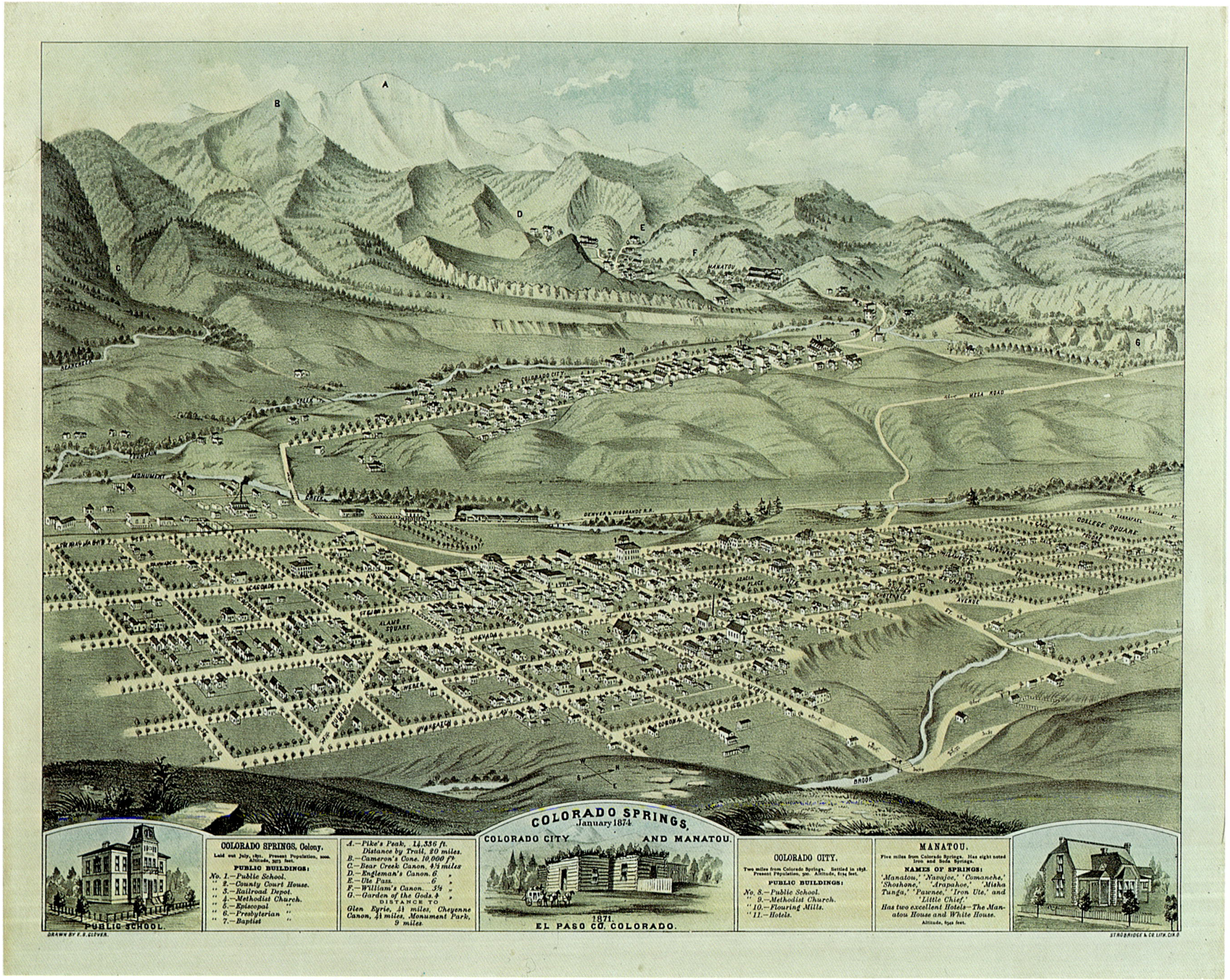

PLATE 22. *Colorado Springs, Colorado City and Manatou. January 1874.* Eli S. Glover. c. 1874. Color lithograph. 16-7/8 x 22-1/4 in. (42.8 x 56.4 cm.) Printed by Strobridge & Co.

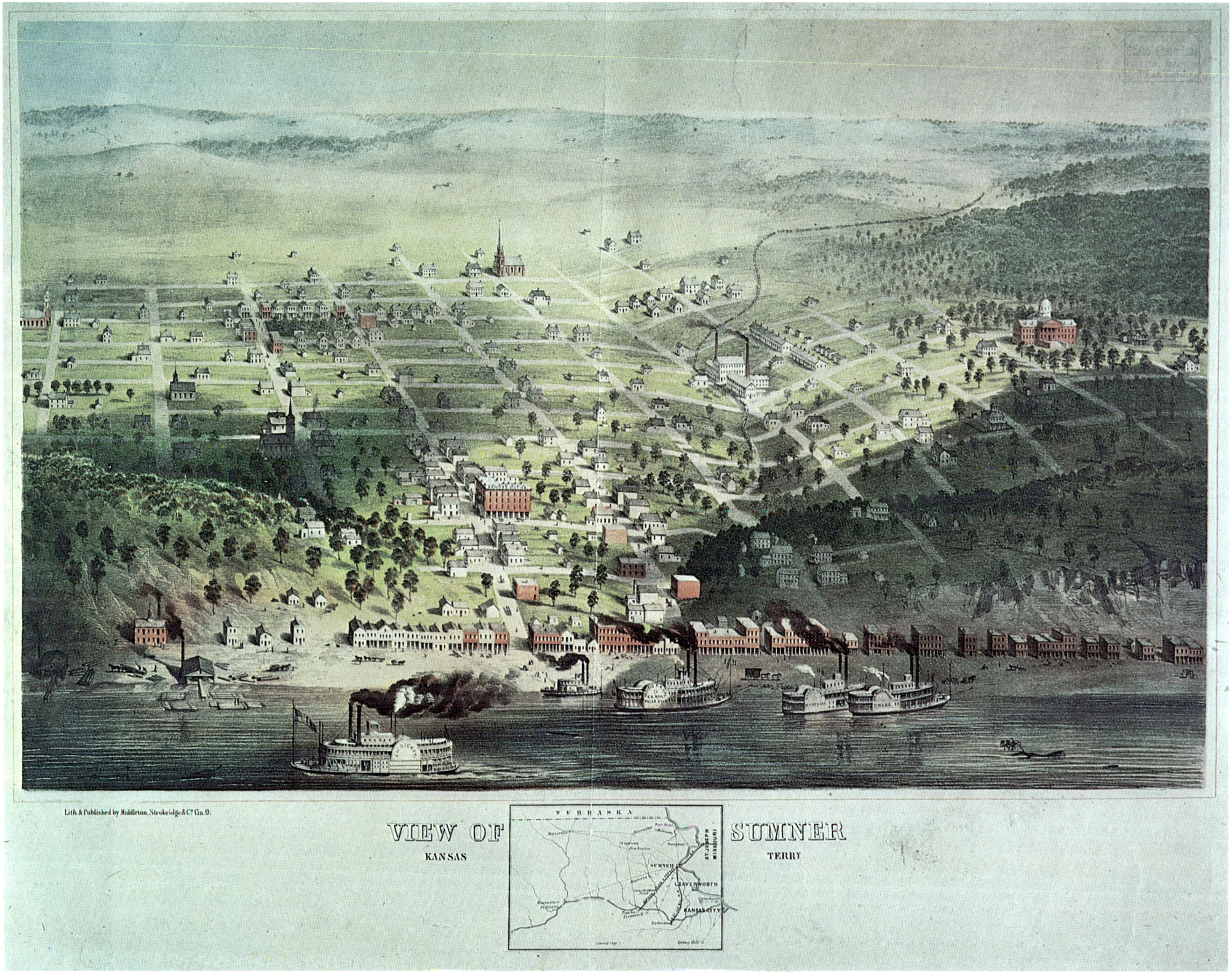

PLATE 23. *View of Sumner Kansas Terry.* Unsigned. c. 1857. Color lithograph. 17-13/16 x 28 in. (45.2 x 71.0 cm.) Printed and published by Middleton, Strobridge & Co. Courtesy Kansas State Historical Society, Topeka.

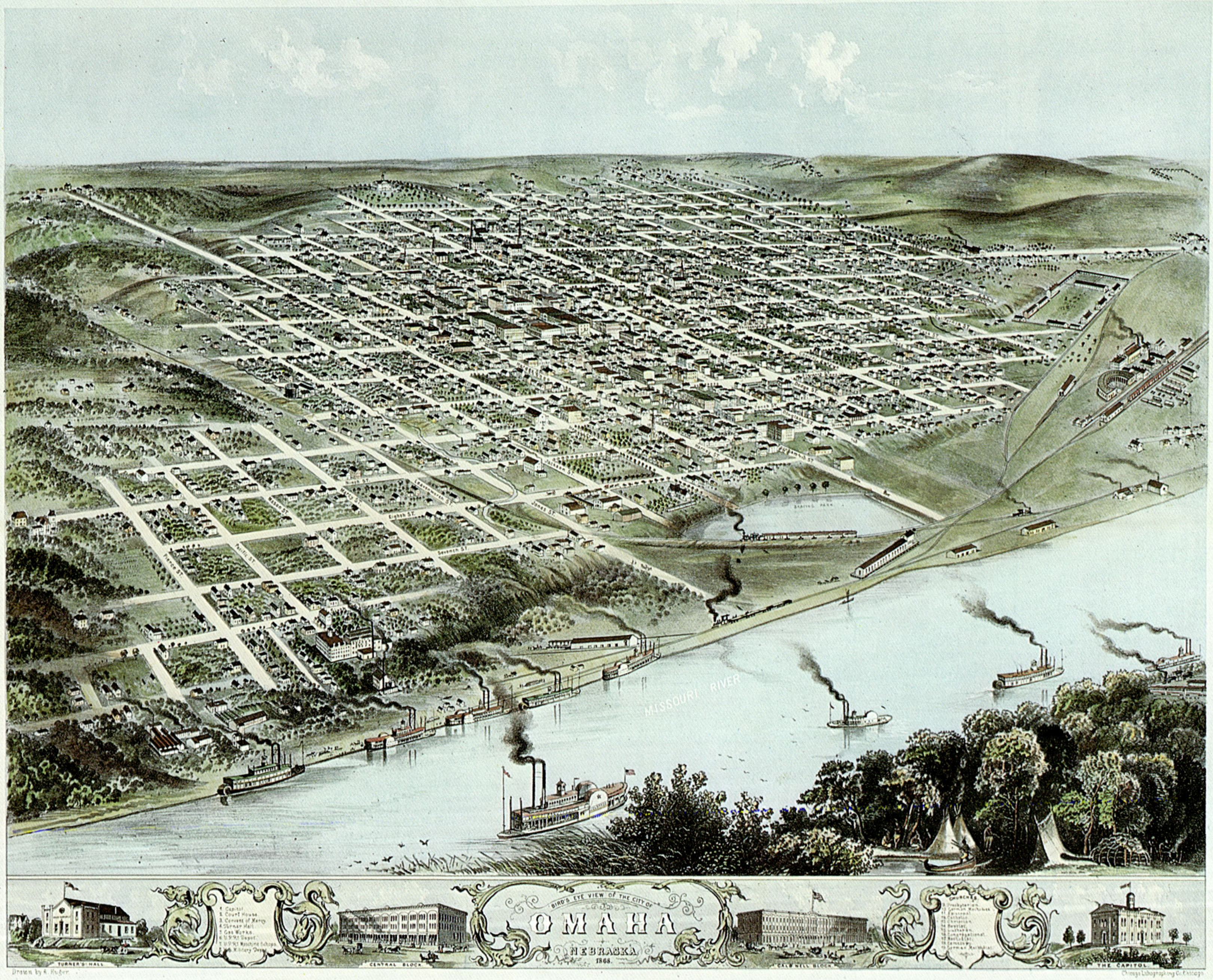

PLATE 24. *Bird's Eye View of the City of Omaha Nebraska 1868.* Albert Ruger. 1868. Toned lithograph (hand colored). 22-1/16 x 28 in. (55.9 x 71.0 cm.) Printed by Chicago Lithographing Co.

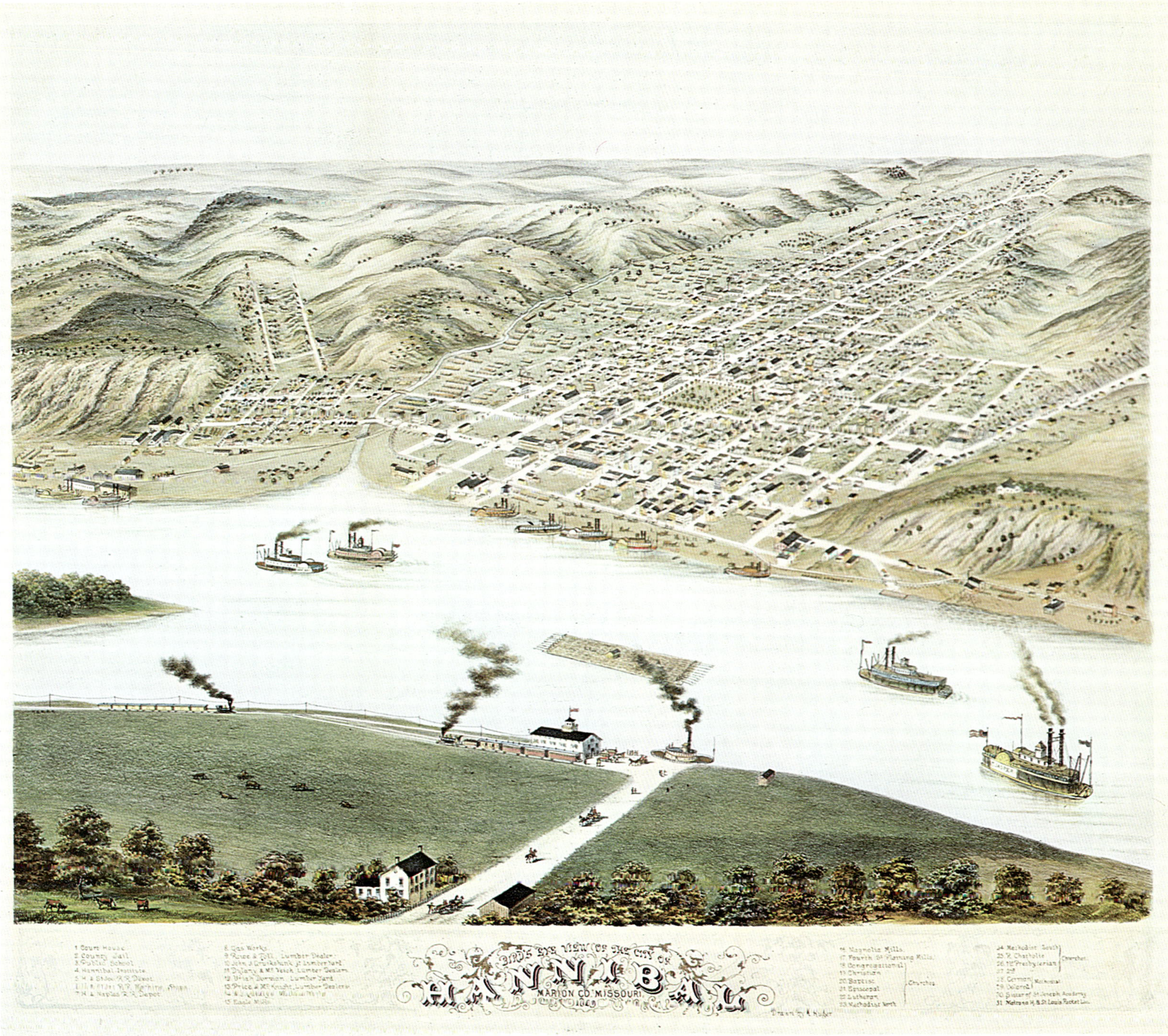

PLATE 25. *Bird's Eye View of the City of Hannibal Marion Co. Missouri. 1869.* Albert Ruger. 1869. Color lithograph (hand colored). 20-1/8 x 25-3/4 in. (51.1 x 65.4 cm.).

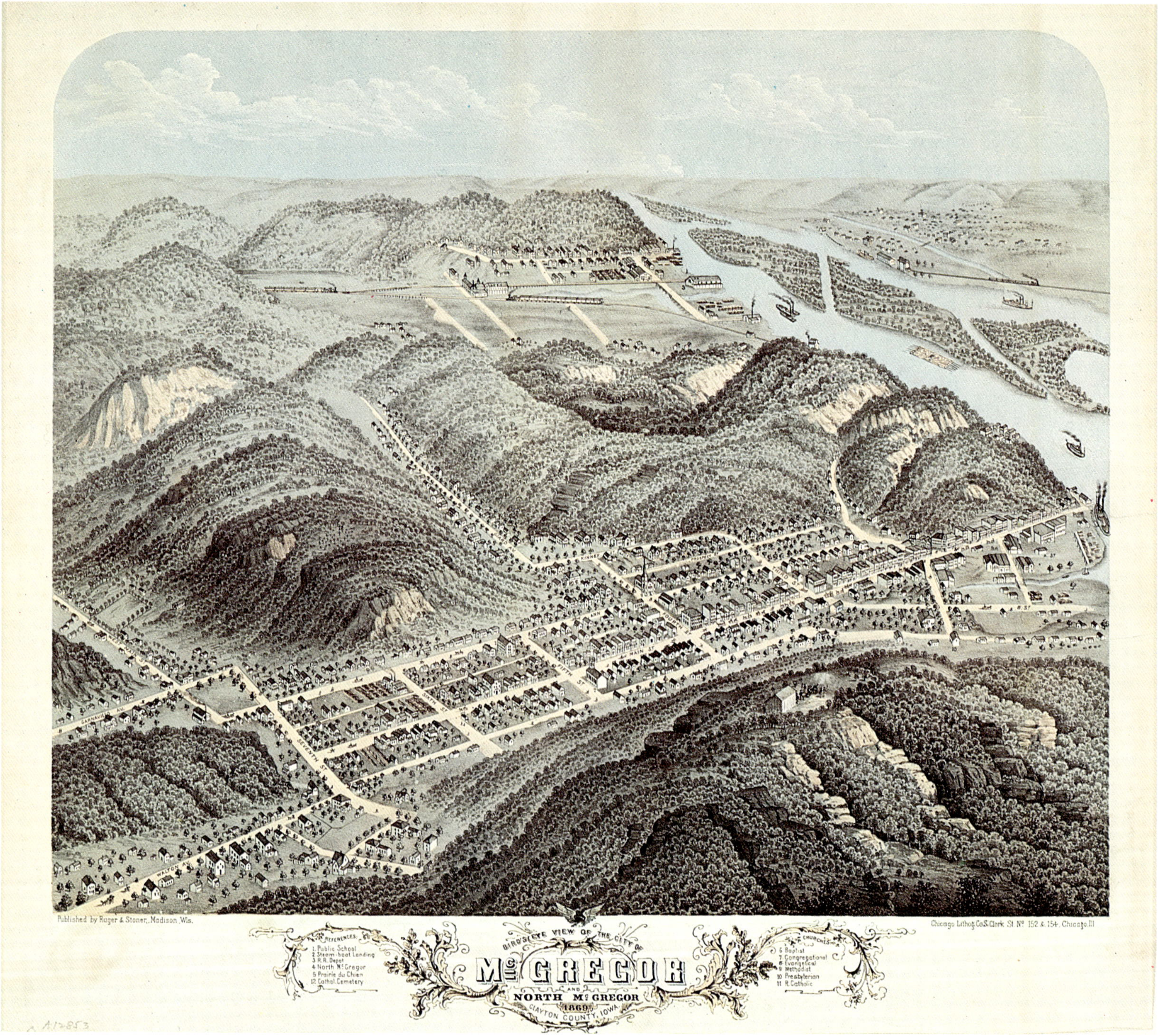

PLATE 26. *Bird's Eye View of the City of McGregor and North McGregor 1869 Clayton County, Iowa.* Unsigned [Albert Ruger]. 1869. Color lithograph. 18-1/16 x 22 in. (45.8 x 55.8 cm.) Printed by Chicago Lithog. Co. Published by Ruger & Stoner.

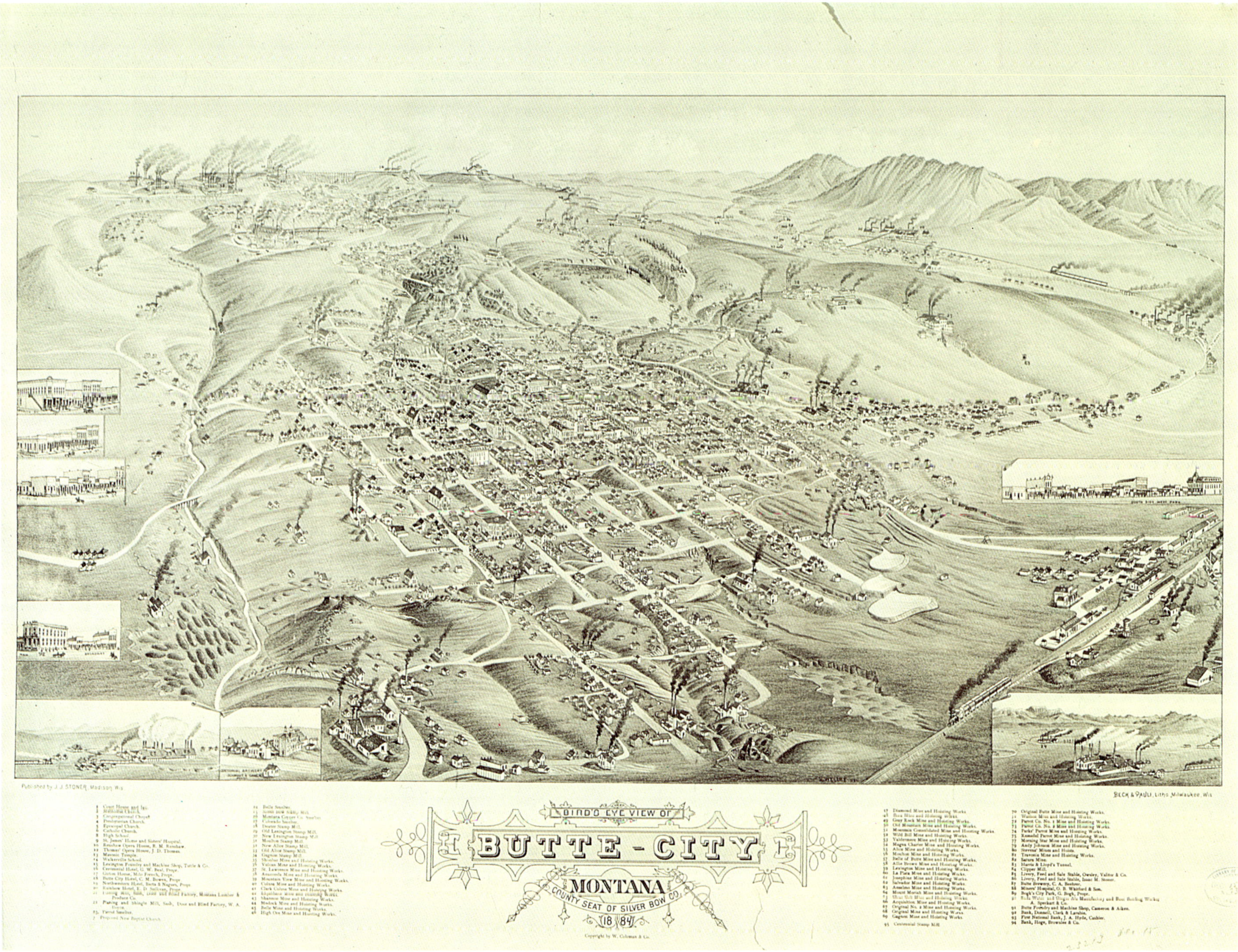

PLATE 27. *Bird's Eye View of Butte-City Montana County Seat of Silver Bow Co. 1884.* Unsigned [Henry Wellge]. Lithograph. 16 x 28-5/8 in. (40.6 x 72.6 cm.) Printed by Beck & Pauli. Published by J. J. Stoner.

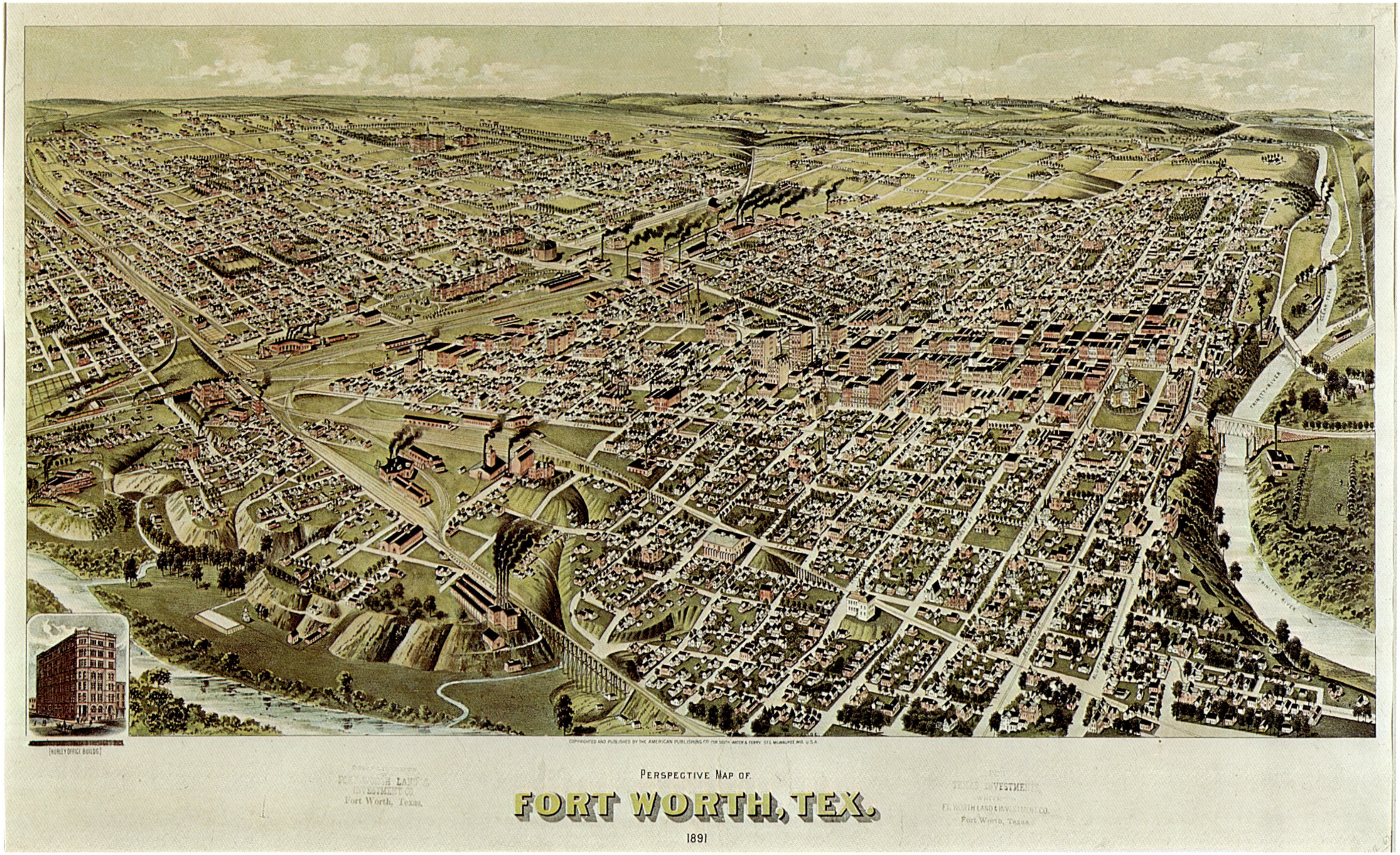

PLATE 28. *Perspective Map of. Fort Worth, Tex. 1891.* Henry Wellge. 1891. Toned lithograph (hand colored). 17-1/16 x 33-1/4 in. (43.3 x 84.5 cm.) Published by American Publishing Co.

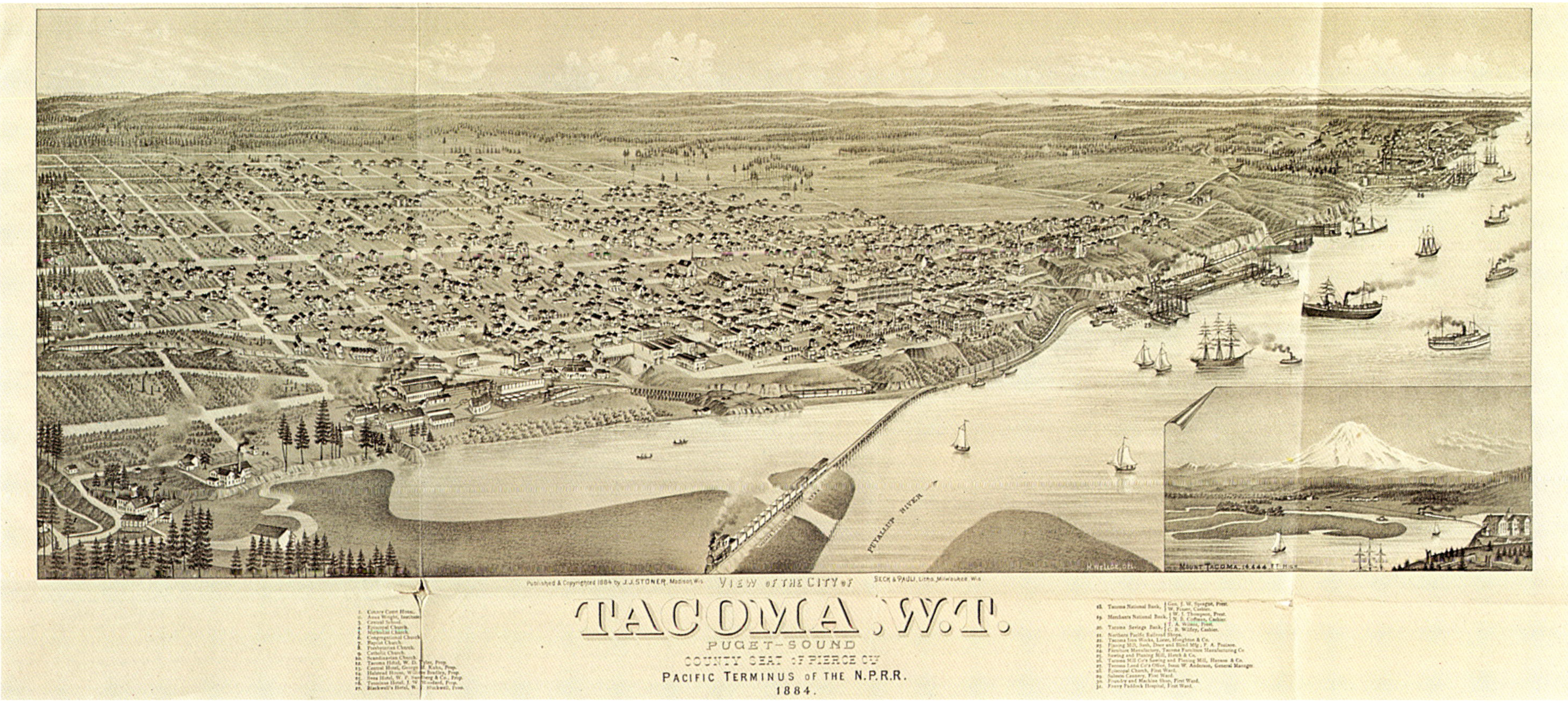

PLATE 29. *View of the City of Tacoma, W. T.* Henry Wellge. 1884. Toned lithograph. 12-1/8 x 32-1/2 in. (30.7 x 82.5 cm.) Printed by Beck & Pauli. Published by J. J. Stoner.

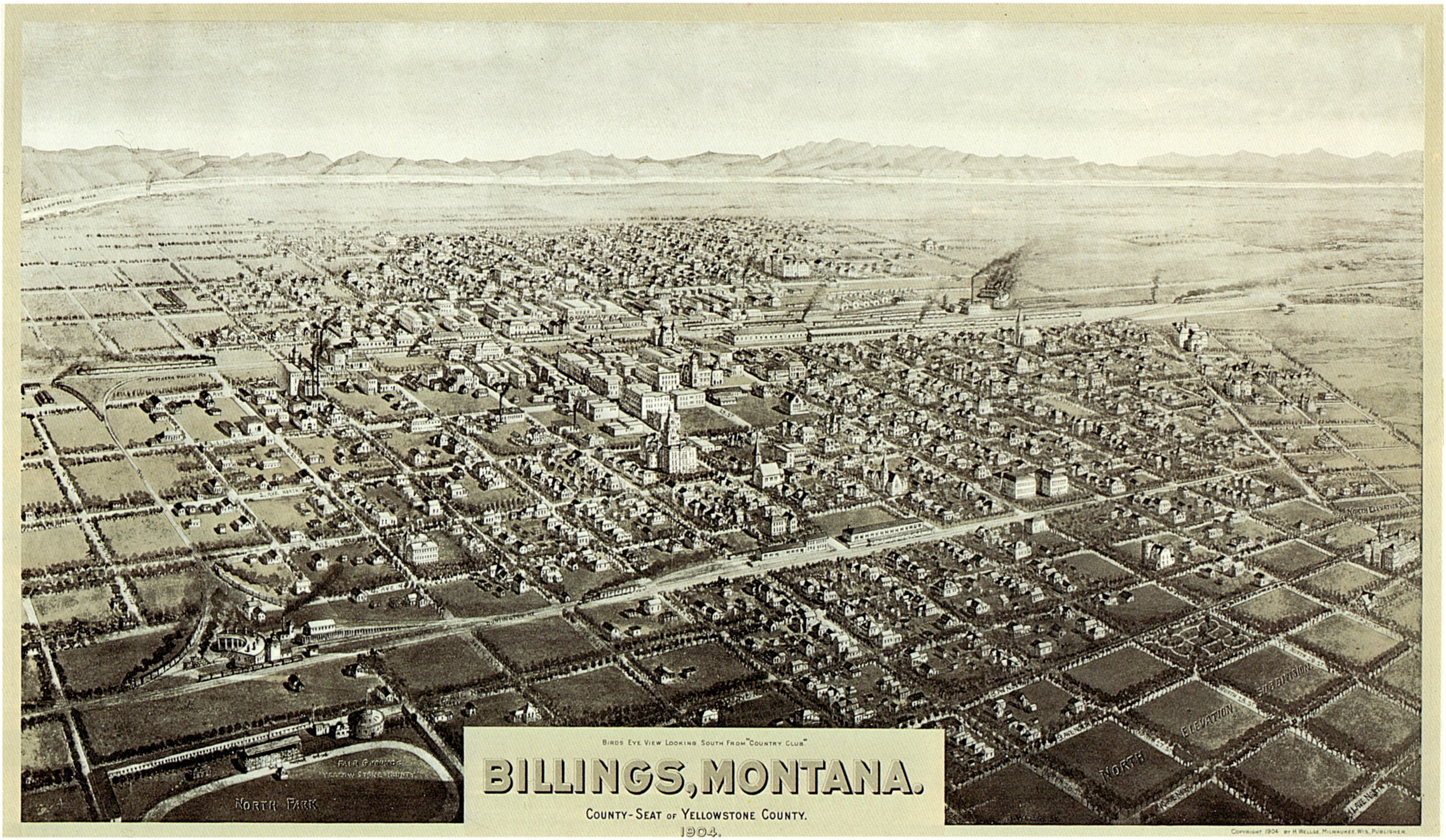

PLATE 30. *Billings, Montana*. Henry Wellge. 1904. Toned lithograph. 16-11/16 x 29-1/8 in. (42.4 x 74.0 cm.)

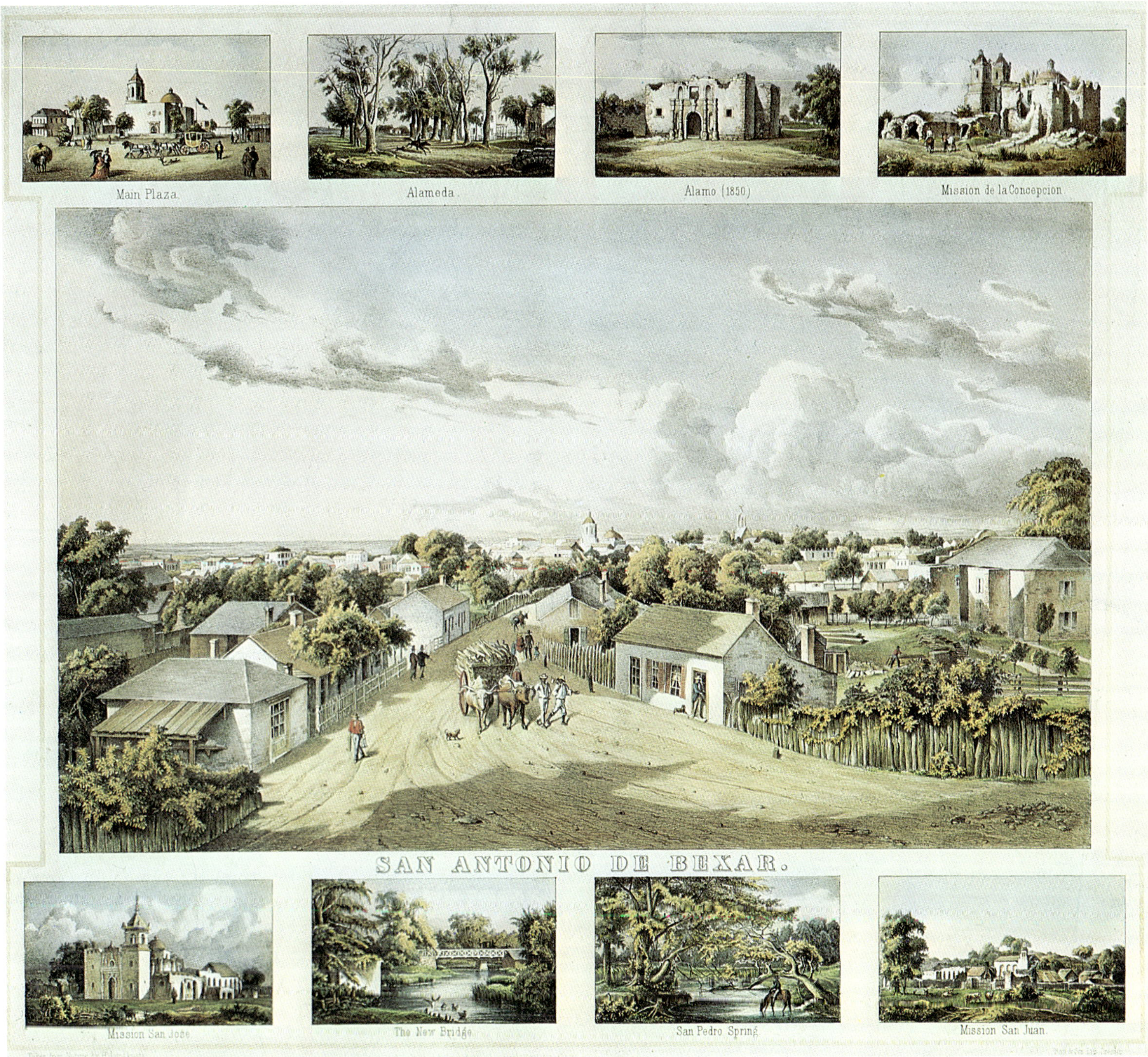

PLATE 31. *San Antonio de Bexar*. Hermann Lungkwitz. c. 1860. Color lithograph (hand colored). 16-13/16 x 19 in. (42.7 x 48.2 cm.) Printed by Rau & Son.

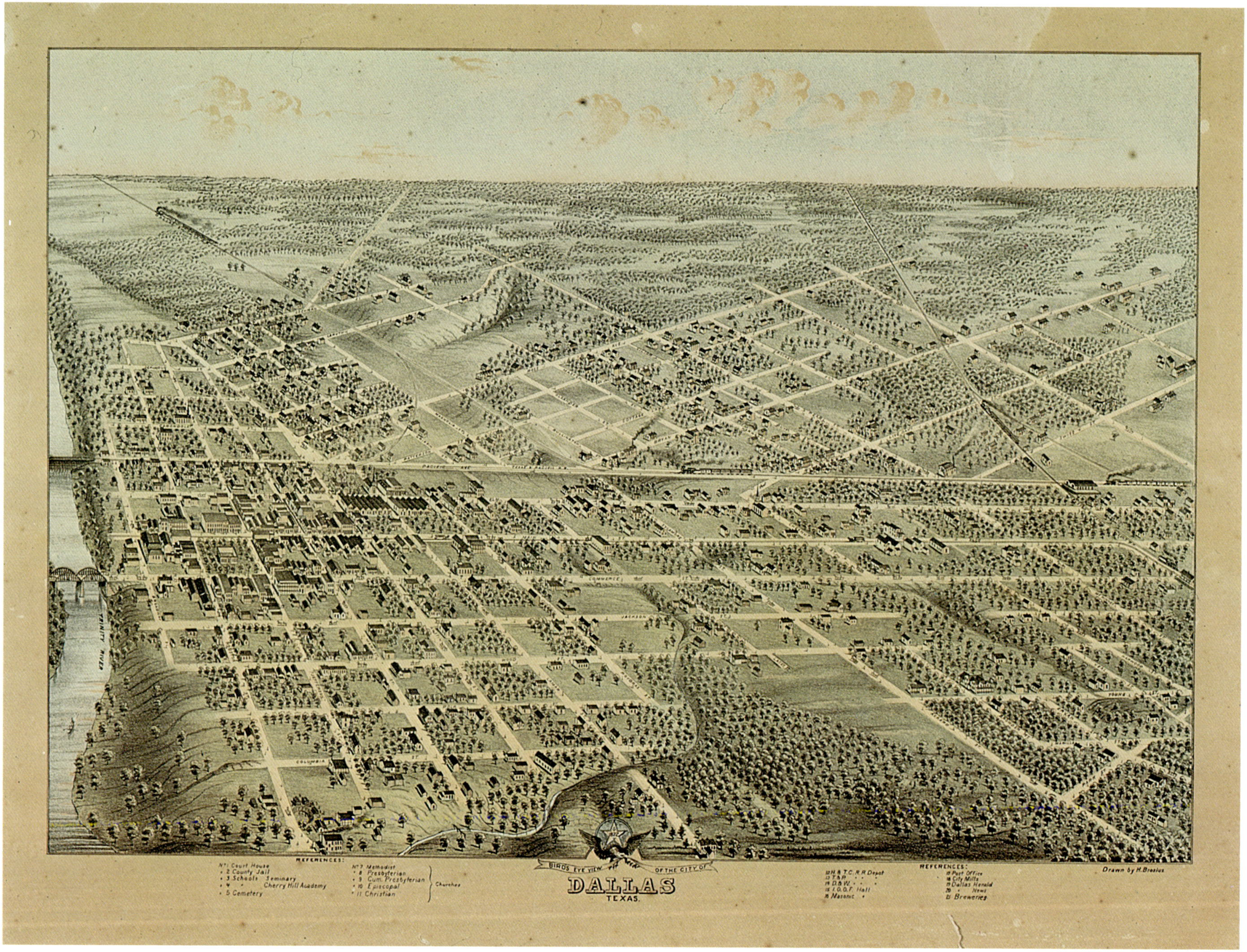

PLATE 32. *Bird's Eye View of the City of Dallas Texas*. Herman Brosius. 1872. Color lithograph. 15-13/16 x 22-7/8 in. (40.1 x 58.1 cm.) Courtesy Dallas Historical Society.

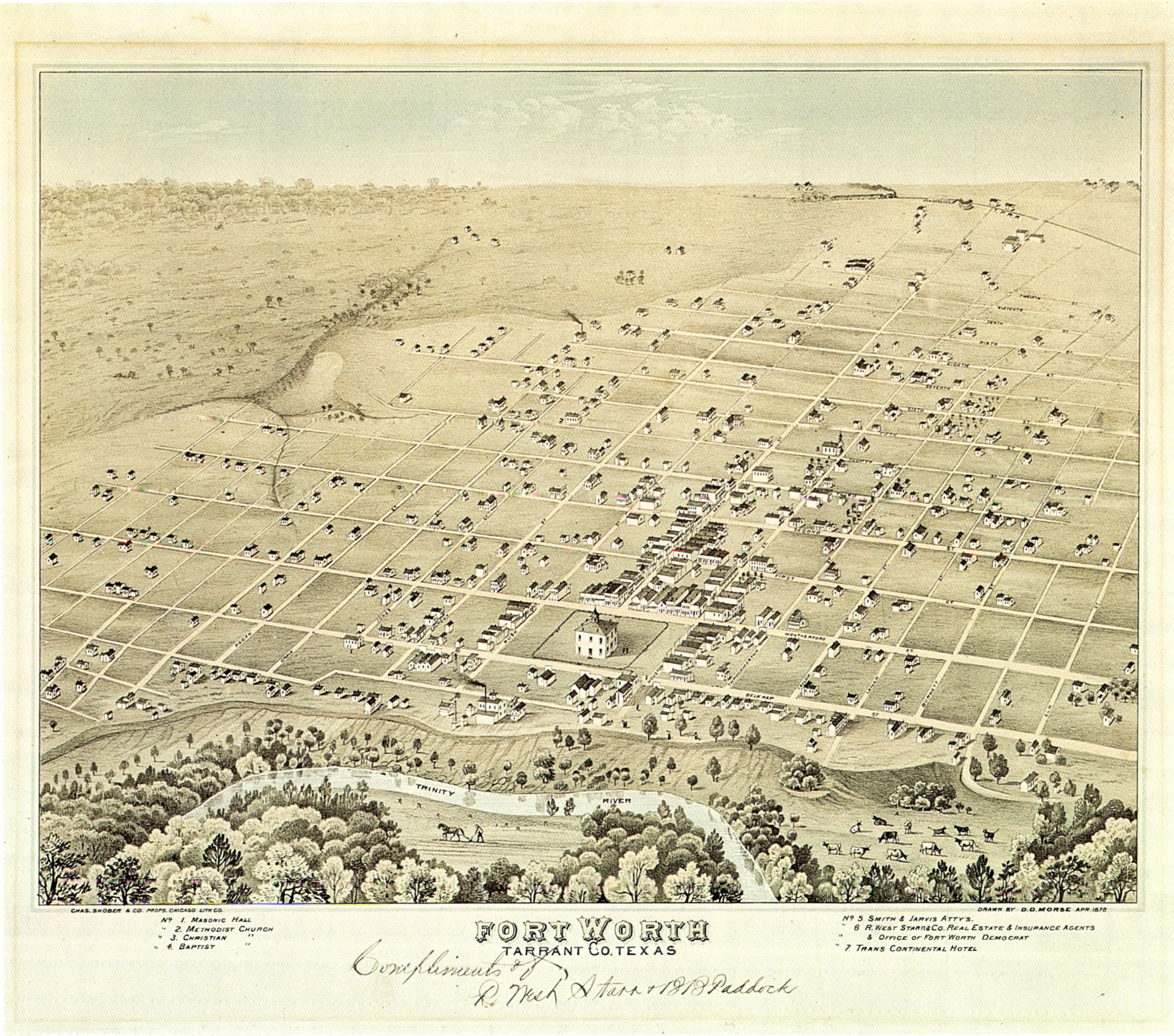

PLATE 33. *Fort Worth Tarrant Co. Texas*. D. D. Morse. 1876. Color lithograph. 14-1/8 x 18-13/16 in. (35.9 x 47.7 cm.) Printed by Chas. Shober & Co.

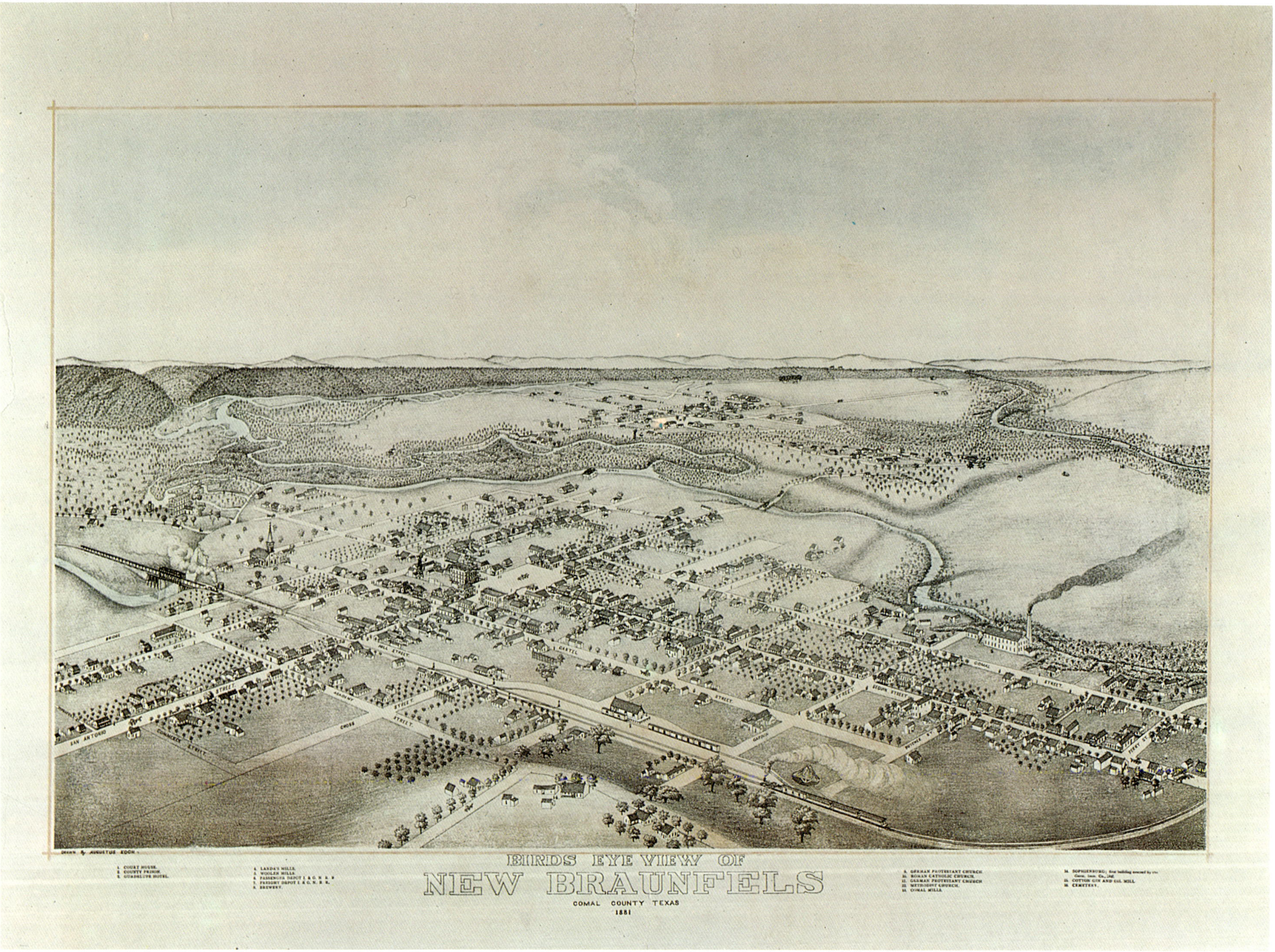

PLATE 34. *Bird's Eye View of New Braunfels Comal County Texas 1881.*
Augustus Koch. 1881. Toned lithograph. 17-15/16 x 28-1/2 in. (45.5 x 72.3 cm.)

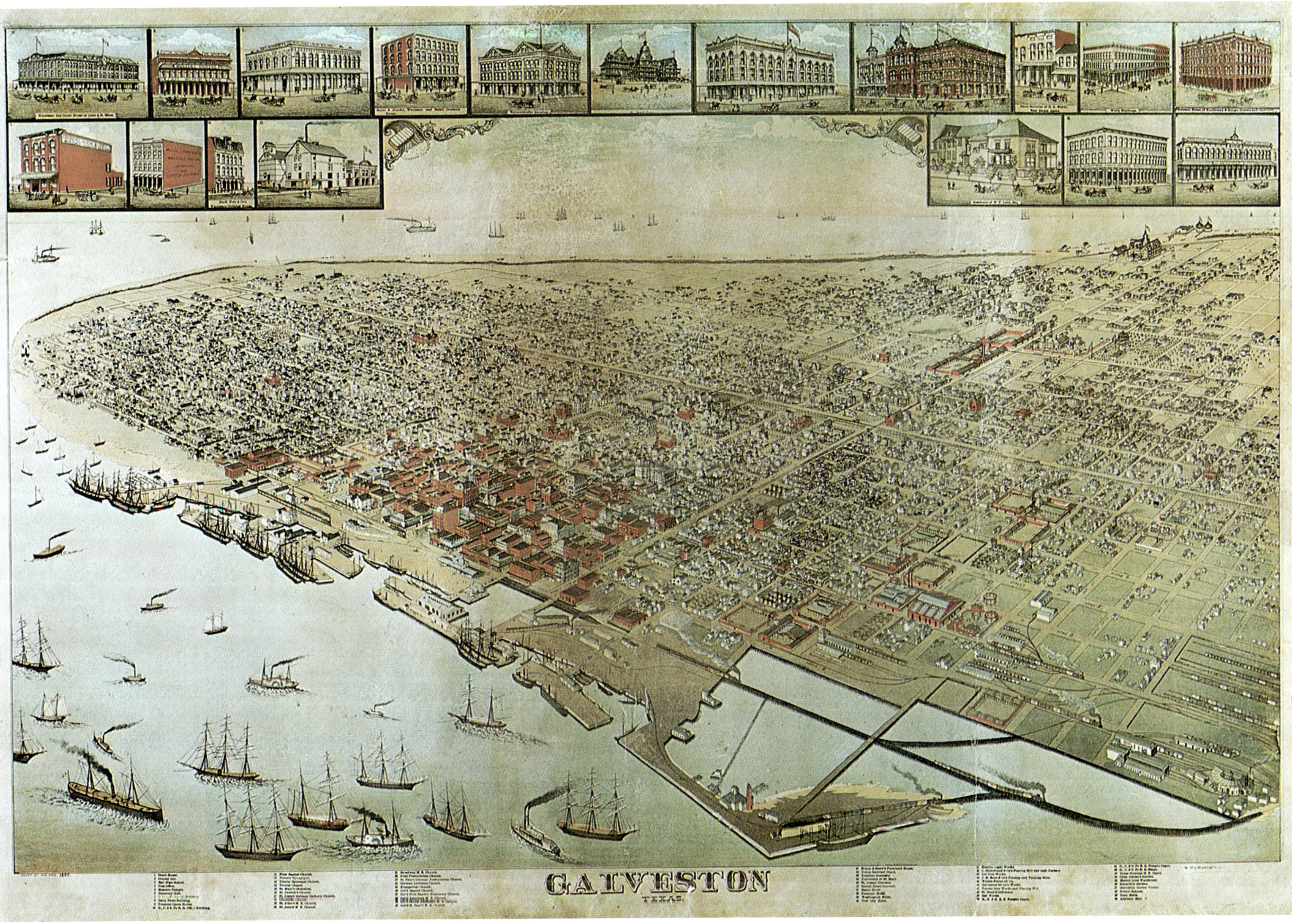

PLATE 35. *Galveston Texas*. Augustus Koch. 1885. Color lithograph. 26 5/16 x 40-1/8 in. (66.8 x 101.9 cm.)

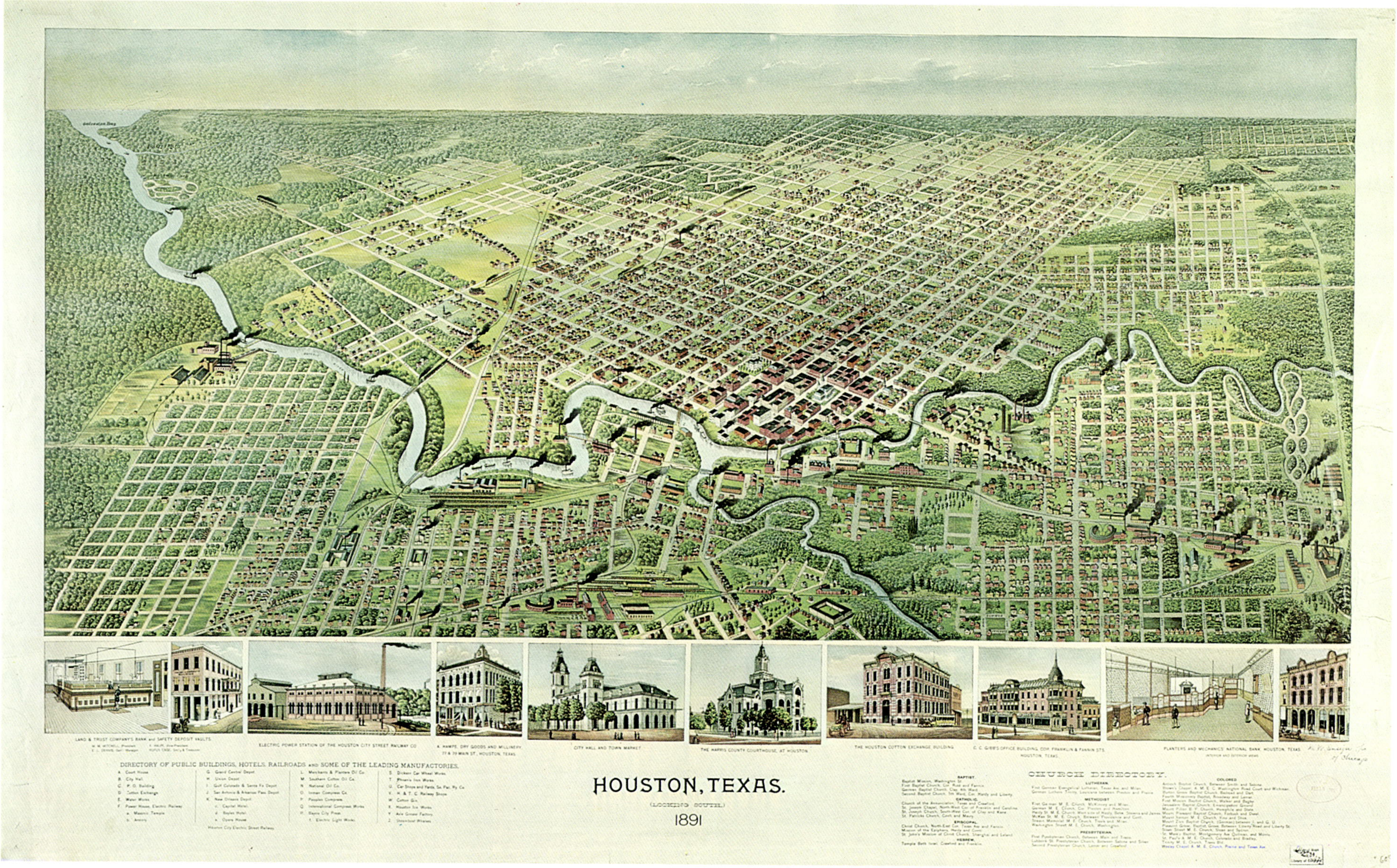

PLATE 36. *Houston, Texas. (Looking South.) 1891.* Unsigned. 1891. Color lithograph. 23 x 42-5/8 in. (58.4 x 108.2 cm.)

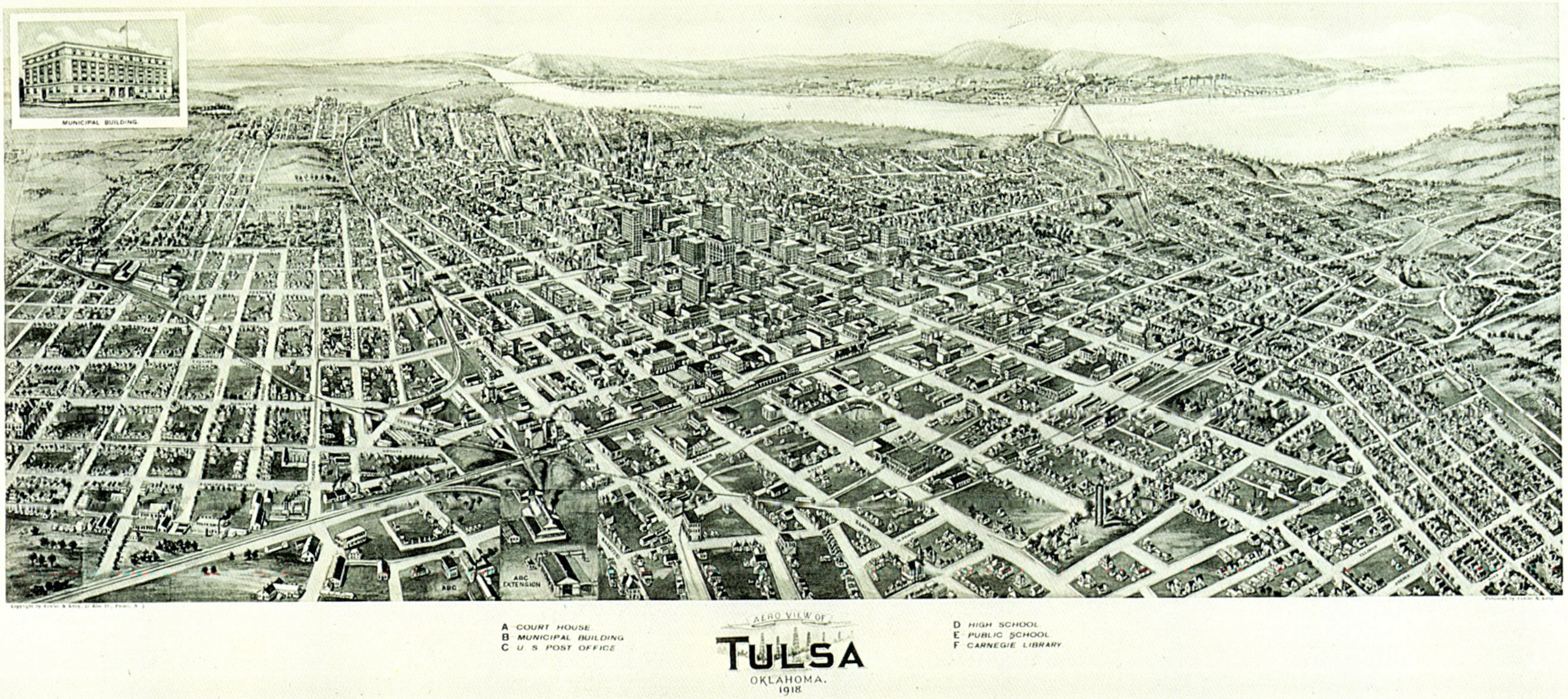

PLATE 37. *Aero View of Tulsa Oklahoma, 1918.* Thaddeus M. Fowler. 1918. Monotone rotogravure. 13-3/16 x 35 in. (33.4 x 88.8 cm.)

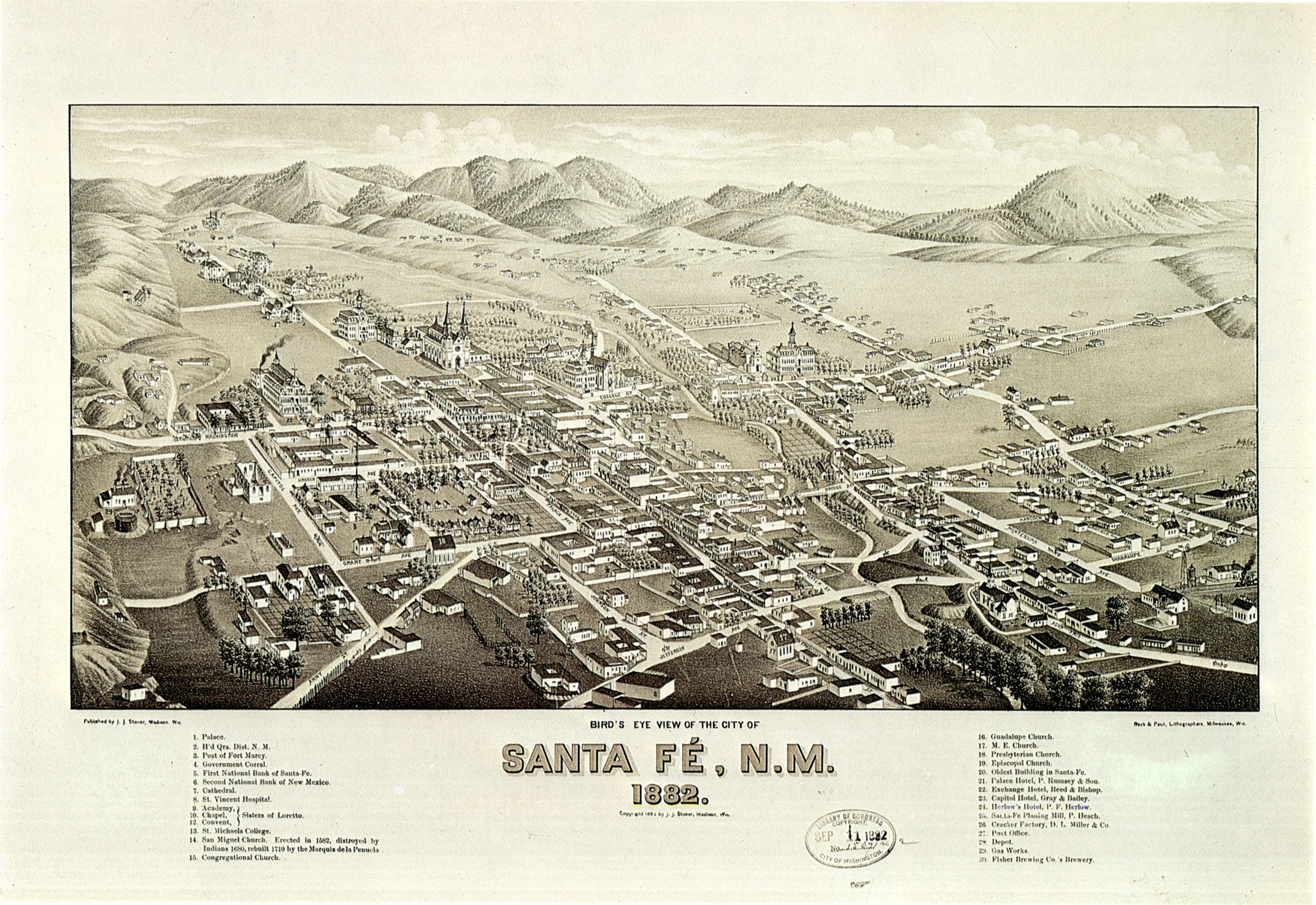

PLATE 38. *Bird's Eye View of the City of Santa Fé, N.M. 1882.* Unsigned [Henry Wellge]. 1882. Toned lithograph. 9-9/16 x 19-1/16 in. (24.2 x 48.3 cm.) Printed by Beck & Pauli. Published by J. J. Stoner.

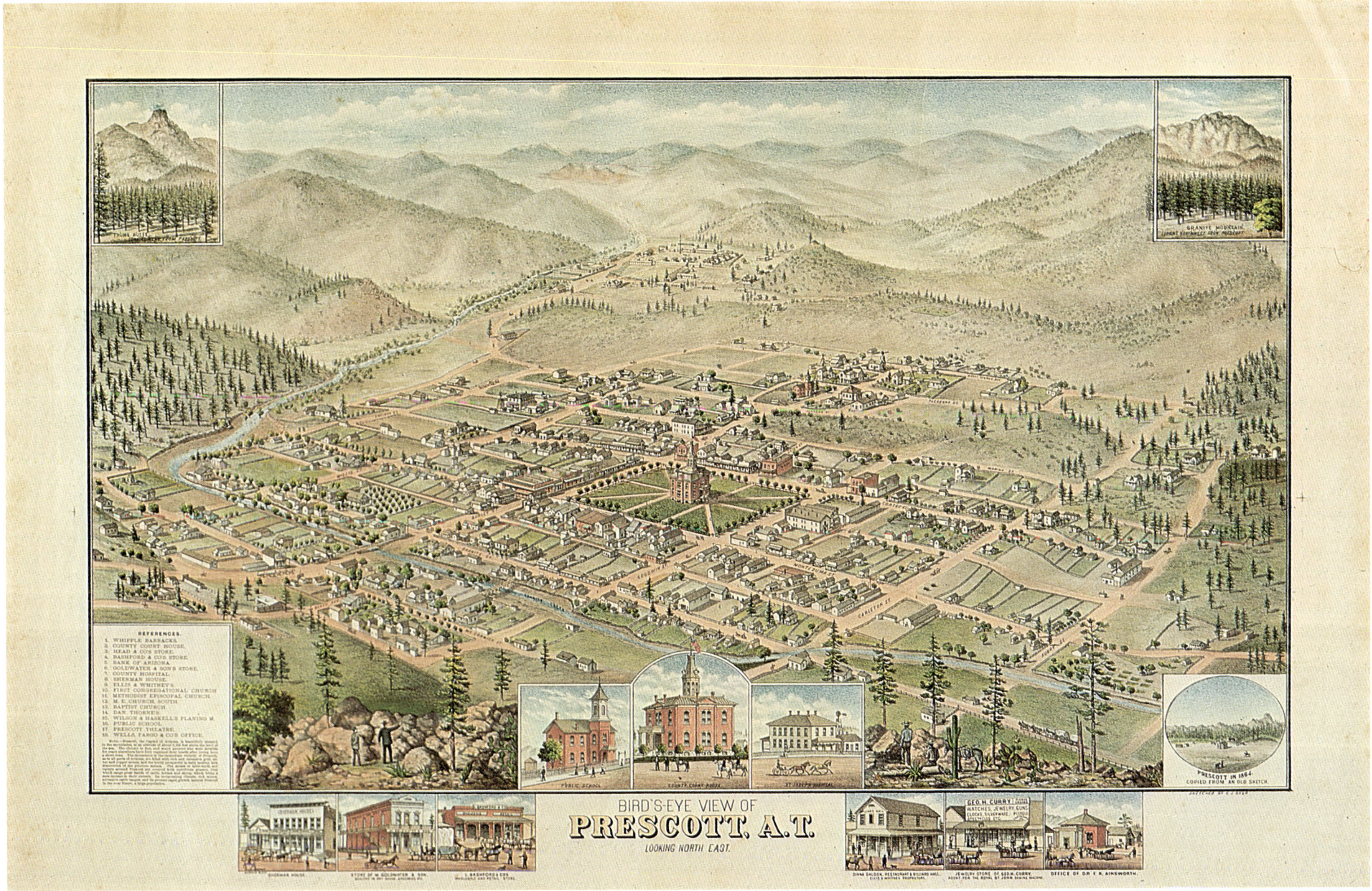

PLATE 39. *Bird's-Eye View of Prescott, A. T. Looking North East*. C. J. Dyer. c. 1885. Color lithograph. 19-1/8 x 29-1/2 in. (48.5 x 74.9 cm.)

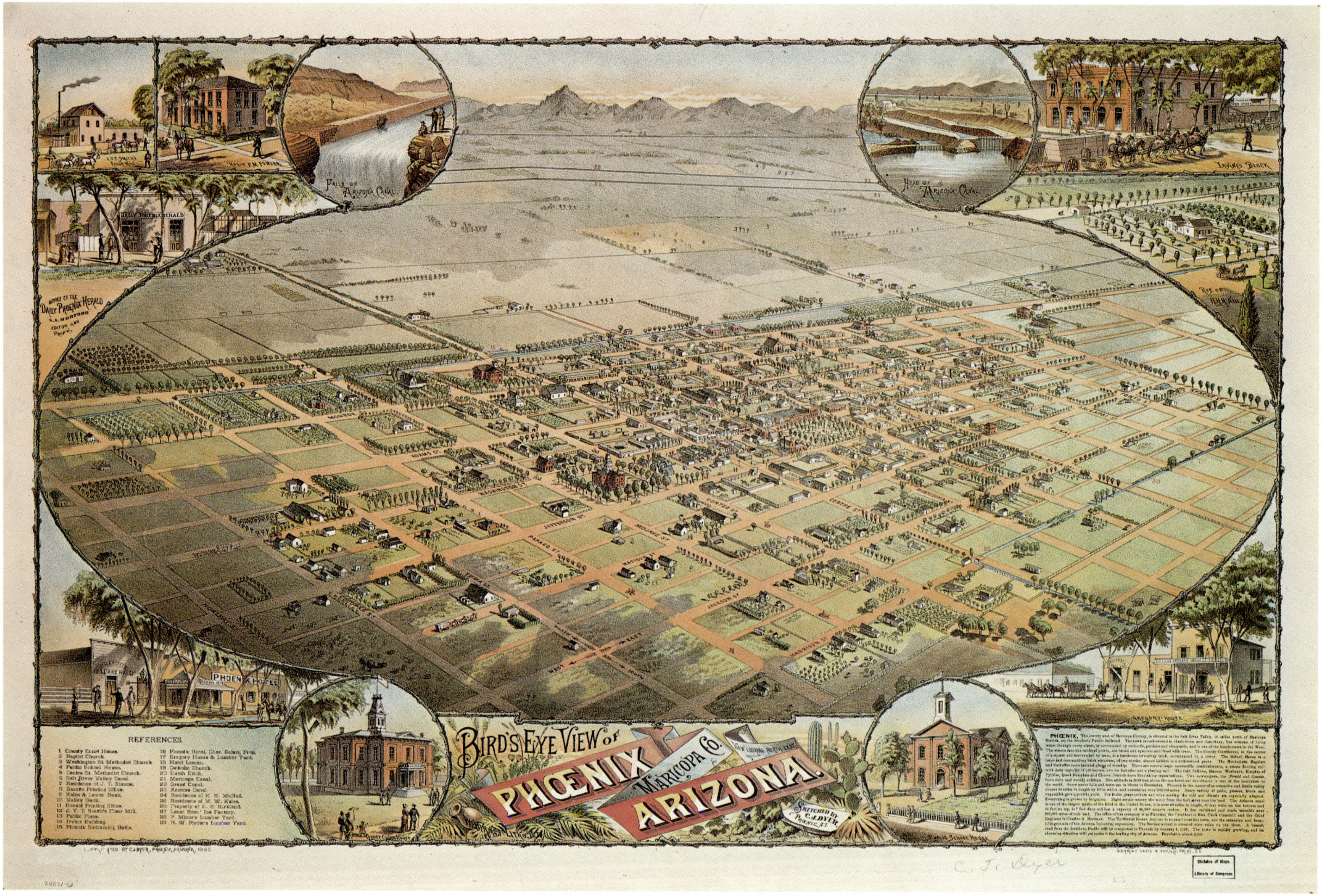

PLATE 40. *Bird's Eye View of Phoenix Maricopa Co. Arizona. View Looking North-East*. C. J. Dyer. 1885. Color lithograph. 22 x 33 in. (55.8 x 83.8 cm.) Printed by Schmidt Label & Litho Co. Courtesy Library of Congress, Washington, D.C.

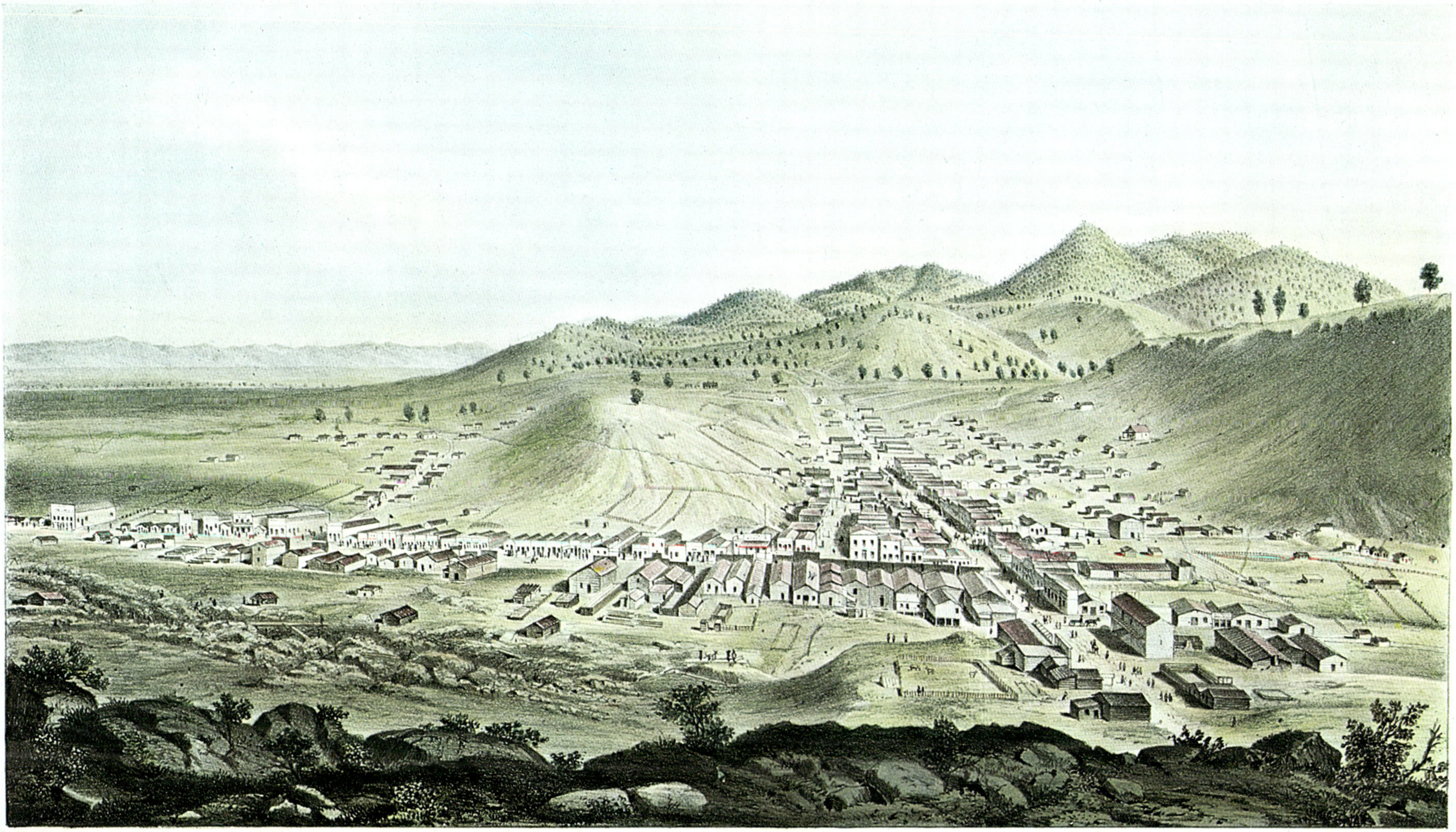

Sketched after Nature by G. R. Bechler

Herline & Hensel, Lith. 632 Chestnut St. Philad.a

HELENA.

(in 1865)

(Montana Territory.)

PLATE 41. *Helena. (in 1865) (Montana Territory.)* Gustave R. Bechler. 1866. Color lithograph (hand colored). 12-3/4 x 22-7/8 in. (32.5 x 58.0 cm.) Printed by Herline & Hensel.

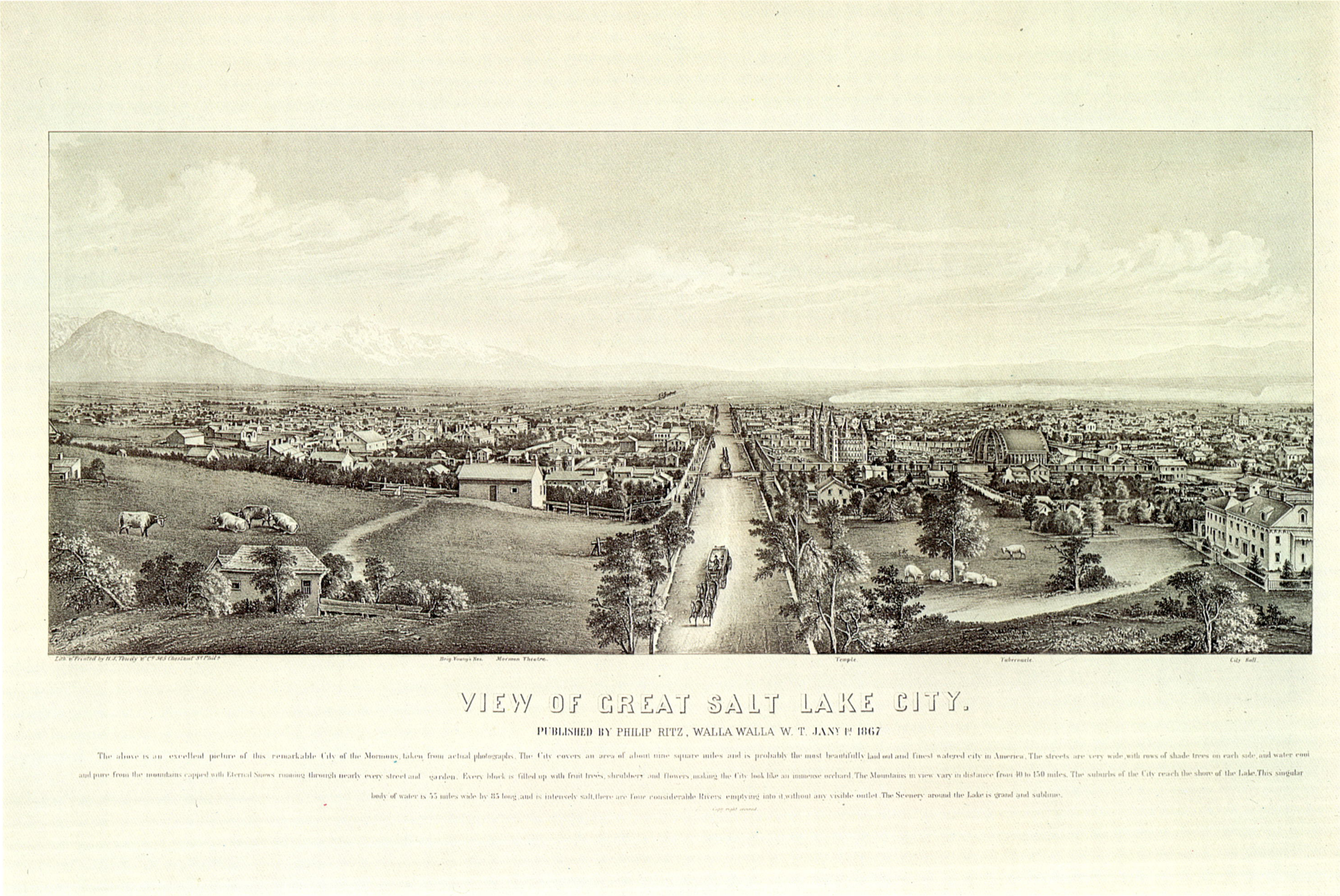

PLATE 42. *View of Great Salt Lake City*. Christian Inger. 1867. Toned lithograph. 11-9/16 x 28-1/2 in. (29.3 x 72.3 cm.) Printed by H. J. Toudy & Co. Published by Philip Ritz.

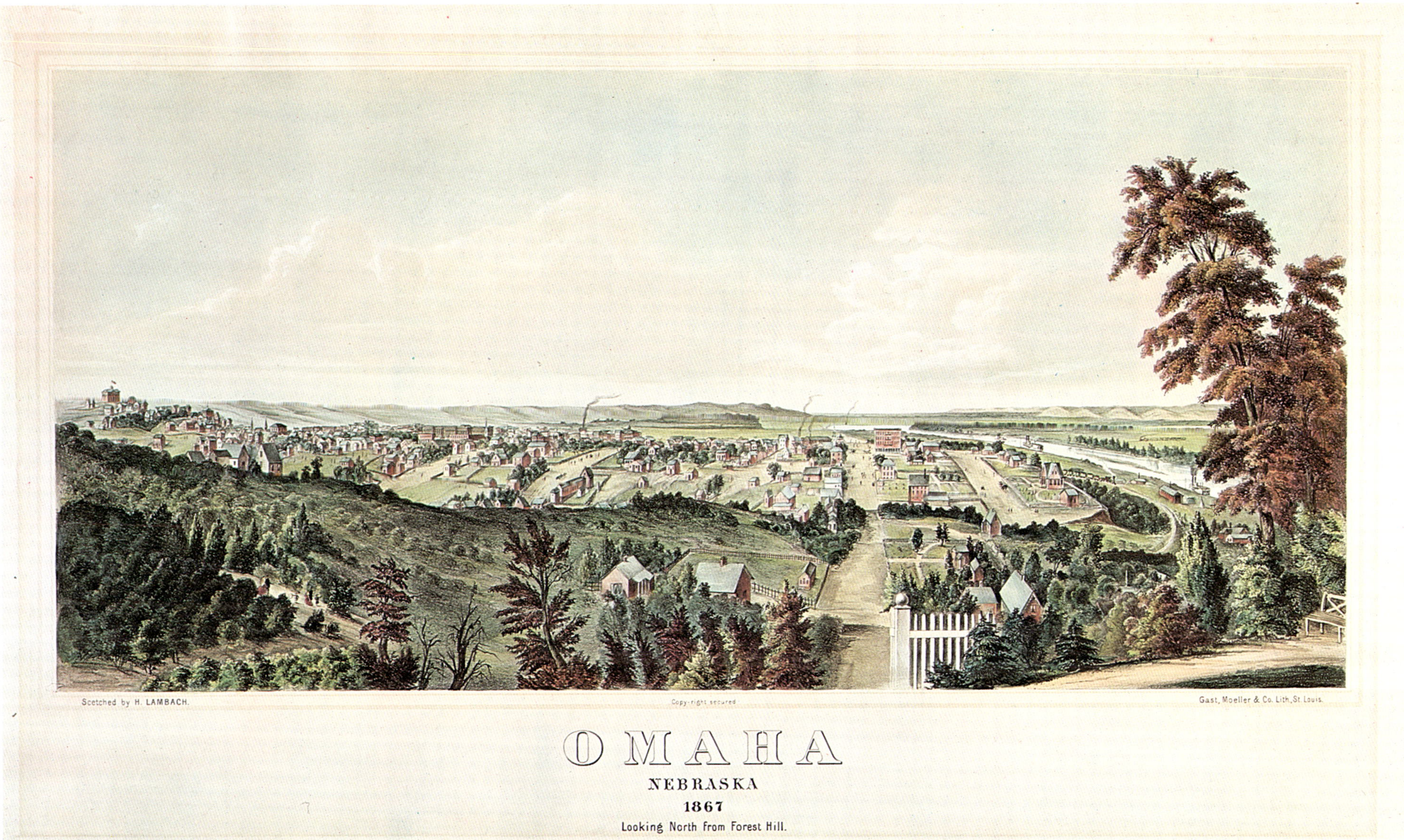

PLATE 43. *Omaha Nebraska 1867*. H. Lambach. 1867. Color lithograph (hand colored). 12-13/16 x 26-7/8 in. (32.5 x 68.2 cm.) Printed and published by Gast, Moeller & Co.

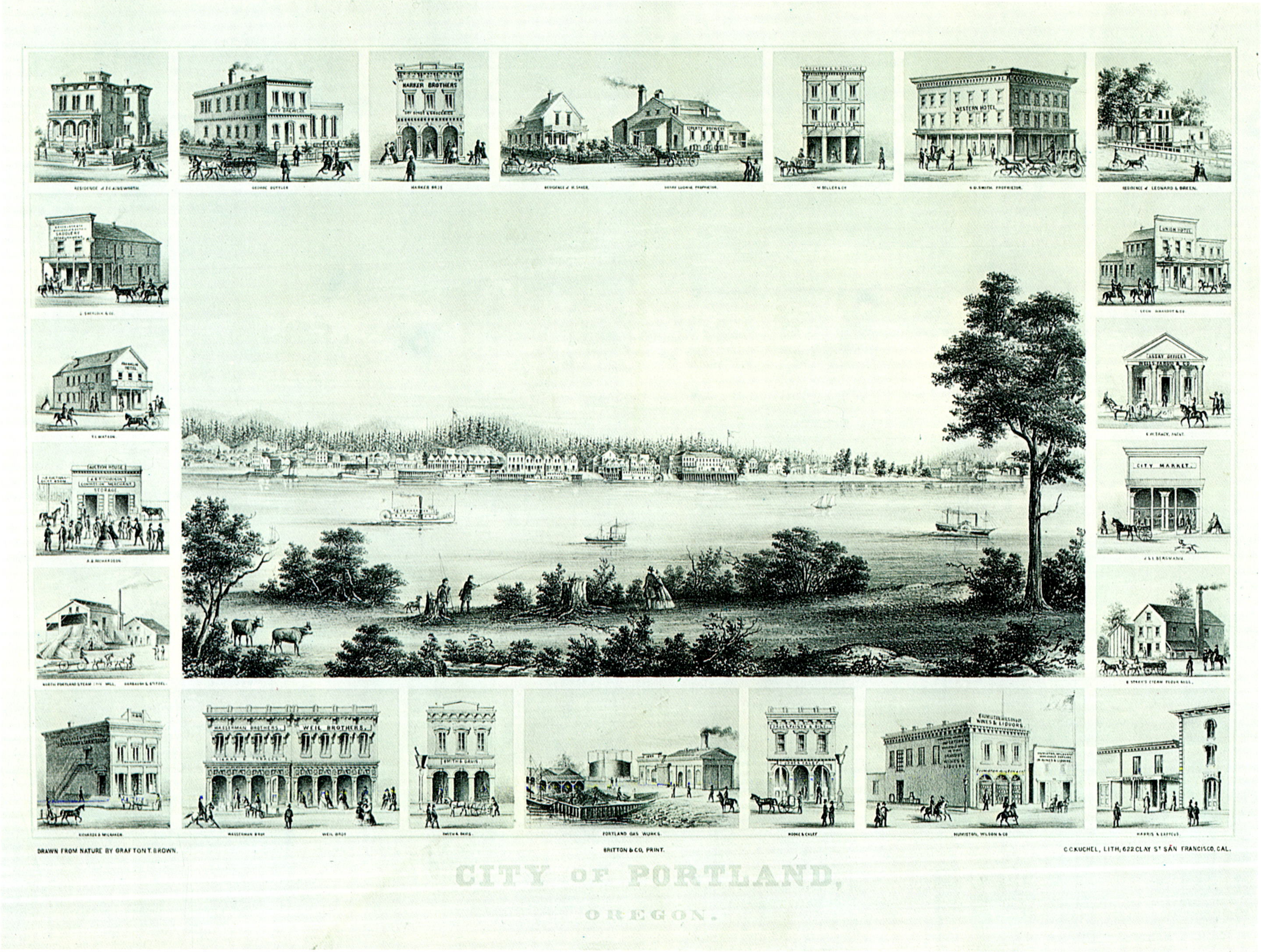

PLATE 44. *City of Portland, Oregon*. Grafton T. Brown. c. 1861. Toned lithograph. 19-1/6 x 29-1/2 in. (48.4 x 74.9 cm.) Printed by Britton & Co. Published by C. C. Kuchel.

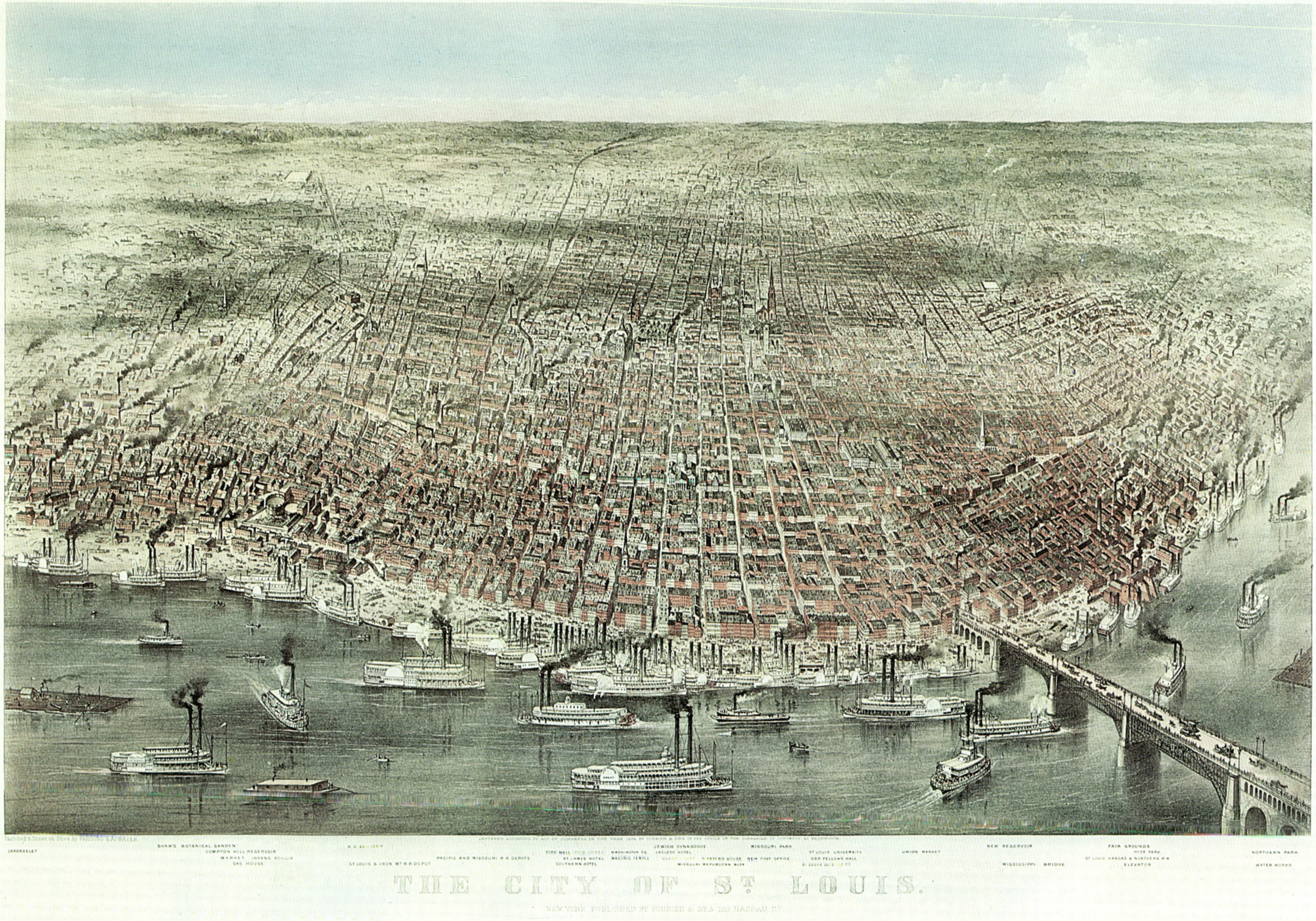

PLATE 45. *The City of St. Louis*. Charles Parsons. 1874. Color lithograph. 20-1/2 x 32-5/8 in. (52.0 x 82.7 cm.) Published by Currier and Ives.

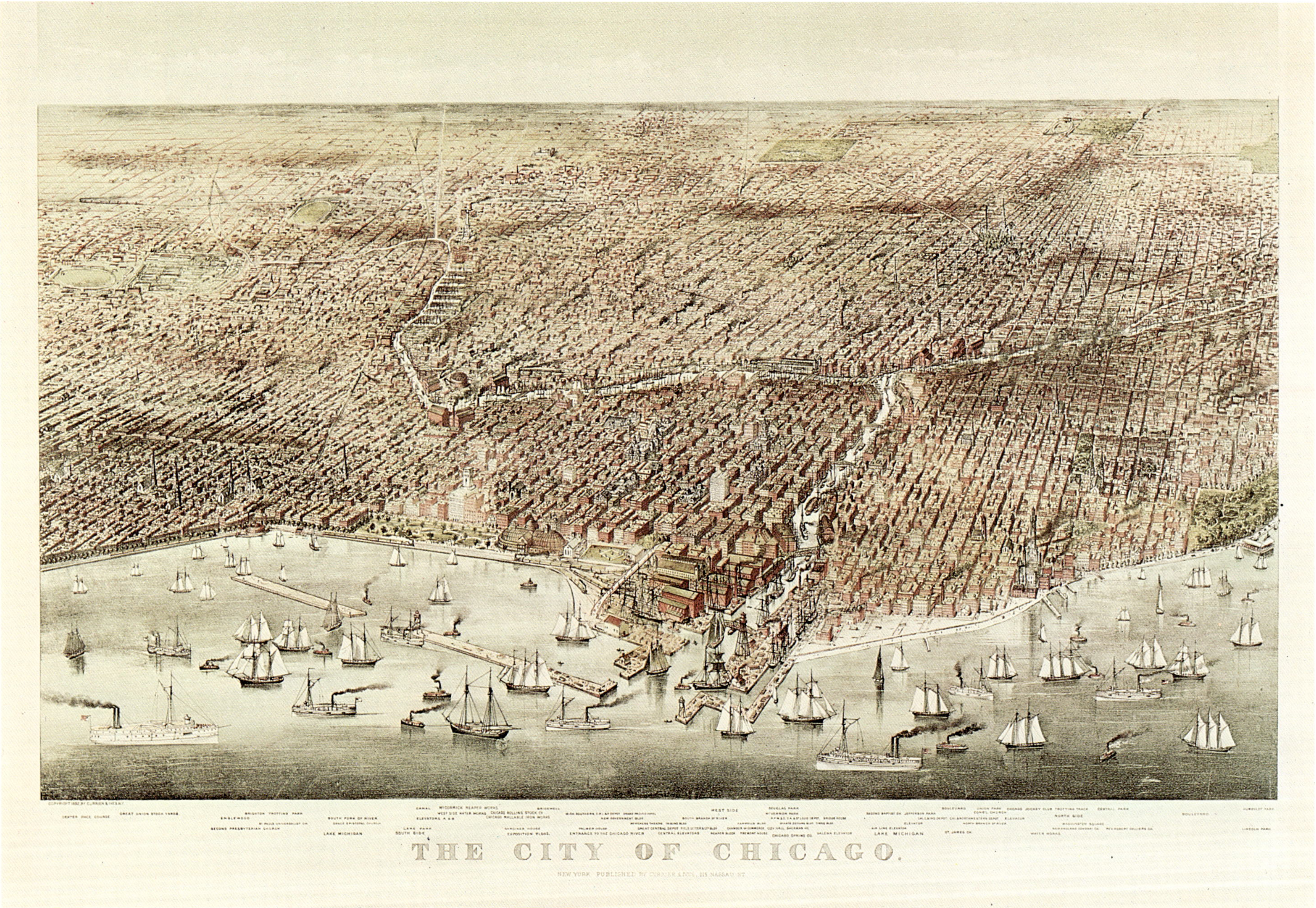

PLATE 46. *The City of Chicago*. Unsigned [Charles Parsons]. 1892. Color lithograph. 20-3/4 x 32-1/2 in. (52.5 x 82.5 cm.) Published by Currier & Ives.

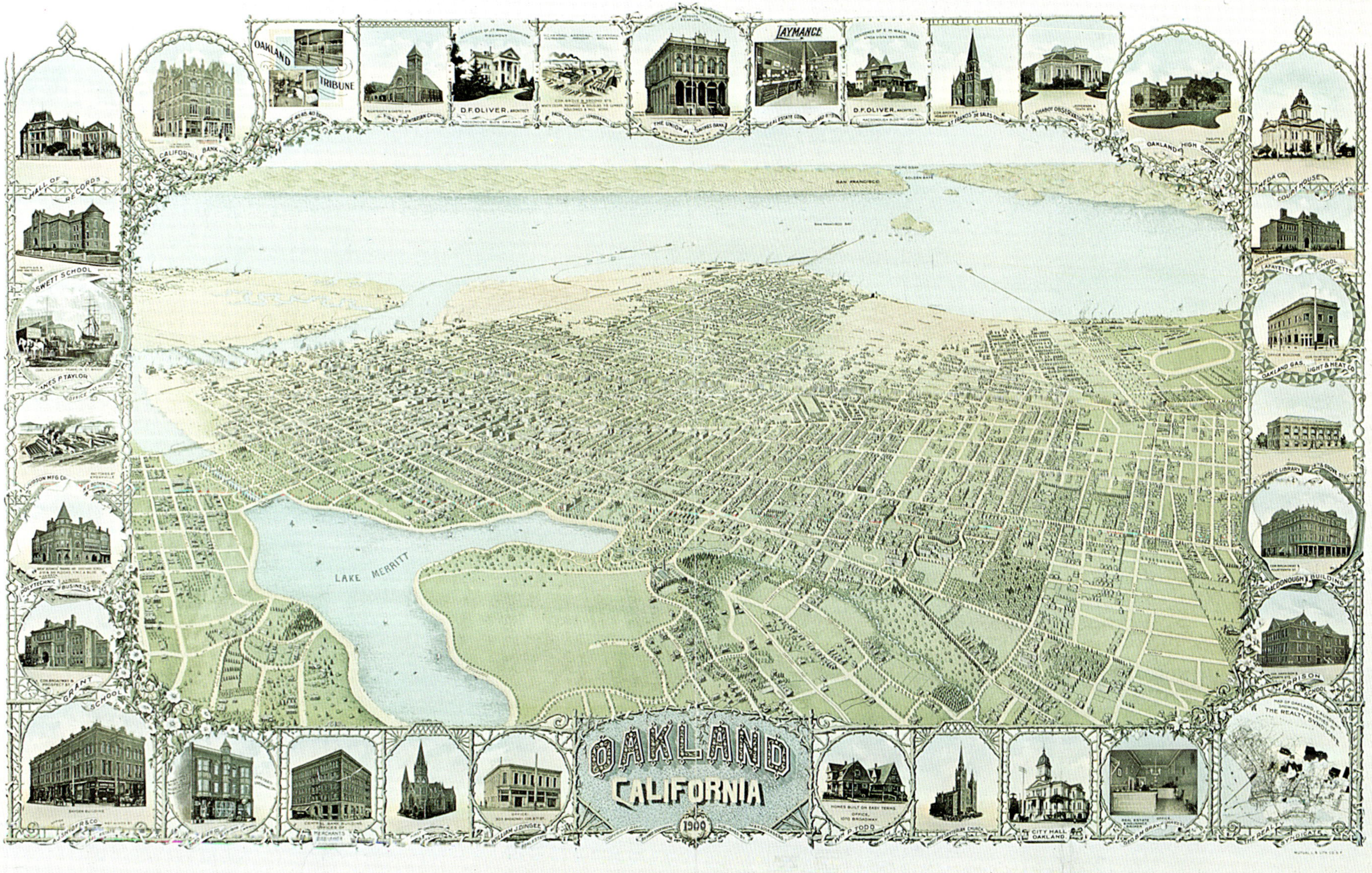

PLATE 47. *Oakland California 1900*. F. L. 1899. Color lithograph. 26-13/16 x 43-1/8 in. (68.0 x 109 5 cm.) Printed by Mutual L. & Lith. Co. Published by F. & H. Soderberg.

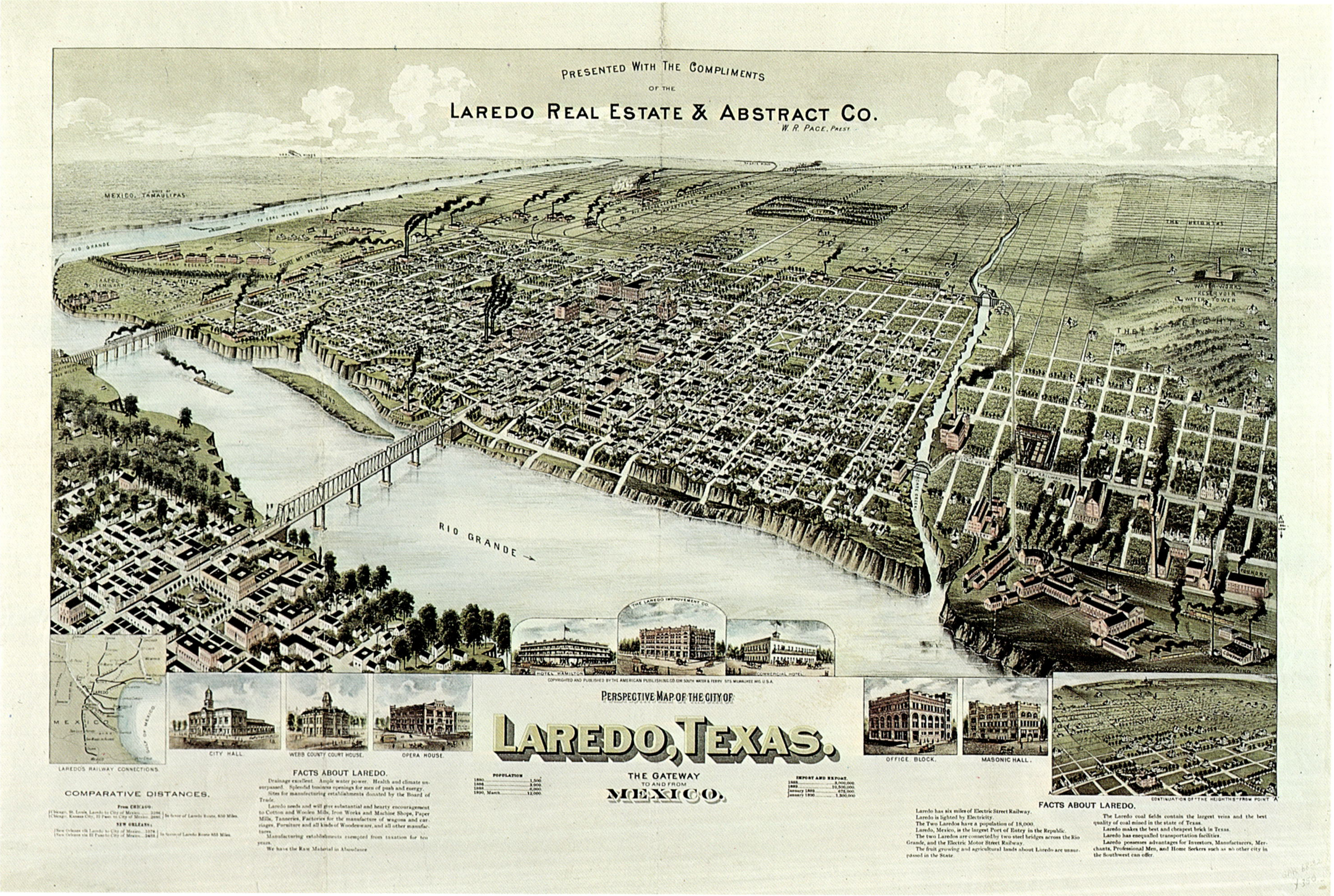

PLATE 48. *Perspective Map of the City of Laredo, Texas*. Unsigned [Henry Wellge]. 1892. Color lithograph (hand colored). 19-11/16 x 33-1/8 in. (50.0 x 84.1 cm.) Published by American Publishing Co.

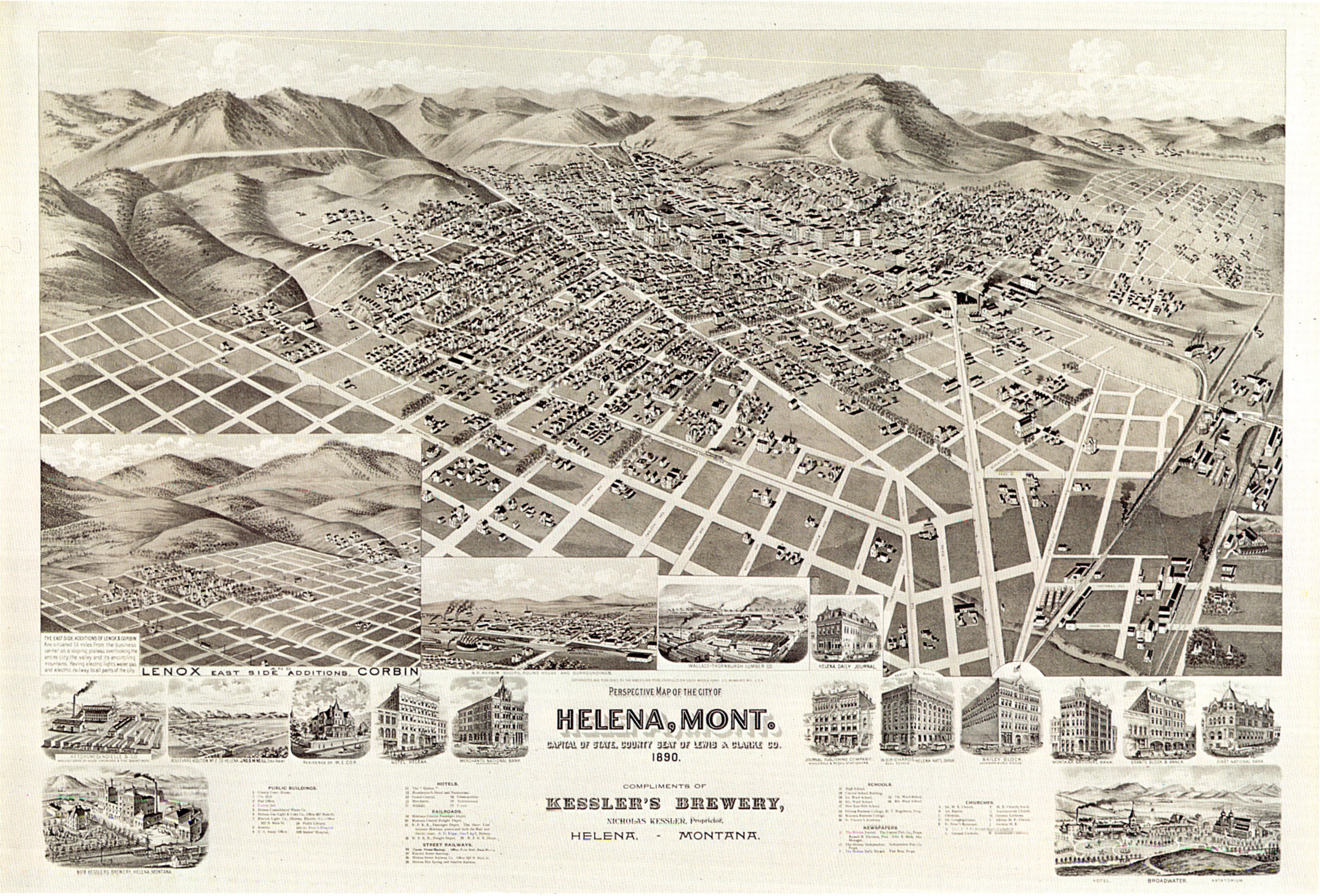

PLATE 49. *Perspective Map of the City of Helena, Mont.* Unsigned [Henry Wellge]. 1890. Toned lithograph. 26-1/4 x 39-3/8 in. (66.7 x 100.0 cm.) Published by American Publishing Co.

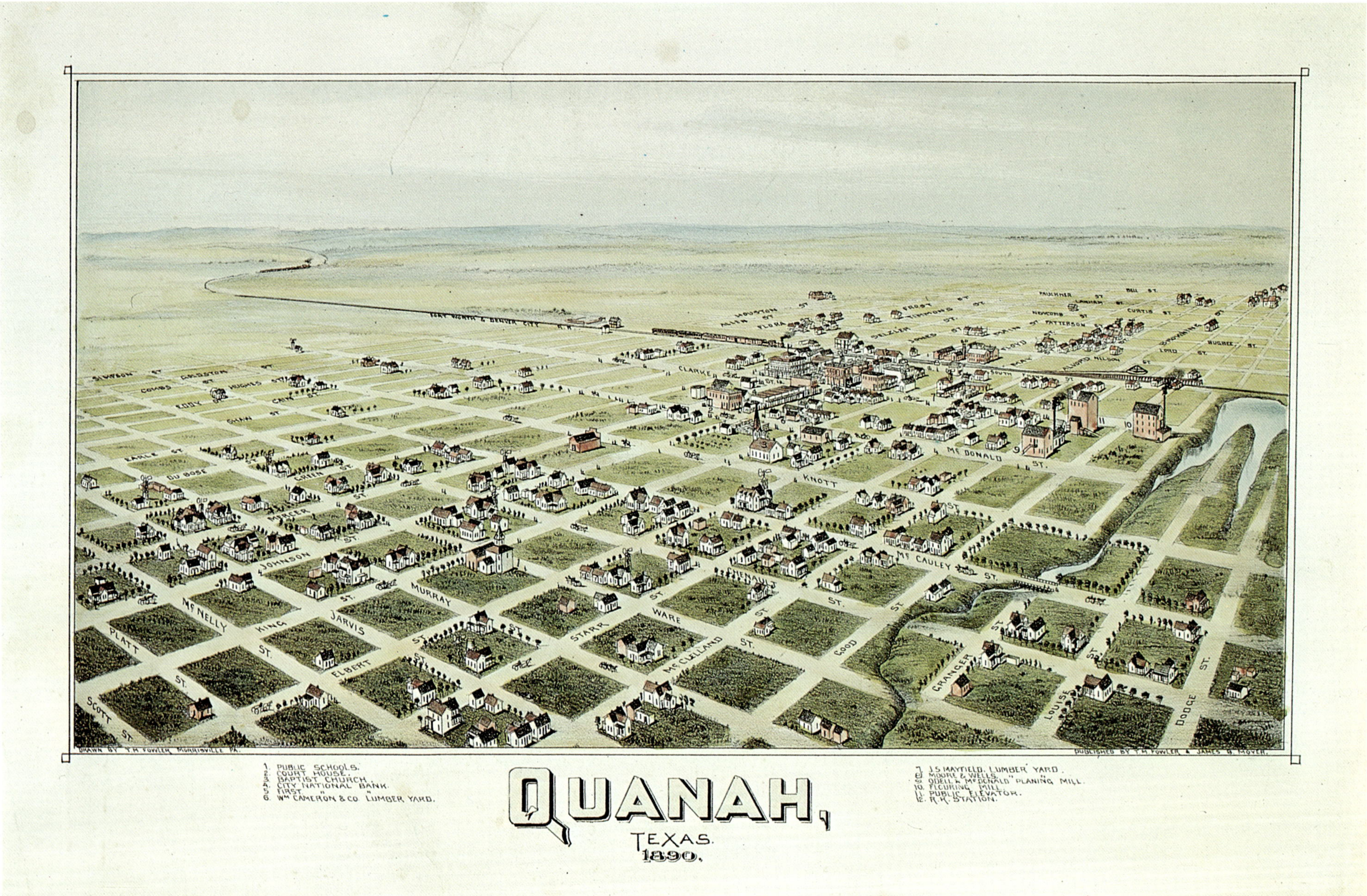

PLATE 50. *Quanah, Texas. 1890.* Thaddeus M. Fowler. 1890. Lithograph (hand colored). 10-7/16 x 19-1/4 in. (26.5 x 48.9 cm.)

EXHIBITION CHECKLIST

Illustrations are denoted by an asterisk.

Lithographer. Unsigned. 1875. Chromolithograph. 12 x 20 in. (30.4 x 50.7 cm.) Printed and published by L. Prang & Co. Courtesy Smithsonian Institution, The National Museum of History and Technology, Washington, D. C.

Birds Eye View of Aberdeen, Dak. Henry Wellge. 1883. Toned lithograph. 15 x 25 in. (38.1 x 63.5 cm.) Published by Hagerty & Marple. Courtesy Library of Congress.

Birds Eye View of Atchison Kansas. Augustus Koch. 1880. Color lithograph. 21-5/16 x 33-15/16 in. (54.1 x 86.1 cm.) Published by Ramsey, Millett & Hudson. Courtesy Kansas State Historical Society, Topeka.

* *City of Austin the New Capital of Texas in January 1, 1840*. Edward Hall. 1844, in *A History of Texas, or the Emigrant's Guide to the New Republic*. Lithograph (hand colored). 4 x 7-3/16 in. (10.1 x 18.2 cm.) Courtesy Amon Carter Museum Library. PLATE 1.

Bird's Eye View of the City of Austin Travis County Texas. Augustus Koch. 1873. Color lithograph. 19-3/4 x 28-1/8 in. (50.1 x 71.4 cm.) Courtesy University of Texas Archives, E. C. Barker Texas History Center, Austin.

Austin, State Capital of Texas. Augustus Koch. 1887. Toned lithograph. 28-1/4 x 41 in. (71.7 x 104.1 cm.) Courtesy Austin-Travis County Collection, Austin Public Library.

Bellvue. Mr. Dougherty's Agency on the Missouri. Carl Bodmer. 1840, in Maximilian, Prince de Wied-Neuwied: *Voyage dans l'interieur de l'Amérique du Nord . .* . Aquatint and etching. 7-5/8 x 10-3/4 in. (19.3 x 27.3 cm.) Courtesy Amon Carter Museum.

* *Billings, Montana*. Henry Wellge. 1904. Toned lithograph. 16-11/16 x 29-1/8 in. (42.4 x 74.0 cm.) Courtesy Amon Carter Museum. PLATE 30.

View of the City of Bismarck, Dak. Unsigned. 1883. Toned lithograph. 16 x 26 in. (40.6 x 66.0 cm.) Printed by Beck & Pauli. Published by J. J. Stoner. Courtesy Library of Congress.

View of Boise City, Idaho From the Court House. E. Green. c. 1850. Toned lithograph. 10-1/4 x 36-1/2 in. (26.0 x 92.6 cm.) Printed by Britton & Rey. Courtesy Amon Carter Museum.

Bird's-Eye View of Brigham City, and Great Salt Lake, Utah Ty. 1875. Eli S. Glover. 1875. Lithograph. 13-5/16 x 22-3/16 in. (34.6 x 56.3 cm.) Printed by Strobridge & Co. Courtesy Amon Carter Museum.

* *Bird's Eye View of Butte-City Montana County Seat of Silver Bow Co. 1884*. Unsigned [Henry Wellge]. Lithograph. 16 x 28-5/8 in. (40.6 x 72.6 cm.) Printed by Beck & Pauli. Published by J. J. Stoner. Courtesy Amon Carter Museum. PLATE 27.

Birds Eye View of Carson City. Augustus Koch. 1876. Color lithograph. 15-5/8 x 24 in. (39.7 x 60.9 cm.) Printed by Britton, Rey & Co. Courtesy Nevada State Museum, Carson City.

Central City; From the Side of Mammoth Hill Looking Up Gregory and Eureka Gulches. Alfred E. Mathews. 1866, in *Pencil Sketches of Colorado*. Color lithograph. 9-1/8 x 16 in. (23.1 x 40.6 cm.) Printed by J. Bien. Courtesy Western History Department, Denver Public Library.

* *Central City and Blackhawk, Colorado 1873*. Eli S. Glover. c. 1874. Color lithograph. 16-7/8 x 22-1/4 in. (42.8 x 56.4 cm.) Printed by Strobridge & Co. Courtesy Amon Carter Museum. PLATE 20.

Premiere Vue D'Aigleville, Colonie du Texas ou Champ D'Asile. Ambroise Louis Garnerey. 1830. Aquatint and etching (hand colored). 9-3/8 x 13-9/16 in. (23.8 x 34.5 cm.) Courtesy Amon Carter Museum.

Clarascum (Cherasco, Italy). Joannes Blaeu. c. 1682, in *Theatrum Sabaudiae*. Copper engraving. 20-1/8 x 23-11/16 in. (51.1 x 60.1 cm.) Courtesy Collection of Professor John W. Reps.

Bird's Eye View of Cheyenne. Augustus Koch. 1870. Color lithograph. 16 x 22-1/2 in. (40.1 x 57.1 cm.) Printed by Chicago Lithographing Co. Courtesy Wyoming State Archives and Historical Department, Cheyenne.

Bird's Eye View of Cheyenne, Wyo. Unsigned. 1882. Toned lithograph. 17-3/4 x 23-1/2 in. (45.1 x 59.6 cm.) Printed by Beck & Pauli. Published by J. J. Stoner. Courtesy Library of Congress.

* *The City of Chicago*. Unsigned [Charles Parsons]. 1892. Color lithograph. 20-3/4 x 32-1/2 in. (52.5 x 82.5 cm.) Published by Currier & Ives. Courtesy Amon Carter Museum. PLATE 46.

Pike's Peak and Colorado City. Alfred E. Mathews. 1866, in *Pencil Sketches of Colorado*. Color lithograph. 9 x 15-3/4 in. (23.0 x 40.0 cm.) Printed by J. Bien. Courtesy Collection of Mr. and Mrs. Mitchell A. Wilder, Fort Worth.

* *Colorado Springs, Colorado City and Manatou. January 1874.* Eli S. Glover. c. 1874. Color lithograph. 16-7/8 x 22-1/4 in. (42.8 x 56.4 cm.) Printed by Strobridge & Co. Courtesy Amon Carter Museum. PLATE 22.

Columbia January, 1852. George H. Goddard. 1852. Lithograph. 9-5/8 x 15-1/8 in. (24.3 x 38.3 cm.) Printed by Pollard & Britton. Courtesy Amon Carter Museum.

Bird's Eye View of Columbus. Augustus Koch. 1874. Toned lithograph. 11-11/16 x 17-7/8 in. (29.7 x 45.4 cm.) Courtesy Nebraska State Historical Society, Lincoln.

* *Constantinople.* Hartmann Schedel. 1493, in *Liber Cronicarum* (Nuremberg Chronicle). Woodcut. 9-1/4 x 20-5/8 in. (23.5 x 52.4 cm.) Courtesy Collection of Professor John W. Reps. FIGURE 1.

Bird's Eye View of Coronado Beach, San Diego Bay and City of San Diego, Cal. in Distance. E. S. Moore. c. 1887. Lithograph. 21 x 28-1/4 in. (53.3 x 71.7 cm.) Printed by Crocker & Co. Published by Coronado Beach Company. Courtesy San Diego Historical Society, Library and Manuscripts Collection.

Cripple Creek. Unsigned. 1896. Color lithograph. 27-1/8 x 36-5/8 in. (68.9 x 93.0 cm.) Printed by Western Litho. Co. Courtesy Amon Carter Museum.

* *Bird's Eye View of the City of Dallas Texas*. Herman Brosius. 1872. Color lithograph. 15-13/16 x 22-7/8 in. (40.1 x 58.1 cm.) Courtesy Dallas Historical Society. PLATE 32.

* *Dalles, Wasco Couniy, Oricon, 1858.* Charles C. Kuchel and Emil Dresel. 1858. Color lithograph (hand colored). 13-3/4 x 20 in. (34.8 x 50.7 cm.) Published by W. L. Demoss. Courtesy Amon Carter Museum. PLATE 14.

Deadwood, Black Hills, Dakota. W. F. Herancourt. 1884. Wood engraving. 12-7/16 x 20-7/16 in. (31.5 x 51.9 cm.) Courtesy Amon Carter Museum.

Delft. Frederick de Wit. c. 1680, in *Theatrum Icongraphicum Omnium Urbium et Praecipuorum Oppidorum Belgicarum XVII Provinciarum per Accurate Delineatarum*. Copper engraving (hand colored). 15-1/4 x 19-3/8 in. (38.7 x 49.2 cm.) Courtesy Collection of Professor John W. Reps.

Denison, Grayson County, Texas 1891. Thaddeus M. Fowler. 1891. Lithograph. 20-7/8 x 33-9/16 in. (53.0 x 85.2 cm.) Courtesy Amon Carter Museum.

Denver, City of the Plains. Alfred E. Mathews. 1866, in *Pencil Sketches of Colorado*. Color lithograph. 8-1/8 x 15-7/8 in. (20.6 x 40.3 cm.) Printed by J. Bien. Courtesy Western History Department, Denver Public Library.

Perspective Map of the City of Denver, Colo. Henry Wellge. 1889. Toned lithograph. 27-1/2 x 42-1/2 in. (69.8 x 107.9 cm.) Published by American Publishing Co. Courtesy Library of Congress.

Bird's Eye View of Dodge City, Kans. Unsigned. 1882. Lithograph. 6-7/16 x 12-11/16 in. (16.3 x 32.2 cm.) Printed by Beck & Pauli. Published by J. J. Stoner. Courtesy Kansas State Historical Society, Topeka.

Eugene City, Lane County, Oregon. 1859. Charles C. Kuchel and Emil Dresel. 1859. Lithograph. 13-3/4 x 20-5/8 in. (34.9 x 52.3 cm.) Published by Danforth & Bro. Courtesy Amon Carter Museum.

* *Flint-Shire.* John Speed. 1611, in *The Theatre of the Empire of Great Britain.* Copper engraving (hand colored). 15-1/4 x 20-3/16 in. (38.7 x 51.3 cm.) Courtesy Collection of Professor John W. Reps. FIGURE 4.

* *Die Stat Florenz.* Sebastian Münster. 1550, in *Cosmographiae Universalis.* Woodcut. 8-7/8 x 14-1/4 in. (22.5 x 36.2 cm.) Courtesy Collection of Professor John W. Reps. FIGURE 2.

* *Forrest Hill Placer County 1857.* Charles C. Kuchel and Emil Dresel. 1857. Color lithograph (hand colored). 14-15/16 x 19-7/8 in. (37.9 x 50.4 cm.) Printed by Britton & Rey. Courtesy Amon Carter Museum. PLATE 6.

Arcis Carolinae delineatio (Fort Caroline, Florida). Jacques Le Moyne. 1591, in Theodore de Bry: *Grand Voyages.* Copper engraving (hand colored). 6-1/8 x 8-1/8 in. (15.5 x 20.6 cm.) Courtesy Collection of Professor John W. Reps.

* *Fort Worth Tarrant Co. Texas.* D. D. Morse. 1876. Color lithograph. 14-1/8 x 18-13/16 in. (35.9 x 47.7 cm.) Printed by Chas. Shober & Co. Courtesy Amon Carter Museum, gift of Mr. and Mrs. Will F. Collins. PLATE 33.

* *Perspective Map of. Fort Worth, Tex. 1891.* Henry Wellge. 1891. Toned lithograph (hand colored). 17-1/16 x 33-1/4 in. (43.3 x 84.5 cm.) Published by American Publishing Co. Courtesy Amon Carter Museum. PLATE 28.

Fresno California. Lawrence. 1901. Color lithograph. 25-1/2 x 42 in. (64.7 x 106.6 cm.) Printed by Britton & Rey. Published by L. W. Klein. Courtesy Library of Congress.

* *Galveston Texas.* Augustus Koch. 1885. Color lithograph. 26-5/16 x 40-1/8 in. (66.8 x 101.9 cm.) Courtesy Amon Carter Museum. PLATE 35.

* *View of Georgetown Colorado, 1874.* Eli S. Glover. c. 1874. Color lithograph. 15-1/2 x 20 in. (39.3 x 50.7 cm.) Printed by Strobridge & Co. Courtesy Amon Carter Museum. PLATE 21.

Perspective Map of Great Falls, Mont. 1891. Unsigned. 1891. Toned lithograph. 18-11/16 x 32-3/4 in. (47.4 x 83.1 cm.) Published by American Publishing Co. Courtesy Amon Carter Museum.

* *Bird's Eye View of the City of Hannibal Marion Co. Missouri. 1869.* Albert Ruger. 1869. Color lithograph (hand colored). 20-1/8 x 25-3/4 in. (51.1 x 65.4 cm.) Courtesy Amon Carter Museum. PLATE 25.

* *Helena. (in 1865) (Montana Territory.)* Gustave R. Bechler. 1866. Color lithograph (hand colored). 12-3/4 x 22-7/8 in. (32.5 x 58.0 cm.) Printed by Herline & Hensel. Courtesy Amon Carter Museum. PLATE 41

* *Perspective Map of the City of Helena, Mont.* Unsigned [Henry Wellge]. 1890. Toned lithograph. 26-1/4 x 39-3/8 in. (66.7 x 100.0 cm.) Published by American Publishing Co. Courtesy Amon Carter Museum. PLATE 49.

* *La Terra De Hochelaga Nella Nova Francia.* Giovanni Battista Ramusio. 1556, in *Delle Navigationi e Viaggi.* Woodcut (hand colored). 10-5/8 x 14-1/2 in. (27.0 x 36.8 cm.) Courtesy Amon Carter Museum. FIGURE 5.

Honey Grove, Tex. Henry Wellge. 1885. Lithograph. 12-11/16 x 16-7/8 in. (32.3 x 53.0 cm.) Printed by Beck & Pauli. Published by Norris, Wellge & Co. Courtesy Amon Carter Museum.

* *Houston, Texas. (Looking South.) 1891.* Unsigned. 1891. Color lithograph. 23 x 42-5/8 in. (58.4 x 108.2 cm.) Courtesy Amon Carter Museum. PLATE 36.

View of Indianola. Taken from the Bay, on the Royal Yard, on Board the Barque Texana. Sept. 1860. Helmuth Holtz. 1860. Toned lithograph. 14-1/4 x 23-1/4 in. (36.2 x 59.0 cm.) Printed by Ed. Lang. Courtesy Amon Carter Museum.

Kansas City Missouri. Albert Ruger. 1869. Color lithograph. 22 x 28 in. (55.8 x 71.1 cm.) Printed by Merchant's Lith. Co. Published by Ruger & Stoner. Courtesy Library of Congress.

* *Perspective Map of the City of Laredo, Texas*. Unsigned [Henry Wellge]. 1892. Color lithograph (hand colored). 19-11/16 x 33-1/8 in. (50.0 x 84.1 cm.) Published by American Publishing Co. Courtesy Amon Carter Museum. PLATE 48.

View of Lawrence Kansas. Unsigned. 1858. Lithograph. 15 x 23-1/8 in. (38.0 x 58.6 cm.) Printed by Middleton, Strobridge & Co. Courtesy Kansas State Historical Society, Topeka.

Lead City, Black Hills, Dakota. W. F. Herancourt. 1884. Wood engraving. 12 x 19-1/6 in. (30.4 x 48.4 cm.) Courtesy Amon Carter Museum.

Bird's Eye View of Leadville, Colo. Henry Wellge. 1882. Toned lithograph. 19 x 26-1/2 in. (48.2 x 67.3 cm.) Printed by Beck & Pauli. Published by J. J. Stoner. Courtesy Library of Congress.

Bird's Eye View of the City of Leavenworth Kansas. Albert Ruger. 1869. Color lithograph. 21-3/4 x 27-3/4 in. (55.2 x 70.5 cm.) Printed by Chicago Lithographing Co. Courtesy Library of Congress.

Bird's Eye View of Lincoln Nebraska. Augustus Koch. 1885. Color lithograph. 20-1/2 x 25-3/4 in. (52.1 x 65.9 cm.) Printed by Ramsey, Millett & Hudson. Courtesy Lincoln City Libraries.

* *Los Angeles, Los Angeles County, Cal. 1857*. Charles C. Kuchel and Emil Dresel. 1857. Toned lithograph. 15-3/4 x 23-1/8 in. (40.0 x 58.7 cm.) Printed by Britton & Rey. Published by Hellman & Bro. Courtesy Amon Carter Museum. PLATE 12.

Birds Eye View of Los Angeles California. Birds Eye View of Wilmington Los Angeles Co. Cal. Birds Eye View of Santa Monica Los Angeles Co. Cal. Eli S. Glover. 1877. Toned lithograph. 21 x 33-1/2 in. (53.3 x 85.1 cm.) Printed by A. L. Bancroft & Co. Courtesy Library of Congress.

Los Angeles, California, 1894. B. W. Pierce. 1894. Color lithograph. 29-3/16 x 43-3/4 in. (74.1 x 111.0 cm.) Published by Semi-Tropic Homestead Co. Courtesy Amon Carter Museum.

* *Bird's Eye View of the City of McGregor and North McGregor 1869 Clayton County, Iowa*. Unsigned [Albert Ruger]. 1869. Color lithograph. 18-1/16 x 22 in. (45.8 x 55.8 cm.) Printed by Chicago Lithog. Co. Published by Ruger & Stoner. Courtesy Amon Carter Museum. PLATE 26.

* *Panoramic View of Milwaukee Wis.* Unsigned. 1898. Chromolithograph. 12-11/16 x 47-3/8 in. (32.2 x 120.3 cm.) Printed and published by The Gugler Lithographic Co. Courtesy Amon Carter Museum. (TITLE PAGE ILLUSTRATION)

Bird's Eye View of Missoula Mon. Henry Wellge. 1884. Toned lithograph. 11-1/8 x 24-1/16 in. (28.2 x 61.1 cm.) Printed by Beck & Pauli. Published by J. J. Stoner. Courtesy Amon Carter Museum.

* *Harbour and City of Monterey, California 1842*. Unsigned. 1850. Toned lithograph. 15 x 29-3/16 in. (38.1 x 74.1 cm.) Printed by D'Avignon. Published by Thomas Larkin. Courtesy Amon Carter Museum. PLATE 4.

* *Moscow*. Georg Braun and Franz Hogenberg. 1575, in *Civitas Orbis Terrarum*. Copper engraving (hand colored). 13-3/4 x 19-1/4 in. (34.9 x 48.9 cm.). Courtesy Collection of Professor John W. Reps. FIGURE 3.

Bird's Eye View of the City of Nebraska City. Albert Ruger. 1868. Color lithograph. 21 x 26 in. (53.3 x 66.0 cm.) Printed by Merchant's Lith. Co. Courtesy Library of Congress.

[*Nevada, 1856*]. Charles C. Kuchel and Emil Dresel. 1856. Toned lithograph. 9-7/8 x 21-11/16 in. (25.0 x 55.1 cm.) Printed by Britton & Rey. Courtesy Amon Carter Museum.

* *Bird's Eye View of New Braunfels Comal County Texas 1881*. Augustus Koch. 1881. Toned lithograph. 17-15/16 x 28-1/2 in. (45.5 x

72.3 cm.) Courtesy Amon Carter Museum, gift of C. W. Geue. PLATE 34.

North Platte, Lincoln County, Neb., Fall of 1888. J. A. Ricker. 1888. Lithograph. 14-9/16 x 23-5/8 in. (37.0 x 60.0 cm.) Published by North Platte *Telegraph*. Courtesy Western History Department, Denver Public Library.

* *Oakland California 1900.* F. L. 1899. Color lithograph. 26-13/16 x 43-1/8 in. (68.0 x 109.5 cm.) Printed by Mutual L. & Lith. Co. Published by F. & H. Soderberg. Courtesy Amon Carter Museum. PLATE 47.

Birds Eye View of Ogden City. Utah, Ty. 1875. Eli S. Glover. 1875. Toned lithograph. 17 x 22-1/2 in. (43.2 x 57.1 cm.) Printed by Strobridge & Co. Courtesy Library of Congress.

Oklahoma City, Indian Territory. 1890. Thaddeus M. Fowler. 1890. Toned lithograph. 15-13/16 x 29-3/8 in. (40.1 x 74.6 cm.) Printed by A. E. Downs. Courtesy Collection of George H. Shirk, Oklahoma City.

* *Bird's-Eye View of the City of Olympia, East Olympia and Tumwater, Puget Sound, Washington Territory, 1879.* Eli S. Glover. c. 1879. Lithograph (hand colored). 16 x 29-13/16 in. (40.5 x 75.7 cm.) Printed by A. L. Bancroft & Co. Courtesy Amon Carter Museum. PLATE 19.

* *Omaha Nebraska 1867*. H. Lambach. 1867. Color lithograph (hand colored). 12-13/16 x 26-7/8 in. (32.5 x 68.2 cm.) Printed and published by Gast, Moeller & Co. Courtesy Amon Carter Museum. PLATE 43.

* *Bird's Eye View of the City of Omaha Nebraska 1868.* Albert Ruger. 1868. Toned lithograph (hand colored). 22-1/16 x 28 in. (55.9 x 71.0 cm.) Printed by Chicago Lithographing Co. Courtesy Amon Carter Museum. PLATE 24.

Aerial View of Omaha. Edward J. Austen. 1905. Oil on canvas. 59-1/2 x 118-3/4 in. (151.1 x 396.9 cm.) Commissioned by Edward Rosewater for Bee Publishing Company. Courtesy Joslyn Art Museum, Omaha. Exhibited only in Fort Worth and Omaha.

Panoramic View of Omaha. Edward J. Austen. 1906. Photographic halftone. 21-1/2 x 42-5/16 in. (54.5 x 107.4 cm.) Printed by Manz Engraving Co. Published by Omaha *Daily Bee*. Courtesy Joslyn Art Museum, Omaha.

* *The American Village* (Oregon City, Oregon). Sir Henry James Warre. c. 1848, in *Sketches in North America and the Oregon Territory*. Toned lithograph (hand colored). 9-13/16 x 13-1/8 in. (24.8 x 33.3 cm.) Courtesy Amon Carter Museum. PLATE 2.

* *Oregon City, Clackamas County, Oregon. 1858.* Charles C. Kuchel and Emil Dresel. 1858. Toned lithograph. 15-15/16 x 25-11/16 in. (40.5 x 65.2 cm.) Published by Charman & Warner. Courtesy Amon Carter Museum. PLATE 13.

Paris, Texas. Unsigned [Henry Wellge]. 1885. Toned lithograph. 19-1/2 x 25-1/2 in. (49.5 x 64.7 cm.) Printed by Beck & Pauli. Published by Norris, Wellge & Co. Courtesy Library of Congress.

Pasadena California, 1893. B. W. Pierce. 1893. Lithograph. 25-3/16 x 40-1/8 in. (64.0 x 101.9 cm.) Published by Wood & Church. Courtesy Amon Carter Museum.

Panoramic View of Pendleton, Or. Henry Wellge. 1884. Color lithograph (hand colored). 11 x 21-7/8 in. (27.9 x 55.6 cm.) Printed by Beck & Pauli. Published by J. J. Stoner. Courtesy Amon Carter Museum.

* *Bird's Eye View of Phoenix Maricopa Co. Arizona. View Looking North-East*. C. J. Dyer. 1885. Color lithograph. 22 x 33 in. (55.8 x 83.8 cm.) Printed by Schmidt Label & Litho Co. Courtesy Library of Congress, Washington, D.C. PLATE 40.

Pikes Peak Panorama. Unsigned. c. 1890. Chromolithograph. 15-3/16 x 41-13/16 in. (38.6 x 106.2 cm.) Published by American Publishing Co. Courtesy Amon Carter Museum.

Bird's Eye View of Port Townsend, Puget Sound, Washington Terri-

tory. Eli S. Glover. 1878. Toned lithograph. 17 x 25 in. (43.1 x 63.5 cm.) Printed by A. L. Bancroft. Courtesy Library of Congress.

* *City of Portland, Oregon*. Grafton T. Brown. c. 1861. Toned lithograph. 19-1/6 x 29-1/2 in. (48.4 x 74.9 cm.) Printed by Britton & Co. Published by C. C. Kuchel. Courtesy Amon Carter Museum. PLATE 44.

Bird's Eye View of the City of Portland, Oregon. C. B. Talbot. 1870. Toned lithograph. 25-3/4 x 37-1/2 in. (65.4 x 95.2 cm.) Printed by G. T. Brown & Co. Published by P. F. Castleman. Courtesy Oregon Historical Society, Portland.

Portland, Oregon. B. W. Pierce. 1890. Lithograph. 30-1/8 x 43-7/8 in. (76.5 x 111.4 cm.) Published by Clohessy & Strengele. Courtesy Oregon Historical Society, Portland.

* *Bird's-Eye View of Prescott, A. T. Looking North East*. C. J. Dyer. c. 1885. Color lithograph. 19-1/8 x 29-1/2 in. (48.5 x 74.9 cm.) Courtesy Amon Carter Museum. PLATE 39.

Birds-Eye View of Pueblo. Eli S. Glover. 1874. Lithograph. 23-1/4 x 26-13/16 in. (59.0 x 68.0 cm.) Printed by Strobridge & Co. Courtesy Western History Department, Denver Public Library.

Pueblo, Colo. Unsigned. 1890. Toned lithograph. 36 x 26 in. (91.4 x 66.0 cm.) Published by American Publishing Co. Courtesy Library of Congress.

* *View of Quanah, Texas. Hardeman County: October 1890.* Thaddeus M. Fowler. 1890. Pencil on paper. 20 x 32-5/8 in. (50.8 x 82.8 cm.) Courtesy Amon Carter Museum. FIGURE 11.

* *Quanah, Texas. 1890.* Thaddeus M. Fowler. 1890. Lithograph (hand colored). 10-7/16 x 19-1/4 in. (26.5 x 48.9 cm.) Courtesy Amon Carter Museum. PLATE 50.

[*Rapid City, Dakota, 1883*]. W. F. Herancourt. 1883. Wood engraving. 11-1/4 x 19-13/16 in. (28.5 x 50.3 cm.) Courtesy Collection of Helen Hill Wrede, Rapid City, South Dakota.

Birds Eye View of Reno Nevada, 1888–1892. Unsigned. 1890. Lithograph (hand colored). 20-7/8 x 34-1/2 in. (53.0 x 87.6 cm.) Printed by M. S. Crocker & Co. Published by C. C. Powning. Courtesy Washoe County School District, Reno.

* *Sacramento City Ca. From the Foot of J. Street, Showing I. J. & K. Sts. With the Sierra Nevada in the Distance*. George V. Cooper. 1850. Color lithograph. 15-3/16 x 23-3/16 in. (38.5 x 58.8 cm.) Printed by Wm. Endicott & Co. Published by Stringer & Townsend. Courtesy Amon Carter Museum. PLATE 3.

A Birds-Eye View of; Sacramento Capital of the State of California. George H. Baker. 1857. Toned lithograph. 27-5/16 x 33-3/4 in. (69.3 x 85.7 cm.) Printed by Britton & Rey. Courtesy Amon Carter Museum.

* *Birds Eye View of the City of Sacramento State Capital of California 1870.* Augustus Koch. 1870. Color lithograph (hand colored). 27-5/16 x 33-1/4 in. (69.3 x 84.4 cm.) Printed by Britton & Rey. Courtesy Amon Carter Museum. PLATE 17.

Pagus Hispanorum in Florida (St. Augustine, Florida). Arnoldus Montanus (Arnald van den Berg). 1671, in *De Niewe en Onbekende Weerld: of Beschryving van America*. Copper engraving (hand colored). 10-7/16 x 14-5/16 in. (27.7 x 36.3 cm.) Courtesy Collection of Professor John W. Reps.

* *City of St. Louis, 1856. Sierra County, Cal.* Charles C. Kuchel and Emil Dresel. 1856. Color lithograph (hand colored). 14-3/16 x 20-3/4 in. (36.0 x 52.7 cm.) Printed by Britton & Rey. Published by Everts, Wilson & Co. Courtesy Amon Carter Museum. PLATE 7.

* *The City of St. Louis*. Charles Parsons. 1874. Color lithograph. 20-1/2 x 32-5/8 in. (52.0 x 82.7 cm.) Published by Currier and Ives. Courtesy Amon Carter Museum. PLATE 45.

Bird's Eye View of Salem, Oregon. Eli S. Glover. 1876. Toned lithograph. 18-9/16 x 29-1/16 in. (47.2 x 73.9 cm.) Printed by A. L. Bancroft & Co. Published by F. A. Smith. Courtesy Library of Congress.

* *View of Great Salt Lake City*. Christian Inger. 1867. Toned lithograph. 11-9/16 x 28-1/2 in. (29.3 x 72.3 cm.) Printed by H. J. Toudy & Co. Published by Philip Ritz. Courtesy Amon Carter Museum. PLATE 42.

Bird's Eye View of Salt Lake City Utah Territory 1870. Augustus Koch. 1870. Color lithograph. 29 x 35 in. (73.6 x 88.9 cm.) Courtesy Library of Congress.

Birds-Eye View of Salt Lake City. Eli S. Glover. 1875. Toned lithograph. 24-1/2 x 32-1/2 in. (60.9 x 82.5 cm.) Printed by Strobridge & Co. Courtesy Library of Congress.

Salt Lake City, Utah. Henry Wellge. 1891. Color lithograph. 24 x 44-1/2 in. (60.9 x 113.0 cm.) Published by American Publishing Co. Courtesy Library of Congress.

* *San Antonio de Bexar*. Hermann Lungkwitz. c. 1860. Color lithograph (hand colored). 16-13/16 x 19 in. (42.7 x 48.2 cm.) Printed by Rau & Son. Courtesy Amon Carter Museum. PLATE 31.

Bird's Eye View of San Diego, California. Eli S. Glover. 1876. Toned lithograph. 19 x 27 in. (48.2 x 68.5 cm.) Printed by A. L. Bancroft & Co. Published by Schneider & Kueppers. Courtesy Library of Congress.

View of San Francisco, Formerly Yerba Buena, in 1846–7. William F. Swasey. c. 1888. Color lithograph. 17 x 20-1/2 in. (43.1 x 52.0 cm.) Printed by Bosqui Eng. & Print. Co. Courtesy Library of Congress.

San Francisco in July, 1849. George Henry Burgess. c. 1885. Oil on canvas. 62 x 144 in. (157.4 x 360.0 cm.) Courtesy John Howell—Books, San Francisco. Exhibited only in Fort Worth.

San-Francisco 1849. Henry Firks. 1868. Toned lithograph. 15-1/2 x 32 in. (39.3 x 81.4 cm.) Printed by G. T. Brown & Co. Published by W. H. Jones. Courtesy The Mariners Museum, Newport News, Virginia.

* *San Francisco*. S. F. Marryat. 1851. Lithograph (hand colored). 16-1/2 x 25-7/16 in. (41.9 x 64.5 cm.) Printed by M. & N. Hanhart. Published by Henry Squire & Co. Courtesy Amon Carter Museum. PLATE 5.

* *Birds Eye View of the City of San Francisco and Surrounding Country*. George Henry Goddard. 1868. Color lithograph (hand colored). 27-5/16 x 40-3/8 in. (69.3 x 102.5 cm.) Printed by Britton & Rey. Published by Snow & Roos. Courtesy Amon Carter Museum. PLATE 15.

The City of San Francisco. Charles Parsons. 1878. Color lithograph. 23-3/8 x 33 in. (59.3 x 83.8 cm.) Published by Currier & Ives. Courtesy The Mariners Museum, Newport News, Virginia.

View of San Gabriel, Cal. Unsigned. c. 1892. Toned lithograph. 14 x 20-1/2 in. (35.5 x 52.0 cm.) Published by D. D. Morse. Courtesy Library of Congress.

* *San Jose, 1856. County of Santa Clara, Cala.* Charles C. Kuchel and Emil Dresel. 1856. Color lithograph (hand colored). 19-7/8 x 25-3/4 in. (50.5 x 65.4 cm.) Printed by Britton & Rey. Courtesy Amon Carter Museum. PLATE 11.

Bird's Eye View of San Luis Obispo, Cal. 1877. Eli S. Glover. c. 1877. Toned lithograph. 12-1/2 x 23-7/8 in. (31.7 x 60.5 cm.) Printed by A. L. Bancroft & Co. Courtesy Amon Carter Museum.

* *Bird's Eye View of Santa Barbara, California, 1877.* Eli S. Glover. c. 1877. Color lithograph (hand colored). 17-3/16 x 30-1/16 in. (43.7 x 74.3 cm.) Printed by A. L. Bancroft & Co. Courtesy Amon Carter Museum. PLATE 18.

Santa Clara, 1856. Charles C. Kuchel and Emil Dresel. 1856. Toned lithograph. 9-7/16 x 17-5/8 in. (23.9 x 44.6 cm.) Printed by Britton & Rey. Courtesy Amon Carter Museum.

* *Bird's Eye View of the City of Santa Fé, N.M. 1882.* Unsigned [Henry Wellge]. 1882. Toned lithograph. 9-9/16 x 19-1/16 in. (24.2 x 48.3 cm.) Printed by Beck & Pauli. Published by J. J. Stoner. Courtesy Amon Carter Museum. PLATE 38.

*A View of Savanah as it stood the 29th of March, 1734. Peter Gordon. c. 1734. Engraving. 15-7/8 x 21-7/8 in. (40.3 x 55.5 cm.) Courtesy Amon Carter Museum. FIGURE 6.

Bird's-Eye View of the City of Seattle. Eli S. Glover. 1878. Toned lithograph. 19-1/2 x 30-1/2 in. (49.5 x 77.4 cm.) Printed by A. L. Bancroft & Co. Courtesy Library of Congress.

Bird's Eye View of the City of Seattle, WT. Henry Wellge. 1884. Lithograph. 13-7/16 x 32-5/8 in. (34.0 x 82.8 cm.) Printed by Beck & Pauli. Published by J. J. Stoner. Courtesy Seattle Historical Society.

Birds Eye View of Seattle and Environs. Augustus Koch. 1891. Color lithograph. 34 x 50-1/2 in. (86.3 x 128.2 cm.) Printed by Hughes Litho. Co. Courtesy Library of Congress.

**Shasta, 1856. Shasta County, California.* Charles C. Kuchel and Emil Dresel. 1856. Color lithograph (hand colored). 16-7/16 x 24 in. (41.7 x 60.8 cm.) Printed by Britton & Rey. Published by A. Roman. Courtesy Amon Carter Museum. PLATE 10.

**Birds Eye View of the City of Stockton San Joaquin County. California. 1870.* Augustus Koch. 1870. Color lithograph (hand colored). 22-5/8 x 28 in. (57.5 x 71.1 cm.) Printed by Britton & Rey. Courtesy Amon Carter Museum. PLATE 16.

**View of Sumner Kansas Terry.* Unsigned. c. 1857. Color lithograph. 17-13/16 x 28 in. (45.2 x 71.0 cm.) Printed and published by Middleton, Strobridge & Co. Courtesy Kansas State Historical Society, Topeka. PLATE 23.

A View of Sutter's Mill & Culloma Valley. Unsigned. n. d. Color lithograph. 17-3/4 x 24-3/4 in. (45.1 x 62.8 cm.) Printed by Sarony & Major. Courtesy Amon Carter Museum.

View of New Tacoma and Mount Rainier. Eli S. Glover. 1878. Toned lithograph. 17 x 25 in. (43.1 x 63.5 cm.) Printed by A. L. Bancroft & Co. Courtesy Library of Congress.

**View of the City of Tacoma, W. T.* Henry Wellge. 1884. Toned lithograph. 12-1/8 x 32-1/2 in. (30.7 x 82.5 cm.) Printed by Beck & Pauli. Published by J. J. Stoner. Courtesy Amon Carter Museum. PLATE 29.

**Todds Valley, Placer County, California. 1857.* Charles C. Kuchel and Emil Dresel. 1857. Color lithograph (hand colored). 14-1/4 x 20-3/4 in. (36.2 x 52.7 cm.) Printed by Britton & Rey. Published by Read & Hall. Courtesy Amon Carter Museum. PLATE 9.

Bird's Eye View of the City of Topeka. Albert Ruger. 1869. Color lithograph. 20 x 26 in. (50.8 x 66.0 cm.) Printed by Chicago Lithographing Co. Courtesy Library of Congress.

Birds Eye View of Topeka Kansas. Augustus Koch. 1880. Color lithograph. 21-3/8 x 33-15/16 in. (54.3 x 86.2 cm.) Printed by Ramsey Millett & Hudson. Courtesy Kansas State Historical Society, Topeka.

**Aero View of Tulsa Oklahoma, 1918.* Thaddeus M. Fowler. 1918. Monotone rotogravure. 13-3/16 x 35 in. (33.4 x 88.8 cm.) Courtesy Amon Carter Museum. PLATE 37.

**Union, On Humboldt Bay, Humboldt Co. Cal. 1857.* Charles C. Kuchel and Emil Dresel. 1857. Color lithograph (hand colored). 14-3/16 x 20-13/16 in. (36.0 x 52.8 cm.) Printed by Britton & Rey. Published by B. Henry Wyman. Courtesy Amon Carter Museum. PLATE 8.

Birds Eye of the City of Vallejo and U. S. Navy Yard, Mare Island. Augustus Koch. 1871. Color lithograph. 32 x 35-1/2 in. (81.2 x 90.1 cm.) Printed by Britton & Rey. Published by Snow & Roos. Courtesy Chicago Historical Society.

Virginia City. Alfred E. Mathews. 1868, in *Pencil Sketches of Montana.* Toned lithograph. 9 x 17-1/4 in. (22.8 x 43.5 cm.) Courtesy Amon Carter Museum.

Birds Eye View of Virginia City. Augustus Koch. 1875. Color lithograph. 24 x 28-1/2 in. (60.9 x 72.4 cm.) Printed by Britton & Rey. Courtesy Library of Congress.

Waco, Tex. Henry Wellge. 1866. Toned lithograph. 18-11/16 x 30-1/2 in. (47.4 x 77.5 cm.) Printed by Beck & Pauli. Published by Norris, Wellge & Co. Courtesy Amon Carter Museum.

Bird's Eye View of Walla Walla, Washington Territory, 1876. Eli S. Glover. 1876. 19 x 28-1/2 in. (48.2 x 71.1 cm.) Printed by A. L. Bancroft & Co. Published by Everts & Able. Courtesy Library of Congress.

Zurich. Matthäus Merian. 1642, in Martin Zeiller: *Topographia Helvetiae, Rhaetiae et Valesiae.* Copper engraving. 10-3/4 x 14-1/8 in. (27.3 x 35.8 cm.) Courtesy Collection of Professor John W. Reps.